# Bond of Friendship

by

## Gordon Wilson

Publisher

Best Books Online
Mediaworld PR Ltd

**ISBN 1-904502-38-5**

Gordon Wilson was born in Yorkshire and whilst growing up, he helped his father in his fruit and veg business.

Discovering he had itchy feet he decided to join the forces and travel the world, it was 22 years before he came back to Yorkshire.

Going back to his education he became a local magistrate before deciding to stand for election as a local councillor to try and make a difference and help others.

After losing friends who had been on the nuclear test sites at Maralinga in South Australia, to various cancers, and whilst he himself was being treated for a very aggressive cancer, he decided to write this book.

Gordon would like to thank his wife, Jean, son, Mark, daughter-in-law, Debbie and his four grandchildren, John, Josh, Melissa and Paul who gave him the strength to carry on.

Thanks also to Graham & Margaret at Mediaworld and Best Books Online for editing and publishing this book.

*Dedicated to all my friends who served their country and have lost their lives, and the many who are still ill from the devastating Maralinga tests.*

This book was written to help me raise enough money to build a small respite holiday home for British Maralinga nuclear bomb test veterans.

I actually lost a lot of friends who, though a lot older than me, served with me in the forces and were at the nuclear test sites in the middle of the desert in South Australia.

Many of them have died from various cancers and other illnesses, none of them have had any recognition for the service to their country. They are the forgotten few who received no compensation from these tests at all.

# Chapter 1

This is a story about the lives of two young men who grew up together in a town in Yorkshire. Brian and I were drawn together from a very early age and were to become the very best of friends. Brian was someone who did not think things through before doing them, but he was a very good-looking lad who would never be short of a woman or two. I was a thinker and very methodical in what I did. I was not as good-looking as Brian, he had a cheeky grin and a searching mind. We became very supportive of each other, sharing interests in our teenage years.

The adventure started one day when we were sat on a wall throwing stones into the drain below trying to hit a bottle that was floating past.

Brian said, "Shall we go away for a couple of days?"

At fourteen years old it would be quite an adventure. The furthest we had been before was a bike ride to the coast and that was about fifteen miles away. This time Brian wanted to see a girl who lived in Rotherham. He had met her when he was with his parents at a caravan site on the coast, he'd had a great time and wanted to see her again.

So we decided to try and get some money to hire a couple of bikes from Reg. He was a man who built bikes and hired them out, all the youngsters used to hire bikes from him, not having the money to buy one of their own. We decided to go and ask our mothers for some money so off we went to my house first, we should have known better, as the answer was 'piss off' with no explanation. The thing was, she had no money, therefore could not help us. A shoe followed us as we made off up the terrace, with a lot of abuse behind it. All my mother wanted was for me to get a full time job to bring some money in. She was not satisfied with the money that I gave her from the part time job I had after school, I was working for an electrical engineer who had offered me a full time job if I went to grammar school after passing my eleven plus.

All mother wanted was for me to leave school as soon as possible and get a full time job, but my father wanted me to go to grammar school then on to college, but he dare not say too much because he would get it in the neck. I was the oldest of four children, two boys and two girls, but I was the one who had to do all the work in the house, or so it seemed to me.

Going on toBrian's house, his mother said that she would have given us something but money was very tight that week as she had to pay a lot of bills. Brian was the youngest in his family, he had an older brother and a sister.

We decided to go on to the drain bank where a rag and bone merchant's back wall ran along the bank. It was a visit that we had made a few times in the past when we didn't have any money. The man had ripped us off when we had taken rags round there before, never giving us a fair price, so we had loosened some bricks in the wall of his yard where we could rake out some rags and woollens and stuff them into a sack. We had to keep an eye on the fisherman who was there fishing for eels in the drain so he didn't spot us. After we had filled the sack we put the bricks back for another day pushing the long grass of the drain bank back up to the wall to hide our secret hole.

So, with a job well done, we scooted round to the front of the yard to resell old Jarvis his own rags.

He grunted and groaned as he told us to throw them on the scales, muttering that the price of rags and wool had dropped, something he always said, but he gave us half a crown for them and we were very happy with that and the outcome of our little deal.

Laughing to ourselves, we made our way round to Reg's to hire a couple of bikes. We picked two that looked okay to us and we paid him sixpence each, which left us with one and six, thanks to Jarvis the rag and bone merchant. With a smug look on our faces we sped off on our bikes to tell our mothers that we were going away for a couple of days. We also needed to pick up a couple of blankets and a few odds and ends that we thought we would need for our trip.

I went to my house and Brian went to his and we arranged to meet in fifteen minutes at the top of my street as Brian only lived two streets away. As I went through the front door my mother asked me where I had been and before I could answer she had taken her shoe off and cuffed me with it, saying, "Next time tell me where you are going. I want you to go to the shops for me, then clean the bedrooms and get the tea ready for your sisters."

My two sisters were totally different to each other, this proved to be true later in life, one of them was a real worker, the other one was to become the 'posh one' and it still remains that way today.

My mother used to knock me about a bit and would not let me further my education, I always had to stay in and look after my sisters and young brother.

My father was a gentle man who used to play music and act as compare around the clubs. He could play all kinds of musical instruments and he also used to repair clocks and radios for our neighbours. He never raised his hand to any of us and, though he didn't show it, I am sure he loved us all in his own way.

After a few clips round the ear from my mother, I told her that I was going camping with Brian then I legged it out of the house, followed by a lot of verbal from my mother. I gathered my bike and raced round to Brian's even though we had arranged to meet at the top of my street, I thought it was best to get well away at this time.

Brian's mum was different again and told us to look after each other. Brian had borrowed his brother's tent so we loaded up the bikes, tying everything on with some string. Then, saying goodbye to Brian's mum we set off on our trip. We had no idea how long it would take us but we were not bothered, we decided to ride until it became dark, not realising that this was to be the start of many journeys that we would take together in the coming years.

We were heading towards Goole on the A63 then on to the A614 to Bawtry where we would pick up the A631 to Rotherham, we did not know if this was the fastest way to get there but that is the route we had chosen together. We were clowning about on the bikes, swaying all over the road, as we passed the time away, it was very warm so we decided to stop and have a drink of water which we had brought with us, pulling off the road we took our shirts off and laid in the nearby field.

We were chatting about what we wanted to do when we left school, Brian said that he wanted to go into the army. I was not too sure as

3

I had set my mind on being an electrical engineer but there was not much chance of that with my mother wanting me to go out to work. I turned to Brian and said, "If that is the case I will join the forces with you and see what the world has to offer us both."

At least we would get to travel around the world, we hoped. We lay idly chatting about everything and nothing before we realised we had better get on or we would never get there before it got dark, so we set off on our bikes once again. As we were passing one field Brian said to me, "Look there is a field of peas, let's get some to eat for later tonight when we make camp."

So we threw our bikes on the floor and began to gather as many peas as we could, filling our pockets and a bag that we had with us. Feeling pleased with ourselves we mounted our bikes and set off once more on our journey.

We arrived near the town of Goole after crossing the bridge over the River Humber, where we paused to toss a few rocks into the water. We decided to buy some chips from a shop that we came across, asking the owner to put a load of scraps (pieces of batter) over the chips. Sitting on a wall, we began to eat them with some of the bread that Brian's mum had packed for us. The chips were very welcome, but we thought that we better not hang around too long as we still had a good way to go. So, finishing the chips we put the paper in a nearby bin and set off once more.

Brian and I were as close as any friends could be and we were always discussing what we could do together. Let's say we really cared about each other, Brian was a little frightened of the dark, but I said we were together and would look after each other, which is what we did for many years to come. It was getting late as we watched the sun going down, we did not think that we were near Rotherham, so we decided to keep going until it was too dark to ride.

It was getting too dark to see as we neared a village where we spotted a wall with some grass behind it, so we decided to pitch our tent there near to the wall to give us a bit of shelter from the wind. We erected the tent and, with both of us feeling very tired, we dived into it rolling in our blankets.

We settled down to talk for awhile but we must have dropped off to sleep within seconds. The next thing we knew was the sun beating down on the tent and the birds singing away woke us up. Before we ventured out we lay there talking for a few minutes to gather our senses. On crawling out of the tent, to our amazement we found we had pitched it on the edge of a graveyard. Brian said, "I would not have slept if I'd known that."

"Me neither, Brian," I said and we both burst out laughing.

We were both dry and very hungry so we fastened the tent up and walked into the village to look for a shop to get something to eat and drink. The only one open was a newspaper shop so we went inside and asked the lady behind the counter if she had any bread that we could buy.

She said that there was none left until she got her delivery. She asked us where we'd come from and what we were doing in the area. When we told her she said, "what brave young men," which made us feel good, then she said that she would give us some cakes that she had left in her flat above the shop.

We felt lucky to have met this kind lady and we stood in the shop while she went upstairs to get us the cakes, a man came in and we told him that she would not be long.

She came down with the cakes for us and wished us well. Then she asked us if we went to church?

"Yes," we said. "We had a good relationship with our vicar at the church back home. He's called Father Scott and he's always there to listen to us and help us, if he can, in anything that we wanted to do."

The lady wished us good luck as we thanked her once more and set off back to the tent to eat the cakes and have some water.

After we had had our fill, we packed up the tent and proceeded on our way to Rotherham feeling content with ourselves. We passed a sign on the road that told us we only had a few more miles to go and we laughed and joked as we rode along on the way to find Brian's young woman.

Finally we entered Rotherham and asked the first person we came across where the street was that we were looking for. The man told us that it was not too far away, and after about five more minutes we found it and we wondered what sort of a reception we would get from the girl that Brian had met at the seaside.

We knocked on the door and this big lady answered. "What can I do for you?"

With that Brian chipped in and said, "We're calling on your Sally."

He knew her to be Sally's mum after seeing her at the seaside caravan.

"Well," she said, "Sally has just gone to the shops for me, would you like to come in and wait for her?"

"Yes, please," we replied.

"Come in, would you like a drink of pop and a piece of homemade bacon and egg pie?"

"Yes, please," we eagerly answered.

She seemed a very nice lady, telling us to sit down while she brought us the drink and pie. Just as she came back, in walked Sally who was a bit taken aback to see us sat there. Brian introduced me to her then she told her mum that she had met Brian at the caravan site that they had been to.

When her mum realised how far we had come she said, "There's no way you can go home again today, you can stay here for the night in my son's bedroom, he's away in the forces. Been in the Navy for two years and loved every minute of it."

We thanked her for the offer saying we would love to stay. Once we had eaten Sally said to her mother she was going to take us to meet her friends.

Typically, some of the lads there tried to rub us up the wrong way, one of them in particular was really nasty telling us to "piss off back to where we'd come from."

Sally and a couple of others told us to take no notice of him because he was fond of Sally and was jealous of Brian invading his patch. Anyway he started throwing his weight around and wanted Brian to fight him, I knew that Brian wasn't a fighter so I told this lad to back off and he then turned on me, telling me to mind my own business.

I looked at him and said. "We've not come all this way for trouble, so leave us alone."

But it was not to be, he would not stop and he pushed me in the chest to provoke me. I thought 'This is no good, I'm not going to take this when we have done nothing wrong,' But it was obvious he was not going to go away or give up, so stepping back, as though I was going away, I turned and hit him with a short right hand and knocked him to the floor, blood streaming from his nose.

He got up and ran, shouting abuse at us. Sally's friends said that it was just what he wanted because he would not leave her alone even though she had told him she wanted nothing to do with him. We carried on and all had a great time hanging around together before going back to Sally's for the night. Her mother was very good to us and we were lucky that she let us stay the night in her home.

"Sally has told me to sneak into her room later on when everyone is in bed," Brian said.

"You shouldn't abuse her mother's hospitality like that, she's been very kind to us," I remarked.

This was to no avail, and, as we were to find out, this sort of thing was to cause us problems in the future.

After playing cards for a bit and chatting, we went up to her brother's room leaving Sally and her mother downstairs, we got into bed and reminisced about the events of the day and how much we had enjoyed ourselves.

"I'm tired, it's getting late, let's try to sleep," I said.

"I'm going to stay awake," said Brian, "to see if Sally taps on the door to give the all clear as she goes to bed."

Sure enough, just as I was going to sleep, there was a little tap at the door and Brian crept out. I told him to be careful and be back in the room before anyone got up in the morning. "Don't let Sally's mother catch you because she has been so good to us both."

Anyway I must have fallen into a deep sleep because the next thing I knew Brian was shaking me saying it was time to get up if we were to have an early start back home.

We went downstairs and, fortunately, no one had noticed that Sally and Brian had slept together.

There was a nice smell of fresh bread and bacon from the kitchen as we walked down the stairs. Sally's mum was cooking us breakfast.

"Sit down," she said. She mentioned that she would have liked us to have met her husband but he was working away and would not be back until the weekend.

With that Sally came down and joined us for breakfast, we thanked her mother for the fine food and letting us stay the night.

She said, "That's okay, come again, we have enjoyed you both being here."

Saying goodbye we set off on our journey home content that we had enjoyed ourselves, chatting away as we pedalled along, Brian keen to tell me that he and Sally had slept together but nothing had happened between them.

"Well, you were lucky that Sally's mum didn't catch you both in bed together. That would have spoilt the good time we'd had with Sally and her friends, as well as abusing her mother's kindness towards us," I said.

Leaving it at that, we continued our journey home, happy that we had nearly completed our first real adventure together.

Little did we know that our future destiny lay together and how close we were to become in the years ahead, relying on each other more and more.

~*~

We decided to ride our bikes all the way home without staying the night anywhere, because we had to have the bikes back to Reg otherwise we'd have to pay for an extra day. Again we talked about what we would do when we left school, stopping a few times to raid some more pea fields on the way to give us something to eat.

We were making good progress when it started to get dark and it was now raining heavily, so we decided to stop at the next field and put up the tent just inside the gate away from the road, determined to get up at first light and head home. We soon fell asleep and the night past quickly, before we knew it we were woken by the birds. Packing everything away as fast as we could, determined to get the bikes back on time, the tent was wet through but we would dry it when we got home to stop it rotting away. On our way once more Brian commented, "We've been lucky not to get a puncture, with the state of these nearly bald tyres."

We were tempting fate, but it did give us an idea to say to Reg

8

that we had a flat and had to walk for a few miles. He would buy that, we thought. At least we had brought the bikes back for him, not dumping them like some would. So just before arriving at his yard we stuck a thorn in one of the tyres, hoping he would not charge us for another day.

Looking at us feeling sorry for ourselves, he said, "Okay lads, off you go but don't let it happen again, take some tools with you next time you go a long way."

Next we had to face the music at home. We went to Brian's house first, his mum was pleased to see us back safe and sound, offering to put the tent out to dry before Brian's brother needed to use it again.

"You two look as though you need a bath, here," she said, giving us some money. "Go to the slipper baths."

These were public baths where lots of people, who did not have baths at home, went. We liked going there it was good fun, but before that we decided to go to my house and see what sort of reception we would get there. We were just going down the terrace as my mother was coming out of the house, she shouted, "Where the bloody hell have you two been, get in the bloody house."

We shot into the house hoping that we could sneak out again and go to the baths, we ran in the front door and out the back and down the passage that ran all the way along the row of houses heading for the slipper baths that were four streets away. We were looking forward to having a long soak in a deep bath, well as long as we could, because you were timed.

In we went, Brian paid for the two baths and asked if we could have them next door to each other. The attendant gave us a towel and some soap each and started to fill the baths for us. They were in small cubicles and you had to shout to the attendant for some more hot or cold water, we did this until we had them full to the top. We used to play a game where we would shout 'soap' and toss our piece of soap over the wall to the other and see how many times we were on target. The attendant used to shout at us and tell us to stop mucking about. Fifteen minutes later (and a bit more we got away with) we got dried and dressed then headed back to Brian's to see if we could get something to eat.

His mum gave us a couple of bread cakes each with butter from the bakery in the next street. They were great baked on the bottom of the oven, a bit like a pizza dough of today. We took them in the back yard to eat with a drink of tea she had made for us.

# Chapter 2

In the area where we lived, it was a case of 'don't stray to far from your own territory' as you would sometimes end up in a fight and get a bloody nose for your efforts. That was our problem, we always wanted to go further than we should. It was the start of the wanderlust that was to take over our lives, we often had to run if we thought a situation was more than we could handle.

The good thing about it was that it was always a straightforward fistfight, no kicking or anything else was used. Sometimes it was just one to one and the others stood and watched, and we always used to shake hands afterwards.

After a good summer it was back to school, we liked school because we both played rugby and liked the physical contact of the sport, our school had the best teams in the city for a number of years. The following year we would have to leave school so we had to think of what we wanted to do. I wanted to carry on working for the electrical engineer and Brian was going to work in the local brewery where his brother worked, they paid quite good money.

We finally finished our last year at school with no bother at all and Brian got his job at the brewery and I worked for the electrical engineering firm where the boss had taken a liking to me. As my parents would not let me go to college, I would have to go to night school. I think that I should re-phrase that as it was my mother who would not let me go, I'm sure my father would have been proud for me to do it.

We were still knocking around with a group of girls and boys and one girl in particular was very fond of me. Her father had a building business, she was a great girl and we got on really well together.

Brian and I were counting the months before we could join the forces together. The time eventually came round and we both applied together. We would rush in from work to see if we had any post from the recruiting office and one day, we were filled with joy when we both received the letter to go for selection.

We could not wait as we counted the days before we had to go for the medical, both of us had no doubts about passing, as we were very fit, and true to form we both past with flying colours: 'A1'.

Then it was the interviews, this is where we thought we may get split up, but we decided that, if that was the case, after our basic training, we would apply to be together again.

I was put into the Royal Engineers and Brian into the Royal Signals. We were content with that, at least we had both got in together, though in different regiments. So in a few weeks we were to depart to different parts of the country, me to Farnborough and Brian to Ripon in Yorkshire, which meant I was farthest away.

It was easy for me when the day came to leave home, gathering what few belongings that I had. My mother was not too happy at my going away because she would not get any money or so she thought, but I promised that I would make a money order from my wages for her and that seemed to cheer her up a bit, she even said that she would save a little out of it every week for me when I came home.

The day came round for us both to leave home and we went to the station together before going our separate ways. I had said goodbye to Ann, Elsie and all our friends the night before, and I said to Brian it was a strange feeling to be leaving home but I was excited about it. Brian felt the same and said, "Let's get our basic training out of the way and then apply for another regiment together."

My train came in first and saying goodbye to Brian was probably the worst thing I'd had to do, but we knew that we would meet again soon. I sat on the train and after a while noticed another lad who looked as though he was going into the forces, so I asked him. "Yes, he was," he said his name was Dave and he was going to the same camp as me. We sat together for the journey and we agreed that it was nice to know that we were both from the same city and would be in the same camp together.

After changing trains we arrived at Farnborough, gathering our belongings we left the train to be greeted by a big-mouthed sergeant telling us to form up. That's when we realised that there were other guys who had joined the train to what seemed like hell!

I said to Dave, "I'm determined to stick this out."

"We'll do this together," he said as we both grimaced.

It seemed to give us both a bit of comfort as we looked at each other. 'Big mouth' (the sergeant) then told us to get aboard the truck that was waiting to take us to the camp. He was shouting and screaming at us as we gathered our belongings and got onto the truck which is why we decided to call him 'Mac The Mouth.'

We arrived at the camp and once again heard 'Mac The Mouth' telling us to get off the truck at the double and to line up in twos. This we did with fear in our hearts but we lined up and were marched down to the army stores to collect out kit which was placed in piles for us to gather and take to the billets that we had been allocated to. This was to be our home for the next few weeks and the place where we would get our uniforms and boots up to standard in the time that we were here. It was to be a hard slog for us, turning ourselves into fighting machines who were super fit. Dave and I were pleased that we had been allocated the same billet, it really was good to have someone from the same city, also the fact that we got on so well together in the short time we had known each other.

My thoughts drifted to wondering how Brian was getting on and I hoped that he was okay and that we both would come through to meet up on our first leave after our basic training.

Then we were brought back to reality by 'Mac The Mouth' telling us to start getting our kit in some sort of order. This meant bulling our boots until we could nearly see our faces in the toe cap, and to get the razor sharp creases into the uniforms, we knew that this would take us a few weeks do.

We decided to start on our boots first, this meant burning the toe cap, with a hot spoon warmed on a candle, until it was smooth and gradually rubbing in the polish with some water on a soft cloth, this would take us hours and hours to get the result that 'Mac The Mouth' wanted, he was never satisfied with our efforts.

The next minute he came to tell us to fall in as he was taking us to the mess room for dinner. He took us to the door trying to get us to march in step with each other on the way, but we were a shambles. We went into the mess and selected a table then we went and joined a line to get our meal before sitting back down. As we started to eat, Dave said to me and some of the other guys.

13

"Look at those guys staring at us."

I said they looked as if they have been here a few weeks and were well into their training, we did not make any comments back to them when they called remarks to us.

After dinner we went straight back to the billet and back to the task of getting our kit in some sort of order. We passed the night bulling our boots and chatting away, Dave and I were getting on fine together. 'Mac The Mouth' put his head round the door into the billet and shouted, "Lights out, six o'clock start in the morning." He left saying that he wanted us all in our denim work clothes in the morning, so it was lights out and off to sleep for us all.

It seemed as though we had just gone to sleep when Mac came in and shouted, "Get down to the washrooms and then to breakfast. I want you to be on the parade ground in forty minutes."

This was to become a regular habit. After washing and eating breakfast we formed up on the parade ground. He started by marching us up and down trying to get us in step with each other, shouting and screaming as he did so. We seemed to have two left feet at times but we knew we'd get there in the end. After two hours of square bashing, it was down to the sports hall for some physical training.

The instructor was a nice guy, or he seemed so after 'Mac The Mouth', he asked for volunteers for the boxing team and as Dave and I liked boxing we both volunteered. This was the best thing that we could have done as we were told that we would get special privileges, one being that we were allowed to go running outside the camp, that meant a lot to us: a bit of freedom.

The first week passed and it had not been too bad, we were getting used to it a bit more. Two of the men in our squad had dropped out and gone home, not being able to stand it, but that was because 'Mac The Mouth' never left us alone for more than five minutes it seemed.

The following week we progressed to the shooting ranges, Dave and I were looking forward to this as we both used to go shooting rats at home with air rifles. We were good shots too, as we found out when we got on the range. We became marksmen and received our marksman badges with the 303 Rifle and the Bren gun, these were not easy to get, we were informed so we were proud of ourselves, achieving something on our own.

We also started to represent the regiment at boxing tournaments against other army regiments and also the RAF and the Navy. I must say both myself and Dave were really getting to like the forces, we got a lot out of it as it taught us respect and gave us discipline. The training was becoming easier for us and we were mastering the kit, our boots were also looking good, even 'Mac The Mouth' was mellowing towards us, we started to believe that he was human after all.

We were getting close now to the time of our passing out parade, that meant that we had completed our basic training and we were all looking forward to going home on leave. I was looking forward to seeing Brian and Dave said that he would go out with us when we went home. We both felt so proud when the day came for us to pass out. We all looked good with uniforms pressed to perfection and boots gleaming ready for the march past, this was to be an occasion that would never be forgotten.

Even 'Mac The Mouth' said that we were an example to the new recruits who were watching us and we sure felt very proud that day. We were now ready to be posted to our various regiments and some of us had applied to go on to specialist training.

Dave had decided to do the same as me and I told him that Brian, who he would meet on leave, was doing the same. There were a couple of other lads also who wanted to do the same, but first we had to wait to find out where we would to be posted. Before we went on leave the next day, the list would be put on the board, so that night, we all decided to go out and celebrate our passing out, even 'Mac The Mouth' came out with us. He proved that he was human after all and was really good company. We had come to realise that he had to be the bad guy, as he had to get us into shape in the limited time we had to train.

We all had a great night together, and next morning we went down to the notice board to see where we were to be posted. Dave and I went together apprehensively, but our worries were short-lived as we looked down the list and found that we had both been accepted for parachute training. With a big smile on our faces, I said to Dave, "I just hope that Brian has been given the same posting."

With that good news Dave and I gathered our gear and went to catch the train back to Hull, where we hoped to have some fun with our mates and most of all, I wanted to see Brian and share our adventures with him.

When we finally arrived at our station, I arranged to meet Dave the next day and set off towards home. When I got there I was surprised that everyone was so pleased to see me, but after saying hello I went round to Brian's to see him, being at a camp near home he had arrived the day before.

The first thing I asked him was, "Did you get the posting?" His face lit up, he could not conceal it from me, he did not have to say anything. We were so happy for each other as we sat talking about our training and looking forward to the future together.

I told him that another Hull lad, Dave, was going for the further training with us, and he said he had met a man from Leicester called Trevor and he was going too. At least there would be the four of us who could stick together, and there were two other guys who Dave and I knew from training who were going there too.

Brian said all our pals had gone to the seaside for a few days staying in their parent's chalet, he asked if we should go?

"Yes," I said. "Let's pick Dave up tomorrow and go on the bus."

Next day we met Dave and asked him if he wanted to go with us he said he would love to, so off we went, arriving just in time for the weekend dance at the Pavilion. It was always a good night and there was never too much trouble.

We headed into the Pavilion after walking from the bus and saw that all the girls were sat at one table and some of the guys at another. They all looked happy to see us, and kissed us both as we introduced Dave to them. We were all having a great time until Brian spotted a girl that he had always liked, and made a bee line for her. It was okay for a while, then her ex boyfriend came in and asked Brian in a loud voice, "What the hell you up to with my girl?"

The girl spoke up and said to him, "Your ex girlfriend you mean."

Brian, being very diplomatic, said, "Piss off mate, on your bike."

With that the man went for him and a fight broke out, only this guy's mates went for Brian as well, so, with no hesitation, we all dived in. I hit one bloke as Dave hit another, knocking them both to the floor, and Brian took care of the guy who started it. It was over in a couple of minutes as his other mates just took off and ran out of the place, so it was not much of a skirmish and we just carried on where we had left off.

The night was soon over and the girls asked us if we wanted to stay the night at the chalet. It was that or sleeping on the beach so we said yes.

Ann and Elsie, two of the girls, said it would be okay as their parents were away for a couple of weeks.

There were about eight of us altogether but they said that was fine, so off we went. We played cards half the night before going to bed, Dave, Brain and I shared a bedroom.

Although I had an idea that Ann was fond of me, there was no way that I was going to get tied down with anyone at all. What I wanted was adventure, so really there was no choice, I had made up my mind to enjoy my army life, the last thing I wanted was to get tied up with a woman as I knew it would distract me from what I wanted to do. I know that Ann had feelings for me but I did not lead her on in any way. She was a very nice girl and her dad had pots of money, but my mind was made up.

We all had a lot of fun together before it was time to go back to camp, this time Brian would be coming with Dave and I, Trevor would meet up with us at the camp.

So saying our goodbyes to the girls and our other mates, we set off for the station with just Ann and Elsie who were coming to see us off. Brian whispered to me, "Ann is crazy for you, look at her eyes, she has tears in them for you."

Looking at Ann, I saw the tears, they kissed us goodbye and Ann did tend to linger a little, but I did not want to mislead her, she was a nice girl. She said, "Write soon and come home as soon as you can."

I was committed to the forces and I was determined that nothing would stop me.

The train was ready to pull out as Ann kissed me once more and I could feel the tears on her cheek. Just then the guard blow his whistle and the carriage doors were being slammed shut. We stuck our heads out of the window as the train started to pull out of the station. I shouted to Ann that I would try to get home on leave before we got posted abroad.

Elsie shouted back, "Don't forget me," laughing as she said it.

I continued to wave and so did Dave and Brian until we were out of sight. The three of us sat down and started talking about our leave and what was in front of us, we also had a bit of banter between ourselves. Dave and Brian had a go at me for not taking advantage of Ann, saying that she had the desire for me to love her

I said, "Don't be stupid, how could I be myself in the forces with someone at home waiting for me?"

We teased each other as Dave said, "She would not have to ask me twice." And Brian said the same.

But it was all good natured fun, even though I knew they meant it. We arrived at our station and got a cab to the camp, a bit different from the last time.

~*~

We were beginning to build up a real friendship with each other and we were to find out in the following years that we would need to depend on each other more and more.

We thought that this training would be a little easier for us, now we knew what to expect from basic training, and that would help us get through the extra physical part that we were to endure. We all knew that this was going to be hard, both on our bodies, and the mental aspect of it.

We met up with Trevor and he seemed a nice guy, he was pleased to have someone he knew with him, having done his basic training with Brian, it would help us all through the difficult days ahead, without mates it could be very lonely.

Our living quarters were allocated to us and we were all in the same billet. We settled in okay because everyone was in the same boat having just come from different regiments. It was fairly relaxed on our first day, we just sat around or strolled round the camp finding our way about as we all got to know each other. We chatted about our different aims, saying that we hoped we'd all come through it and stay together. There were another couple of guys in our billet who we got on well with, called Robert and Tony.

After we had settled in the Sergeant, who was going to take us through our training, came and explained what would be expected of us. He wanted total commitment he said, then we would all get on great together, we assured him that he would get that from us.

He then said, "Anyone who has second thoughts, declare it now and don't waste my time."

No one spoke so he said, "Good, that's that out of the way."


We were all really excited about the training which would include parachuting, weapon training and general survival. We were up for this and determined to give it our best shot.

Next day we set off on an early morning, ten mile route march, but we were fit from our basic training and that helped us. This was to become regular fitness and survival training for the next four to five weeks before we started our parachute training. We all enjoyed the training and went down to the shooting ranges on a regular basis, at least we were doing something that we all enjoyed, our level of fitness was getting better and our shooting skills were excellent. This was a really exciting time for us all.

After three weeks our fitness was reaching levels that we never envisaged we could achieve, feeling really good about ourselves, the tempo was building up for us as we progressed to survival and self defence techniques. This meant that we would be taken in a lorry to Dartmoor and left to find our own way back, staying out for three nights in the first instance. This was going to be a tough task as, at this time of the year, it was very cold and damp at night, but this was to build up our friendship and reliance on each other, as well as self survival, if the need arose.

Our first priority was to find somewhere to sleep for the night so we split into two groups. Dave and Robert found a place that had a few rocks we could use to build a fireplace so that we could have a hot drink and something to eat before we turned in for the night. As the fire started burning well, the night was pulling in fast, we all sat around mulling over the training ahead and the need to build up our respect for each other's skills. We would need these in a big way in the future.

The night was clear as we fell asleep under the stars. Next morning, we were awakened by the birds, we lit a fire, or should I say Dave did, and we had our breakfast as we studied the maps to find the right direction to go across the moors. It started to rain so we packed up and set off, we were all in good spirits, laughing and joking as we made our way. Trevor said, "Let's trap some rabbits tonight and we can roast them for dinner."

It was surprising how well we were bonding together. It was so desolate walking in the rain and we had been going for about ten miles when we decided to set up camp for the day, Trevor and Brian went off to set snares near to some rabbit runs. The rest of us started to build a fire and gather the driest twigs and moss that we could find. Trevor was the best map reader among us so we left that to him, although we would all have to have a go at it. We were all a little dirty but the support and encouragement that we had for each other was great.

We hoped that Trevor and Brian had caught some rabbits, or it would be the corned beef again, after an hour they arrived back with big smiles on their faces and two rabbits, we all cheered and Dave gutted and skinned them and set them to roast on the fire that was burning brightly now.

The rabbit tasted great washed down with a pot of tea, they had reset the snares hoping for more in the morning. With just a couple of nights to go, and hoping that it would clear up for us, we sat chatting about many things including women. Dave said, "Look how warm we would be if we had women to snuggle up to for the night."

Robert laughed, "Dave, is that all you think about?"

"Brian is just as bad," I replied.

Trevor said, "Yes, you should have been with us on our basic training, when we got out of the camp for a night. Brian takes some beating with the women."

Tony had fallen asleep and the rest of us decided to turn in as well.

The next day we cleaned up the camp and buried all our rubbish, before setting off once more. We had decided to move right on to the pick up point, it was a long trek, but as the weather had picked up, we did not mind at all. On the way we found the snares which had three rabbits in them.

Tony said, "I feel bloody dirty and need a hot shower."

"Well at least we have that to look forward to," replied Robert.

The night was closing in and we started to get a bit weary so Trevor said we should do another mile and that would do for today. We looked for a suitable spot to spend the night and get the rabbits cooked, picking up some twigs and stuff for the fire as we made our way along. After half a mile we found a decent spot and stopped for the night. Exhausted, we lit a fire as Dave skinned the three rabbits and cleaned them as best he could. We were getting low on water so Trevor and I went for a walk and found some which had gathered in a hole after the rain. We filled our Billy cans, taking them back to boil up and then wash the rabbits before we roasted them. Dave remarked how good roast rabbit tasted and we all agreed with him.

It was the last night and we all thought that we had done well together, knowing that this exercise was just a taste of what was coming for us. After spending the night on Dartmoor we set off for the pickup point that was only twenty minutes away. Sure enough as we approached the spot there was a truck waiting for us and the Sergeant said to us, "Well done lads."

The easy part was now out of the way, but we were proud of what we had done and looked forward to the next task put in front of us.

~*~

The Sergeant said that we could have a weekend leave and a rail warrant, if we wanted to go home. Dave, Brian and I asked the others what they were doing and they all said going home, so we collected what we wanted to take with us and caught the train home.

Arriving there we said goodbye to Dave, who lived in another part of town, and set off home, looking forward to seeing our friends and having a night on the town. After quickly saying hi to everyone at home, we went round to see Ann and Elsie and Ann's mother invited us all to dinner. Her Dad said. "It's been very quiet round here without you two around."

Her Mum said she had missed us both and Elsie said, "and so have I."

We had a nice dinner and after thanking Ann's mum and dad we decided to get a bus into town to meet up with Dave, sure enough he was there with a nice looking girl on his arm. After the introductions, we went into a dance hall for a drink and finding a table for six, settled down to have a good time, it felt great to be together again, all laughing and having a great time.

The night passed quickly and we decided to walk home together, Ann had told Dave and his girlfriend they could stay at her house if they wanted, so they came with us. When we finally got there we decided to have a drink and a game of cards.

Elsie said, "Why don't you each get a permanent girlfriend, then you will have someone to write to?"

"Nice try, Elsie," I said, "but I will get you someone to write to."

There was no way I was going to get tied down with anyone, I loved the army too much.

"Good, do that," she answered with a tone in her voice that said she was not happy with that answer.


Ann's Mum and Dad treated me like a son they were so very good to me, and Ann was a nice girl but I would not get involved at all. Turning in for the night, the girls slept in Ann's room and the guys had a room each. The next day Ann's father said we could borrow his car and we all went for a ride. It was a good day out at the coast and on the way back we dropped Dave and his girlfriend off with a: "See you tomorrow at the station". Then we set off to Ann's for the rest of the day. We had one night left and decided to stay in and have a drink and play cards together as we had to catch an early train.

Next day Ann's dad said that he would run us to the station and the girls came with us.

Ann said, as she kissed me goodbye, "Write to me, please."

I replied that I would when I could.

Elsie came across and kissed both Brian and I saying, "take care of yourselves."

Ann's dad shook mine and Brian's hand, telling the girls he would wait for them at the car.

Dave, with his girlfriend, arrived just as the guard started to close the carriage doors, so we dived on the train and dropped the windows to say goodbye once more to the girls. I waved to Ann and could see the tears in her eyes as the train pulled out of the station. It was going to be the last time we came home for a long while, but this is what we wanted, it was the adventure that we had been looking forward to. We just hoped that we could stay together as we got on so well with each other. Sleeping on the way we soon arrived back and caught a cab to camp.

Dave and Brian said that they had enjoyed the weekend as we walked into the NAAFI, Trevor and the others were already there, the place was pretty full. We had a game of darts and a few drinks looking forward to our training starting again. We all knew that it was going to get tough from now on.

# Chapter 3

The next day we had to go for another medical to see if we were up to the next lot of training. We wished each other luck, we needed it because, after the tests, we found out that about ten men had been sent back to their original regiments, but all the men that we knew well had got through. It was now going to be really tough for us, as we were to find out in the next few weeks.

Later we were told that we were to go to Wales for some training and were to live in tents for a couple of weeks. Trevor and Brian grumbled that this was going to be rough on us, we had to learn all the basic skills and, at the same time, develop our fitness. Arriving back at camp exhausted, after being out for hours with our packs on our backs, sore and stiff from going down the mountain paths time and time again. It seemed as though we were only having a couple of hours sleep a night, it passed so fast, but we were becoming fitter and fitter as the time went on.

The physical and mental fatigue was really getting to us all now and we wondered how much longer we could stand it. A couple of the guys decided that they'd had enough and could take no more as it was so draining on the bodies resources, and they went back to their original regiments.

Brian said to us one day that he did not know how much longer he could keep it up. We all said we felt just the same, he was not alone and we were all in the same boat. This made him feel a little better, knowing that he was not on his own in this. Our friendship was getting very strong and we helped each other get through the days and nights. At least in a few days we were to move on to the ranges to do some weapon training and general survival techniques, this helped us through the rest of the fitness programme that savaged our bodies.

~*~

We were told that we would be split into small groups of six and were to compete against each other, this was to push each team into giving their best and where we'd begin to come together as a team. We were also going to learn demolition skills. We were on the moors next day practicing our survival and field craft, it was all really exciting now, as we were expanding on our training into other fields which was going to be our work in the future. All this was what we wanted to do, even with the demand on mind and body.

That particular day we were going to learn how to catch small game, in between punishing our bodies once more, we were all quite sure that they were trying to break us down as we were out from early morning until late at night. It was taking its toll on us both mentally and physically, but we were determined to carry on getting fitter and fitter as we went along.

The days went by and we were then told that we had to try to avoid a group of men who had been put in the area to try and capture us, this was going to be our first real test. We were dropped off in a nearby wooded area and were told that we had to make the checkpoint without getting captured if possible, we would be given points for every man who got back. So we decided to split up thinking that maybe then we had a better chance of getting more men back without them being captured, spreading ourselves out we all wished each other luck.

I headed off as fast as I could, hoping that they would not expect me to make such good progress, but I soon realised that I was being foolish because, if this was real combat, I would not be able to do this as the enemy could be just anywhere, but this was different and I guessed you would have to treat each mission as it came. I carried on, as I was making good ground but just at that moment, I caught a movement to my right. Rolling to my left behind a fallen tree, it turned out to be a couple of the men who were looking for us. I lay there in silence watching them from beneath the tree as they moved on, not expecting anyone to have gotten that far just yet. Once they were out of sight I proceeded with caution, stopping every few minutes to listen for breaking twigs or any sort of movement. I was lucky and made good progress, looking at my map and getting my bearings, I reckoned that I had about four miles to go and hoped that I could make it without getting caught. Just at that moment a couple of birds were disturbed just in front of me, I froze and hid behind a tree waiting for what seemed like an eternity, then a man came straight towards me, I did not move as I peered through the leaves towards him as he approached me, I was hoping that I could claim him and take his lanyard rather than him take me. He walked within five feet of me, not noticing my presence, I waited while he had gone by and I crept behind him and stuck my rifle in his back claiming him as my first victim.

I felt so good about it when he said that he had no idea that I was there. I took his lanyard to prove that I had claimed a kill, and left him, as he now had to drop out and return to the checkpoint. I followed behind knowing that he was not allowed to tell anyone that I was there.

Arriving at the checkpoint with no further incidents, I handed in my lanyard to claim my kill, there were a couple of guys there who had been captured. I got a mug of tea and lay back against a tree waiting for the others to arrive back, a couple more came in who had been captured, then, with a big smile on his face, in came Brian, I gave him a big cheer as he joined me with a mug of tea and we sat waiting for the rest of them.

Dave came in next having been captured just as he was approaching the checkpoint. Following him were Trevor and Tony, they'd avoided capture and we cheered them in, along with a few more guys from other teams, who had also escaped. We were just waiting for Robert but unfortunately he had been caught, so we came joint second with another team, we didn't think that was too bad.

This went on for a few weeks more, training and more training. We had to admit we were all becoming very focused on what we were doing and most of all, we were mentally and physically at our peak of fitness.

~*~

Our weapons training was great, we had to make all shots count and learn how to take care of our weapons. Brian and I were two of the best shots in the groups and we were very proud of that, we were told that we could have a weekend pass but could only go into the town nearby.

The next four or five weeks we were to concentrate on our parachute training after which we all decided to go into the town together because it was known that the local guys did not like us talking to their girls. This was a pattern that had gone on for years as these super fit soldiers were a great attraction to the local girls. Well, all done up to the nines in slacks and short sleeve shirts, we felt good going into town, when we arrived at the local dance hall it was heaving with girls and a good few guys, but it looked as though there were more girls tonight. We said to each other, as long as we leave the attached girls alone, we should not have any trouble. We all split up and sat at different tables and the six of us got a table to ourselves in one corner. Dave and I went to the bar to get the drinks for the rest. It was tactical thinking, as we were always thinking about covering our backs everywhere we went, this was to become part of our lives, thinking about everything that we did and always being one step ahead.

We sat chatting to each other as we all scanned the unattached talent in the room. A group of girls who were on their own came over and joined us so we made room round the table and pulled some chairs round for them. We were having a great time, up and down with the girls and a good banter going on between us all. It got to about eleven o'clock when a group of about ten guys came in looking worse for wear, they must have been round the pubs. Brian had gone to get some drinks just as they came in and one of the guys said, "That is my ex girlfriend that you are with," and Brian said, "Yes that is what she is: your ex."

'Poor Brian, caught out again," I thought.

Just then the guy took a swing at Brian, knocking all the drinks over and catching him on the cheek.

The floor cleared quickly as people got out of the way. We sat there and watched as Brian took a step back and hit him with a short blow to the jaw, he went down like a sack of spuds. With that we had to react fast as all the guy's mates were moving in on Brian to give him a good hiding, or so they thought, as we all dived in picking one each first, and then taking the others as they came. We moved so fast it was all over in minutes and the floor was littered with bodies, the rest of them took to their feet and scurried away out of the place. As we picked up the tables and chairs that had been knocked over, the owner came up and said, "Carry on guys, enjoy the rest of the night."

He apologised for the trouble we'd had and told us that they were always causing problems. With that he replaced our drinks for us and we went on to have a good night with the girls. Brian and Dave were trying to get the two girls, they had latched on to, to let them take them home and we all knew what that meant, sex was overruling their brains, but still tonight it would not cause them too much trouble we thought.

Eventually Dave and Brian won the girls over and took them home, we decided to walk the rest of the girls home as they lived in the same street. We had a good chat to each other as we walked through the night then they gave us all a goodnight kiss, asking if they would see us next weekend?

We said, "If we are allowed out, yes sure."

Arriving back at camp at about three in the morning we were soon in our billets and fast asleep. The next morning we had not heard Brian or Dave come in and, looking at their untouched beds, we guessed that they must have struck lucky and stayed with the girls, we knew that we would meet up with them later in the day somewhere.

After a good shower we all went down to the NAAFI for something to eat and a game of pool or darts, just to pass the day before we went out again that night. Trevor said to the three of us, "Shall we go early and eat out before we go to the dance hall?"

So we went to a little restaurant near the dance hall, Tony and Trevor went and found a table, while we went to the boy's room, then we had a decent meal together before going into the dance hall to, hopefully, meet up with Dave and Brian.

When Robert and I went to the bar to get the drinks, the owner said to us, "Welcome back lads, I know that you will not start trouble." he was right we were very disciplined and would only react to protect ourselves.

Sitting at the same table as the night before, we could observe all who came into the place, we had been there about an hour when in walked some of the girls who were with us the night before. They said, as they pulled up their chairs that their two friends and ours would be in soon.

Tony whispered, "They must have got their feet under the table then."

Thirty minutes later, in walked Dave and Brian with big smiles on their faces and the two girls on their arms. We found out that one of the girl's parents had gone away for a few days so the four of them had gone to her house.

We were all having a great time together as we got on so well, and the night passed by without any trouble at all. We were so pleased that we were having a good weekend so far, that we arranged to meet the girls the next day and all go into the countryside to have a bit of fun, play games in general and just lounge around together. The night was over and Dave and Brian were going back to the girl's house they said they would meet up with us about lunchtime next day.

Meeting in the square the following day, it was a pleasure not to be laden down with full equipment.

We found a place that the girls had pointed out to us near to a small stream and, settling down, chatted away to each other. It was so peaceful, between games of soccer and cricket, the day passed quickly and it was goodbye to the girls and back to camp for us.

We all remarked on what a good few days we had enjoyed and that we were all relaxed and ready for the parachute training that was to come. We were all really looking forward to the training as things were getting easier for us as we got stronger both mentally and physically. We were adapting well to our new life in a positive way even though a lot of the men had fallen by the wayside.

In between the parachute training we were going to go through an interrogation programme that was not for the faint hearted and very scary to say the least. Unfortunately, one man who we had taken to, in one of the other groups, had hit a rock on a parachute drop and broken his leg, so that was the end of Mike's participation in the course, he would have to join a later one if he could, we all felt sorry for him because he was a nice guy but there was nothing that anyone could do.

Before finishing the course we had made some drops at night and also under fire, Trevor said that he had overheard that we were to go to the Far East to do some real survival work and jungle training. We'd never ever dreamed that we would be going there, and we were really looking forward to it. Trevor turned out to be right as we were told to go and pick up our tropical gear and report to the medical officer for our injections which were to be spread over a few days.

Two weeks later we were taken to an airfield and boarded a Royal Air Force Hastings aircraft for the Far East, stopping at various locations on the way. The first one being Italy then on to Habbania in Iraq and then Ceylon, this was where we were to stay for some training in the hot, sweaty jungle.

When we alighted from the plane, our clothes just stuck to us, we were taken to some British barracks near to the airfield, we were lucky as Dave and Tony had spotted a swimming pool for the service personnel and after being given our rooms, we were told that we could have a couple of days to acclimatise to the area. With that we all decided to go for a dip in the pool, as usual I wanted to be first in, but what a shock, as I dived in I felt as if I could not breath, the water was so hot! I struggled to the surface, it was overpowering to say the least. I tried not to show that there was anything wrong as I came to the surface and swam to the edge of the pool, this was so that the rest would just dive in and have the pleasure of my experience also. I watched as they all dived in together and then all came up gasping for air as I was sat there laughing at them.

Brian said, "You bastard."

They headed for me and chased me only for all five of them to get my legs and arms, carry me to the edge of the pool, and heave me right into the middle for another dose of the sauna which is what it felt like. But as usual it was all in good fun, and later we just lay around the pool teasing the scorpions with twigs from the trees. We did some silly things at times.

As the night came in on us, we decided to go to the mess room and bar for food and drinks.

We were soon stacking away the cool beer, not realising the strength of the local brew. Feeling under the influence, we decided to go to bed, not forgetting to pull our mosquito nets over us to save getting bitten to death as we were watching the small lizards running up the walls.

Next morning we went for breakfast and realised what a nice little posting this was for the RAF personnel who were based here, it seemed a nice relaxed camp. Unfortunately, we were not going to be staying there for too long, and the time that we would spend there would not be all taking it easy because we had work to do, but at least when we came back we would have these relaxed facilities.

We were going to be 'blooded' in a big way and the games were over for us, so after relaxing for a couple of days the real work started as we were taken into the jungle and had to find our way back without being spotted by the observers. This may have seemed like fun, but it certainly was not, with the map readings that we had been given, and having to hack our way through dense bamboo and undergrowth, also there were very swampy areas where leeches stuck to you wherever they could get a hold. The weight of our clothes and kit hindered us and we could hear all sorts of eerie sounds around us. It was so humid as we made our way back to the air force base.

After a few hours Tony said, "I can't go on much farther, I am bushed,"

Trevor replied, "If I am right there's only a few hundred yards to go before we hit the edge of the camp."

Good old Trevor, we all cheered as we came to a break in the dense undergrowth. This was our first day, and it had been made easy for us, or so we were told, we all looked a sorry sight covered in mud and wet through.

So, we had arrived back utterly exhausted from our short trip and just wanted to get out of our clothes, shower and go for some food and a few beers. When we went into the mess room some of the Royal Air Force guys, who were sat near to us, said that they could not understand why we wanted to torture our bodies so much. We just shrugged our shoulders and said this was what we had chosen to do.

We all then had a few drinks together and one of the young girls who was serving in the bar brought us some more drinks over, Robert said, "Look at Brian, drooling over her and Dave's not to far behind."

At that we all laughed and the RAF guys said that the girls were out of bounds to us, not that anyone would tell you guys.

Brian put his arm round her and told her to get a drink for herself and sit down. He really was the limit as, within two minutes, his hands were all over her.

Tony said he felt sorry for her but Robert said, "Don't be, look at her, she seems to be enjoying the attention that she's getting."

Dave was also trying to chat up one of the other girls. After a few drinks and playing cards we decided to turn in for the night leaving Brian and Dave in the mess chatting to the young girls.

On the way to our huts we sat on the edge of the jungle on a fallen tree just listening and marvelling at the sounds of the jungle, gazing into the night sky it was so warm and the stars seemed so bright as we sat there wondering what was in store for us all in the future.

Just then Brian walked by with the young girl hanging onto his arm, followed by Dave with another one, like two lambs to the slaughter. We had been warned about mixing with the girls but it 'would have been easier talking to the tree in front of us,' Trevor said with a laugh.

As we walked by their huts there was not a sound, just the magic of the jungle night. Saying goodnight to each other we all turned in.

Morning came round too fast, it was heaving down with rain as I headed towards the mess knocking on the doors as I passed. When I came to Brian's hut there was no answer, same with Dave's. Trevor was nearly ready and Robert and Tony had already gone to breakfast.

The mud was thick as we made our way to the mess and the rain did not look like stopping. Then we heard a shout and there was Brian and Dave, trying to catch us up, both of them just in a pair of shorts. We all entered the mess together, wondering what was in store for us today. Whatever we had to do that day would not be very pleasant, as the rain had brought the mosquitoes out in force, buzzing about in the damp and humid air. Going into the mess we sat down with Robert, Tony and a couple of the RAF guys, they loved to talk to us and asked what we were doing today as they manned the airfield.

First, we all had to listen to Brian and Dave's version of last night with the girls.

The RAF guys said that they would be in big trouble if they were caught with the girls who worked at the camp, but Brian and Dave did not care, and it was like talking to a bloody brick wall where women were concerned. We all said that one day it would get them both into big trouble, but they just laughed and said that they were too careful. I suppose that's life, it would not do for us all to be the same.

We finished breakfast and went to get changed into our kit and were told that we were to build some hides today, we were to create somewhere to vanish into in the jungle, a den, invisible to the human eye. This was to be a life saver to us in the future we were to find out. We were all given two hours to go into the jungle and create this den before they came looking for us.

It was bloody hard going as we made our way in, and we said that we would work in twos and break off at intervals to create our lairs. First two off were Tony and Robert, followed by Dave and Trevor, leaving Brian and me, the last two to break to make our lair. After finding what we thought was a good area in which to build our den, just away from the track we had been travelling on, we decided that this was the spot for us. It was like a small hollow in the ground and we thought with good covering it would be the best we could do. Making sure that the moss and undergrowth that we wanted was taken well away from the den because that would be a dead give away. The leeches and scorpions were a real nuisance to us as we gathered the stuff to cover our hide with. We laid our groundsheets in the hole in the ground then we fashioned some branches that we had trimmed off to form a structure to lay the moss and undergrowth over, being careful to get a good mix of healthy looking and dead moss we laid it over the branches. The finished product looked good to us and there was just enough room to crawl under it but before that we dragged a branch over the ground hoping that would clear any footprints that we had made. We also disturbed some ground about a hundred yards away to make it look as if we had gone further into the jungle making a big circle back to the den we crawled in and waited for them to come and find us, both of us looking different ways through the small gaps in the undergrowth we had made to observe anyone who came by.

The jungle around us had some magical sounds but was a very dangerous place to be. Brian started to tell me about the good time he'd had with the young girl the night before as we knew it would be a good while before anyone reached the point where we had chosen to hide. He said she was coming back again that night, he was just out of this world where women was concerned, everything else took second place. I told him that if he was not careful his luck would run out but he did not say a word.

As we lay there talking in low voices I said, "I hope that the rest of the guys have concealed themselves well."

It was getting near to the time that we thought they would arrive around the area so we decided to be silent as we looked out into the steaming jungle around us not daring to move a muscle as we lay listening for breaking twigs.

It was not long before they came along, chatting away to each other, as we lay so still and silent. Our breathing seemed so loud as they passed us by and we heard one say 'they may have gone further on than this so we will go on for a bit longer then work our way back and spread out'. It was a relief even though they had not stopped near to us. It seemed like an eternity before we spotted them coming back prodding the ground, looking for disturbed undergrowth, as they spread out. They were very well drilled in the search but they were still a good way from us and there was a time limit of three hours on them finding any of us, after that we could all come out, feeling great that we had not been found, hopefully, and beating the challenge. They were now getting a bit too close for comfort and we dare not move a muscle, one of them got so close we could only see his legs. We were on tender hooks hoping that he did not walk over us because that would be it. As he headed our way the heat and humidity was getting to us in the small space that we had made. We were trembling at the thought of him being there and realised that, if it had been the enemy, we would have been dead ducks if we did not move fast and take them all out. But this was a different ball game for us, it was a relief to know that all we had to do was not be found.

We were lucky as he walked about three feet from where we were concealed in the undergrowth, then he began to walk away out of sight. Still not daring to move we looked and listened not knowing if they were hiding, thinking that we may come out once they had passed us, but we were disciplined and did not move.

About another hour had passed when we heard the whistle to say time was up and we could not wait to get out of there and head back to camp, to be congratulated by the captain in charge of the training programme for not getting caught. Unfortunately Dave and Trevor had been found, but Tony and Robert had evaded capture, so in all we did pretty well for a first time with many more to come in different circumstances.

It was great to get into the showers and we must have lost a couple of pounds in weight stuck under the cover in that sort of heat and humidity, but the shower made up for that, it felt good as we burned a few leeches off each other. This was good for team building and the comradeship between us was getting as good as it could ever be between men, it needed to be, as we were to need each other in the next few years, helping each other and giving support when in trouble. It was imperative for us to be a team with no weak links, yet also, to be able to survive on our own in dangerous situations. This was to become part of our lives together.

# Chapter 4

After our shower we decided to go eat and drink in the RAF bar, having a game of cards and darts after our meal. Brian and Dave were thinking of other things because they were not concentrating on what they were doing, trying to get the attention of the little waitresses but there were a good few in that night so they were very busy.

Trevor said, "Give them a chance, they will be over later when it dies down."

They brought us some drinks over and Dave had his hands all over his girl, she kissed him on the cheek and went back to serve others, Brian's girl was at the other end of the bar smiling across at him, so we all continued to have a few drinks and enjoy our game of cards, passing the night away. Later we decided to turn in and headed out of there, leaving Dave and Brian to wait for the two girls to finish for the night.

We had a busy day tomorrow learning about small explosives and other skills that we would need in our movement around the world, our resilience and physical condition was to be paramount, as was our mental condition, all was going to have to be second to none by the time that we had finished our training. Once again it was team building that would carry us through even though we were able to work alone in certain instances.

Going outside into the night we sat, once again, to watch the stars, this was becoming a habit for us, the music of the jungle around us was really an experience. We talked about what we thought we would be doing in six months time after we'd finished our training. I thought of everyone at home and said aloud,

"I'll have to write some letters as I've received many from various people."

Most of the letters were from Ann and Elsie but I still refused to get tied down with anyone. After chatting and daydreaming for about an hour we all decided to turn in for the night, it was easy getting to sleep even though it was very hot and sticky and you could hear the mosquitoes buzzing around you.

After a good night's sleep we met up at breakfast then we went to pick up some gun cotton, plastic explosive and fuses, we were to be trained in causing a distraction but not a great deal of damage, that would come later when we'd also be doing some demolition.

We assembled together with others and split into groups to be given different tasks to do, Brian and Robert said; 'this sounds good,' as we were told that we had to prepare for a quick raid on a rebel post.

Our group was to cause a distraction and another group go in to rescue some prisoners and then we would swap roles. So we set about laying charges on short fuses just as the other group rushed into the makeshift camp to rescue the prisoners. We had to wait for the command and the timing had to be spot on so that everyone moved at the same time as we set the fuses off, we then took up positions to cover the men who had gone in to rescue the prisoners. We hoped that we would be successful in this mission even though it was a mock one for us we treated it as the real thing.

The charges went off at the right time and the guys rushed in and out with the prisoners with great speed and an element of surprise, this was as near to the real thing as we could get. The adrenalin was running high and the hidden strength was coming out. We reformed and the captain assessed how it had gone in all departments. He said that it had gone well, seeing as how it was our first encounter of that sort and he was very happy with the way we had conducted ourselves. We had done remarkably well and he was proud of us all, with this we all felt as though the team spirit we had been working on had shown through in our performance and we were happy with that.

This part of the training was very fulfilling for us and it was the best part so far in our taste of army life, this was partly due to the comrades we had made, being like one big family together, helping each other through the days, and every task being a shared one as we had to trust each other with our lives as the training got more intense.

~*~

Next we were to do some night drops in the jungle and that was to be a daunting exercise for us having also to find our way back to the camp from the drop zone. Each and every one of us would have a job to do this time, I was covering the guys from the front, so that meant that I had to go ahead and make sure it was all clear. Even though we were just on an exercise we had to live the part of the real thing so all the caution and planning had to be right. With limited food and water, we were dropped from a small aircraft into the jungle in full camouflage to blend in with the undergrowth. It was really exciting and it was a big responsibility for me because there would be people in there trying to ambush us as we tried to make our way back. I had my rifle ready and kept away from the tracks as much as I could, even though it took a little longer, we were in radio contact with each other.

As I took five minutes to gather my thoughts, I observed a movement further up the track to my left.

Looking as far as I could through my binoculars, I spotted three men laying in wait for us. So leaving a marker pointing at the men, as we had agreed to do, I proceeded round them hoping that I was quiet enough not to be caught because we were told to try to get back without having to take anyone out if possible. In other circumstances yes, I would have attempted to do this, but hopefully I had no need to.

As I got clear of these guys I radioed back to say that I had placed a marker pointing at the men who were waiting, telling our men to go to the right, round them and follow in my tracks using the markers I had left. I had gone about another half mile when I caught a flash of light in the distance, so I stopped, got out my binoculars and scanned the area ahead, searching the tree tops for any sort of movement. Slowly going backwards and forwards scanning the trees, I observed a movement about three hundred yards away. Keeping my binoculars on the tree, after about ten minutes my suspicion was confirmed, as, all of a sudden, the man moved to get himself more comfortable and gave me a clear view. I did not think it would be appropriate to leave a marker as he was high up and had a pretty good view of all below him, so I dropped my kit and proceeded with just my rifle all the way around crawling for what seemed an eternity. I stealthily came up behind him and got within ten feet of him as he was concentrating on the other direction. I stood up and said to him "I claim this kill." pointing my rifle at his head as I did so. He had no opportunity to do anything else but to come down and give me his lanyard as evidence that I had claimed the kill. This was great I had enjoyed it.

I worked out that we must still have about ten miles to go and we would have to get more vigilant as we went on through the jungle, also as we were to meet up in ten minutes I decided to wait where I was, because there was a good bit of cover but still a good view towards the tracks.

About fifteen minutes had passed when I spotted the men heading my way, I had kept very quiet, watching and listening to the sounds around me, as I thought of home and all my mates, male and female, and wondered what they all would be doing. Mind you I didn't miss being at home as I was so into this life that I had chosen for myself. Shortly, the guys came up to me as I signalled to them it was all clear.

Trevor said, "we may as well have something to eat and drink here as the guy who was to cover this area has been taken out."

Brian had been covering the rear so he was about five minutes after the others, we all hoped that we would succeed today. This sort of training was to go on for a few days yet and we would change roles as we pushed on through the jungle. We were to go on and try all the different terrains. We really were becoming a formidable force and we had a physical and mental fitness to be proud of, that would help us through the conflicts that we may have to deal with in the future. We were all becoming honed to as near perfection as we could and all of us felt good about ourselves.

So we were halfway there in our quest to be the best and be there for each other, we were to have lots more training in many different techniques, it was hard but we were really getting used to it with the fitness and mental strengths carrying us forward and helping us achieve our aims.

~*~

Making our way onwards to the camp we had swapped roles, with Trevor taking up the front and me the rear. It seemed as if we had taken the right option by staying away from the main tracks as we proceeded onwards. I was glad that Trevor had taken over from me, at least now I just had to watch the rear and as we had just passed through it I hoped that everything was clear, unless someone was waiting to get to the rear of us and take us from behind.

Hoping that this would not be the case, I still kept very vigilant as we were covering the ground a little faster it seemed. Just when I thought everything was going well, I heard an explosion in the distance and Brian came scurrying back to tell me that Dave had set off a trip wire and that would alert whoever was out there that we were around. Catching up to the rest, Trevor had come back to see if anyone needed help, and thinking quickly, we decided to cross the track from where the explosion had gone off and make our way steadily to the left hoping that we would not be seen. Lady luck was on our side for sure, as we made very good progress and no one had caught us as we entered the boundary of the camp. The captain was waiting to congratulate us all as we came in, saying, "Well done, once again I am proud of you all, you are becoming quite a team."

Brian and Trevor said 'into the showers guys' and that is where we headed after having a de-briefing session on how we had done.

In the de-briefing room we were told that we would be having a few more days here in the Royal Air Force camp before moving on. The next two days and nights would be spent finding out how we would stand up to a night in the jungle with no cover. This was going to be a test for us as we had to lay out and observe a make shift rebel camp, set up for the purpose, for two days and nights. The men that were in the camp were not going to be told that we were coming but had to be alert at all times as this was also part of their training.

We would have to observe and come back with details of all their movements, day and night, as if they were a real rebel camp where we would have to take and kill everyone in it. We would have to find out how many men were in the camp or around it before we could take it over quietly with minimum casualties to us. With that, we all headed towards the showers.

The next day we had an early start, heading towards our objective. This was going to be an uncomfortable couple of nights for us but very relevant to our training. Not having to travel far but in a different direction to where we had been before, the six of us were so clued up to each other's personalities now that it was an asset to us as we accepted each other for what we were.

Trevor said we had better be quiet now as we had about a mile to go and did not want to make anyone aware of us coming towards them. The camp was set up in a clearing and we decided to break into twos so we could watch each side of the camp. Brian and I went one side, Trevor and Robert another and Tony and Dave would take up the rear, there was plenty of cover around so we quietly found a decent bit where we would have a full view yet could not be seen.

Brian and I lifted a clump of undergrowth that we had spotted and, putting our groundsheet down, thought we had a decent hide. This was going to be a long drawn out exercise but essential for us all. We had enough rations to last us about three days if we were sparing with them, as we observed the comings and goings at the camp, making sure that we did not miss anyone but at the same time not counting people twice.

The first day was okay and as night closed in on us we looked at the men sat around a fire and counted about twelve of them, as we didn't know how many were in the huts as yet, we looked for ways of identifying them so as not to count them twice.

They did not sit out long and disappeared into their huts for the night, that was our sign to get our heads down and try to get some sleep, the next day we observed them coming and going and the same the following night. We were very wet and aching like hell from lying in the damp so we decided that we had seen enough to pull out of the area. We went unobserved by the men in the camp as we left, reporting back that there were at least fifteen guys there. The next day we were told to go back and destroy the camp and everyone in it using blanks of course, so after having a good night in the canteen and a good sleep in a comfortable bed, we then headed into the jungle using the rifles that were to become our live or die friends.

The Colt MI6 was one such rifle and the Browning hand gun was to be another weapon that we were to use and have as part of our body. The weapon that I loved the most was the sniper rifle l96A1, this was both light and accurate up to about three thousand feet, I just felt at home with it and it was to become my friend and companion in the years to come. I loved to use this weapon and always had my leather lace to hold it still near to a tree or anywhere that I could attach it to. The Colt MI6 was to be used in general jungle fighting but my little baby was for sniper duties.

So in the next week we had shot off so many rounds in practice we were unable to count them. Brian, Trevor and I were mainly to use the sniper rifles as we were by far the most accurate shots, also it was about supporting each other, that was the team work coming through. We all had our strengths and weaknesses but together we became a team. It was surprising how far Dave, Brian, Trevor, Robert, Tony and I had come, developing into men who showed no fear. Mentally and physically we were at our peak, the army had taught us to respect people and property. We had nearly come to the end of our training and were to be given some leave and flown to Changi Barracks in Singapore, we were looking forward to having some good nights out. We decided to have one more night having a good booze up with the Royal Air Force lads who had become our friends in the time that we had spent there.

# Chapter 5

Next morning we were flown to Singapore's Changi barracks, this is where we had the privilege of being allocated the officer quarters. These were a bit up market to what we were used to but we were pleased to be there. The beach was nearby so we had ten days to enjoy ourselves in Singapore. This was to be a real experience for us because it was such a beautiful place to be and was a dream come true for us, we would have never visited this place if it had not been for the forces. After dumping our kit in our rooms we decided to explore the camp before doing anything else, this we did and ended up in the bar having a drink. We were told that we could drink in the officer's bar but we declined and said this would do us fine thanks.

Deciding to have an early night we turned in ready to hit the town tomorrow, this was going to be quite an experience for us, a leave in a different country so far from home.

We all sat at some tables in the bar and looked out over the gardens, it was so warm and such a beautiful night, as we sat there talking and wondering what Singapore had to offer us in the way of fun. We knew very little about it as no one we knew had been there before, but we were sure that we would enjoy our stay, you could bet your life that we were going to make the most of it as we sat there drinking bottles of Tiger Ale, this, we were to find out, was mighty strong beer and we put away bottle after bottle not realising the strength of it. That was until Tony got up to go to the toilet, he walked about two feet and then staggered uneasily on his feet and walked straight into a table falling head over heels. Thinking he had just stumbled we laughed, but when he tried to get to his feet we realised that something was wrong and as we got up to help him we all had to hold on to the chair backs, we looked at each other and laughed again, as we realised that it was the beer, we were all unsteady on our feet due to having too much to drink.

The guy behind the bar realized we were in trouble and said that he would help us to our rooms. He shouted to one of the girls to come and man the bar while he helped us, telling us as he did so how strong the beer was and advising us to try not to move around too much until we were more steady on our feet. I can only speak for myself but as I lay on the bed the whole room started to spin, this was the worse I had ever felt as I lay there wondering how the others were, thinking to myself how easy it was to get in a mess, what would have happened if we had gone into the city and drunk just the same? We would have been in a right state and in a strange place, it was a good job that we had decided to stay in that first night in Singapore, at least we had learnt our lesson on home ground so to speak. I finally got to sleep after staggering to the loo a few times, the bed had stopped spinning round.

Next morning the heat was terrific because I had forgotten to draw the curtains and the sun was streaming through the windows, but all I wanted was a drink of water, this I quickly got and felt a little better afterwards. So a lesson was learnt and I knew that I would be more careful in future with the local brew and treat it with the respect that it deserved. I got a shower and felt better still as I set off to the canteen to get a mug of tea or something.

There were a few guys in there, head in hands feeling sorry for themselves as did I, but we raised a laugh between us as I asked Brian how he felt, his reply was: "bloody awful, never again." but that's what we all said at the time. After about five mugs of tea and some toast we decided to go get another shower and liven ourselves up a bit more, if we possibly could, and go into Singapore itself.

It was hot and sticky outside but we were looking forward to having some fun, we decided to meet in an hour's time and one of the RAF lads was to take us all into the city. We were told by an officer that we had to be looked after while we were in the Changi Barracks, and that he had instructions to give us all the help we needed and a free hand.

An hour later, as we drove into the city, we were feeling much better in ourselves. The driver told us that he was taking us to the Raffles Hotel. We had heard that it was supposed to be a bit flash, full of well-to-do Brits.

We admired the view as we drove in the truck to the hotel. On arriving it was like a great big colonial palace and true to form it was full of Brits having tea, typical of the filthy rich, all full of themselves, what a bloody life they were living, compared to the poverty at home they did not know how the other half lived. They looked across at us as we strode into the big room with all the fans going, it was real splendour for sure.

We sat down and had some coconut milk each, as we were leaving the beer until later in the day. We decided not to stay there but Brian had spotted a couple of young fillies and walked over to them to ask if they would show us round the town, telling them that we had just got there and did not want to get lost. He was so lucky! These young women agreed to show us around, it turned out that they lived out here with their parents and it seemed as though they were bored with the company that was around, they told us that there was always some old guy trying to get them into bed, it seemed to us that they knew the score okay.

Well we ordered a couple of cabs to take us into the centre of Singapore where all the bars and shops were, we went down to the waterfront and looked out to Sentosa Island.

As we sat at a bar having a drink, Dave said that he was going to go round the town with an RAF lad who was stationed at Changi Barracks, Dave was another one for the women and he said he wanted to try the local talent out. He and Brian had a mutual respect for each other but did not want to go round the town together just yet, so Dave set off with the RAF guy, we knew that he would be okay as he could look after himself and he had the RAF lad with him who had been stationed here for quite a good while, so they said their goodbyes and went off on their own.

The two girls turned out to be good company, Brian said to Trevor and me that we were on to a winner here. One thing about Brian, not a minute was wasted, he was as bad as Dave when it came down to women, the thought of getting laid was his number one priority nothing stood in his way when there was a chance of a new conquest. They were both very pretty girls but he said to me he wanted the one with the large breasts, mind you the other one wasn't to badly endowed either, but he had made up his mind and was homing in on her. She was called Mary and her mate was Susan. As we sat in the humidity watching the world go by and chatting

45

away to the girls, some of the guys who had been in the bar next door said they were asked, as they ordered a drink, if they wanted to choose a young woman each and have a room at the hotel?

Susan said that this was normal in all the bars, they had girls on tap with the drinks.

"Well," the guys said, "what a place, we are going to have one sure sexy leave."

Most of the men drifted off to the various bars around the town, Brian and I were content to sit there with Mary and Susan watching the world go by. We were both quite happy to spend tonight in the town with the two English girls, Brian's hands were wandering all over Mary and she did not seem to mind, Susan asked me to go for a walk downtown, I think she was a little uneasy with what was going on. We politely asked Brian and Mary if they wanted to come and they declined saying they would wait there for us, so saying that we would catch up with them later, we set off for a walk together, Susan took hold of my hand and it felt nice as I grasped her hand back.

We walked along the front heading for a little restaurant that Susan said was good. It was a nice feeling having a woman with me after all the training and being focused on what we were doing. It was good to partly relax, we were taught never to relax fully until we knew for sure that it was safe to do so. As we went into the restaurant Susan gave me a peck on the cheek, I felt relaxed with her and not threatened by her wanting more than friendship. So we sat at a table in the corner out of the way where I could see who came into the place.

The menu was quite extensive and I ordered a lobster and Susan ordered the same, the waiter then brought us a drink each, I had a small beer and Susan had a vodka and orange.

We talked about where we lived in England and other stuff from home, Susan had been in Singapore for about two years now, she told me that she was used to travelling about with her parents, I told her that I was making the forces my career.

She said I would enjoy it here in Singapore with all the girls that were available for English guys, I replied that I was quite happy with her company and that was the truth. She smiled and kissed me

46

on the cheek, it felt good and I kissed her back, lingering on her lips, I could feel the warmth of her body as she put her arms round me in the dimly lit restaurant, and I just knew that this was going to be a good leave for me.

'Eat your heart out Brian,' I thought, you see, he knew that I had to like someone before I could even think of kissing them and Susan and I had that instant friendship together, whereas he just wanted to get them into bed regardless, another conquest, it was just like Dave and that's what Mary would be to him, just one on a very long list.

We were getting on very well just enjoying each other's company, just then the meal was delivered and we ordered another drink, the lobster looked great and was circled by large prawns, we got stuck into it and it tasted as good as it looked. We said that after the meal we would go and try to find Brian and Mary and have a couple of drinks with them.

This was a very nice place to be with a beautiful woman on your arm, and Susan was so very attractive and looked well in all departments, especially with the tan, she was a nice woman to be out with.

When we had finished the meal she leaned across and kissed me full on the lips with a long lingering kiss. It felt so good and I was beginning to get aroused, what full-blooded guy wouldn't with a girl like this? As we got up and paid for the meal she grasped my hand and held it tight, saying what a good time she was having. I told her that I was enjoying her company as well, we walked out of the restaurant with eyes only for each other.

As we were leaving we were hit by the humidity outside, but as I looked up into the sky I knew that this was going to be a great leave with no need to look at the local girls at all, Susan had everything a guy could ask for.

We headed back to the waterfront to look for Brian and Mary, on reaching the bar where we had left them, we entered and looked around. The owner told us that they had left not long after us. We looked at each other and burst out laughing, both of the same mind, and at the same time saying, "I know where they've gone."

It was strange how easy we got on with each other and being so relaxed together, it was as though we had known each other for a long while. We decided to go for a slow walk along the front holding hands and stopping to kiss each other, it seemed so natural.

Calling a cab we went back to Changi to have a drink there, sitting at a table overlooking the beach, it was so peaceful. Shortly afterwards Brian and Mary came in and waved to us as they walked towards us, both with a smile on their faces. We knew what that meant as they sat down beside us, Brian whispered in my ear that he had been to bed with Mary, as if we didn't know! Anyway we ordered some drinks and had a game of cards, talking as we played seven card brag, in all we had a pleasant evening together.

About two hours later the girls said that they would have to go home so we kissed them goodnight and ordered them a cab. Susan said she would call me in the morning and I said, "Great look forward to hearing from you."

Mary said the same to Brian but he said that he had some work to do and would see her tomorrow night, she looked at him puzzled, but I realised, I don't know why, what he was up to. He would be going to taste the local dishes - the female kind. With that the girls went and we decided to have one more drink, Brian then started to tell me about how fast Mary had taken her clothes off when they went back to his room and how hot she was, right to the fine details of what she did to him. He asked me if Susan and I had sex, to which I answered, "No, but we had a good night together," he looked at me and dare not contradict what I had said this time.

He then said he was going round the town tomorrow to have a bit of the local talent, he asked if I was going and I said I was meeting Susan and we were going to go round Chinatown. As usual he called me a fool when there was all that different talent in the place, but I said, "You do what you want mate, but be careful." I just knew he would get us into trouble one day.

We had one more drink and decided to turn in for the night saying we would meet at breakfast, as I lay on my bed I thought what a nice life it was out here and how Susan and I had got on so well, I wondered to myself would we go to bed together during my leave here? I must have fallen asleep then because next I knew was Brian knocking on my door, I quickly pulled on some pants and a tee shirt and went to breakfast.

As we sat there Brian was asking Trevor, who had come to sit near to us, how he had got on the night before and where he thought was the best places to go. Trevor said virtually every bar that you went in to, the owner asked if you wanted a girl or girls with your drink. Brian's face lit up, Trevor looked at me and said, "Brian you will wear yourself out and get into trouble."

I just laughed and said to Trevor that Brian had been with Mary last night and was now fed up with her, I personally thought that Brian was insecure and had to prove himself with as many women as possible. The barman came through and told me that there was a telephone call for me, I guessed it was Susan to see what we were doing today, I suggested hiring a boat and going for a sail around and she thought that was a good idea.

She then said, "What is Brian doing? Mary has asked me to find out for her."

I said I was not sure but he said he would see her tonight in the bar all being well. So we arranged to meet in an hour and go down to the jetty and get a boat with a canopy so we would be protected from the sun.

I said goodbye and went to tell Brian what Mary had said and how I had answered Susan, so that he knew what had been said. I then told him that Susan and I were going on a boat, even then he tried to convince me to go with him, but I said another day maybe. With that Trevor said he would go with Brian, I was relieved because I felt responsible for him, he would be okay with Trevor because he was not as hasty as Brian and had his head screwed on his shoulders, and not in his trousers like Brian. So with that parting shot we said that we would meet up later that day to go out for a drink into the city, I went back to my room to have a shower and change into some shorts and top.

While I was waiting for Susan to come I was thinking about home and wondering how people were getting on back there, in particular Ann and Elsie. As friends, they were both very loving and caring girls and liked by all. Then there was a knock at the door, it was Susan and did she look stunning in a dress that left nothing to the imagination?

We just looked at each other then walked forward as our arms went around each other and our lips touched in a warm embrace. She felt so good under the dress and I said to her that we had better go before anything happened between us, she just smiled and took my hand and we walked out to the jetty to pick up our boat complete with canopy and cool box with drinks. We made ourselves comfortable and set off up the coast, hoping to find a secluded beach.

After skirting the coastline for a good while looking for a desolate spot where we could relax together and sit and talk, we eventually found a beautiful little cove and we pulled the boat front just onto the beach together, we were really relaxed with each other's company.

We chatted about various things, one of them being Brian and Mary. Susan said she knew Brian was not working and that he would be in the city, chasing the local women, she sure had him weighed up. I told her, although he was my best friend, I had to admit that his brains were always overruled by what he had between his legs and that he was ruthless with women, using them for what he could get, and also he soon got rid of them to try pastures new. We also talked about each other quite openly as we sat and watched the ships passing further out at sea. I told her that there was no way that I was going to get too attached to a woman as the forces were my career, she said she respected that but hoped that we could be very good friends.

We decided to get back on the boat and go further round the coast, hugging the beautiful coastline, it was so relaxing as we cruised along on a very calm sea seeing the odd fin cutting through the waves and looking down into the clear blue waters we could see the many different fish swimming about.

We had the odd touch and leaned towards each other and brushed our lips, I think we were both becoming aroused by the remoteness of the boat and the cover the canopy gave us.

We saw in the distance another stretch of beach with not a soul on it so we decided to make for the shore and go for a walk on the sands. As we ran up to the sand and dragged the boat partly out of the sea, laughing about nothing, just enjoying each other's company, we held hands and started to walk up the beach picking up shells as we went it seemed so good to be alone.

We kept stopping to kiss each other gently and I'm sure we both knew that sometime we would be doing more than just kissing. We sat on the sand after a while and just stared out to sea it was heaven sat there with not a care in the world. We kissed and lay on the warm sand it was not too hot because it was now cloudy, which gave us some shade from the intense sun that was usually beating down.

We both said that we had better stop the cuddles before we went too far, we agreed that this was not the place or the time to make love to each other and so we got to our feet and headed back to the boat. Deciding to head home the day had passed quickly as we went back up the coast to Changi, we just laid there and held hands as we chugged along on the water that was like a mill pond it was so calm and inviting.

We seemed to arrive back faster than it had taken to get to the last beach which we had stopped at, anyway as we docked the boat, we decide to go straight home to get a shower and meet up later, we kissed and said our goodbyes.

~*~

As I was in the shower dreaming to myself, I thought what good company Susan was to be with, I am sure that under different circumstances we could have made something of our relationship, it just seemed so natural for us to be together.

I also wondered if we would ever go to bed with each other, or just enjoy the friendship that we had. Regardless of the sex I was happy just to have someone close to cuddle up to and, most of all, talk to in a way that you can't always talk to some people.

I finished my shower and lay on the top of the bed just drifting in and out of dreams, when there was a knock at the door and it was Brian, I shouted 'come in' as I was interested in finding out how their day had been, he was going to tell me anyway. Brian started by saying that they had decided to go round a few bars to look at the potential women first, I said to him, "That must be a first for you," he would have normally just gone in the first one and picked

51

a woman and that would have been it. But Trevor had told him that the choice was unlimited and would always be there anyway, they had been in about five bars looking at the girls when he saw this most beautiful young girl and "she had a figure to match," he said.

He said to Trevor, "I'm going no further, this is the one for me", as he was led by the girl to a room in the bar. When they got in the room she just shed the robe that she had on, then started to undress him, at the same time kissing him, her hands were so gentle as she stroked his back. He said he thought all his birthdays had come at once as she led him over to the bed and lay down beside him. She started to kiss him all over, working down from the top, Brian said the excitement at what she was doing was the best he had ever experienced. She then began to give him oral sex he stood that for a while then turned her over and entered her, she was so alive, it was definitely the best sex he had ever had as she writhed under him. He said she was so good and just knew what he wanted without being prompted, he was going back to see her again but would go out with Mary and us tonight.

Well that was Brian, always told you everything about his conquests. I said to him, "you will never have any privacy when you meet the girl you want to spend the rest of your life with, you would be telling everyone what goes on. I believe it is between the couple, not for others."

"Have you screwed Susan yet?" He asked, that was Brian, straight to the point.

I told him he should know after all these years that I have always said that things like that are private between two people.

"Anyway," he said. "I hope that you have some fun, you are too serious when it comes down to women, they will always do the dirty on you so don't trust them and have as many as you can, I certainly will."

Well he sure made up for some of us in the women department, but I said every man should do what he wants, so we left it at that. I said I was going to have a shower, he would wait for the girls to come in the bar and asked if I would meet him there?

I said, "Yes, in about thirty minutes", with that I got under the shower and told him to close the door on his way out. He had not been gone two minutes when I heard a knock and shouted "you have been fast", but it was Trevor to ask what we were doing tonight?

I told him that I was going out with Susan but could not afford to get tied down in a relationship because that would be the end of my army career, I think if I wanted to tie myself down in any way at all I would not have joined the forces.

I walked out of the shower and flopped onto the bed and just lay there thinking about the way things were, I knew then this was going to be a hell of a leave without going to the bars with Brian, I told Trevor I'd better get ready and go to meet Susan, Brian and Mary and he was welcome to come out with us.

I quickly got dressed and we set off. I believed the bond between Trevor and I was getting so strong, we were just like two brothers, as we walked in they looked at us and said together, "Where on earth have you two been? We thought you weren't coming."

Realising that we had been over an hour I said, "sorry for that folks."

We smiled at them and said we just got carried away talking, with us being late we decided to go straight into town for a meal at one of the seafront restaurants. As Susan and I walked hand in hand, I could feel the warmth from Susan as she held my hand tightly in hers. She slowly moved her fingers about, there was a nice feeling going through my body as we walked along together. Susan whispered in my ear that she wished we had stayed in tonight and I told her we would not stay out too long anyway. She said that she would tell her mum and dad that she was staying at Mary's because they had gone to Bali for a week. I smiled and said out loud, "I know who will be staying at Mary's and it won't be Susan."

With that Brian said, "Guess it's me then," much to Mary's delight.

So we had our excuse for Susan's Mum and Dad which made us both very happy as we entered the restaurant.

It was amazing the number of young girls on offer in the bars and restaurants all through Singapore. We ordered drinks and a meal, we decided on Chinese so we could have loads of different dishes, the food was mouth watering and there was plenty of it.

Trevor saw Robert and decided to go for a walk with him as he said laughingly, "I feel as though I'm an intruder."

Mary said, "It may be better if we all stay at my house, just in case Susan's mum calls."

Susan looked at me and said, "Is that okay?"

"No problem to me," I replied, "if that's okay with you?"

With that settled we decided to have another drink, we were talking about how we were going to miss Singapore after this leave, but hoped that we would have many more here. The girls said they hoped so too, as Susan stroked my leg under the table.

We paid the bill and decided to get a taxi to Mary's house, and what a shock we had as we entered a big drive and approached a massive colonial house. Getting out of the taxi we entered a wide front entrance with a great big staircase, Brian and I gasped at the splendour that they lived in out here.

We went into this great big drawing room and Mary asked us what we wanted to drink. I said a whisky and Brian had rum, Mary and Susan had vodka each as we made ourselves comfortable on the massive settee.

Susan leaned towards me and kissed me on the lips this began to cause me a problem, what with the drink making me more relaxed. As I looked towards Mary and Brian he was fondling her breasts and she was beginning to put her hand down his trousers.

We interrupted and said to Mary, "which bedroom are we having?"

Assuming that we were sleeping together tonight, she answered, "Use the bedroom that you usually use when you stay, Susan."

So saying good night to Brian and Mary we went up the magnificent staircase to a room nearly at the end which suited us fine, it was massive with a great big bed.

We no sooner got in the room and Susan had laid on the bed and patted it for me to lay beside her. I said that I was hot and sticky and would have a shower, when I came back Susan was fast asleep.

~*~

The next day we went back to barracks knowing that this was nearly the end of our leave, we only had one more day left. I knew that I would miss the island of Singapore but it was to be back to training in Borneo, maybe soon we could come back again. We had arranged to meet up in the bar that night so Brian and I walked there together, when we arrived Trevor, Tony and Robert were already sat there waiting. We had just got a drink when in walked Dave and we all burst out laughing because he looked bloody rough. He turned to us and said, "it was worth it", as we sat him down and got him a drink, he looked even worse close up but he said he had had a whale of a time and could not wait to go back. As he said it, the guy from the RAF walked in and he looked the same as Dave, it appeared that they had got on really well together.

The one good thing about Dave was that he looked out for us, same as we all did for each other, you could not fault him that way. After all, that was the qualities that were seen in us with our different skills and why we were put together, it would not do for us not to get on as we later learned half the battle was mutual respect for each other and to be there when needed, that was drummed into us.

So then we chatted about the different women that Dave and his mate had been with, they said that they could not remember or did not want to, they just said that it had been a great time and they needed a rest. With that we all said at the same time, "You bloody look as though you do!" laughing as we did so.

I turned to Brian and said, "are you jealous?"

He said, "no there will be other leaves, and anyway, I have had a good time also."

He did not want Dave to think he had been outdone by him. It was like a challenge between them where women were concerned but it gave us some entertainment keeping up with their antics, they were always trying to beat each other.

We decided to have a quiet night in the bar that night, this was because we had to have an early start, we called the girls and asked if they wanted to come over and they agreed, so we asked them if there were any other girls that they could bring along, with Trevor, Robert, Tony and Dave being with us, they said that they would do their best. Susan asked me if I would go into town with her at lunchtime so I said that I would pick her up about twelve noon so we could get back for the last night in the bar.

I called for her at twelve prompt and we decided to walk down to the town past Chinatown, it was interesting to see all the stalls selling anything you could think of, it was quite an education as we walked towards the riverside quay. Walking slowly down there we stopped to kiss and hold hands, content with each other's company.

Susan said, "Stop a minute," and she put her arms around me then said, "Please don't forget me, come back as soon as you get another leave."

Kissing her gently on the lips, I pulled her close and said, "If I get leave I will come back to Singapore to see you because we have been good together this last two weeks."

She said, "let's spend the rest of your time here together." Then she dropped the bombshell saying that she loved me. I told her, "I like you a lot but with my army career I can't get involved with anyone, having said that, you never know?"

She took it well saying that she understood what I was saying, I felt really bad about it and told her so. That was my problem, I did not like hurting anyone, also I had made it very clear that I did not want to get committed to anyone because I would have to think about her, and with the job we were in, I did not want distractions as they could be fatal. We walked in silence back to the barracks just holding hands and having the odd brush of our lips. We entered the bar, Mary and some other girls were there with the guys and seemed to be having a good time together, we decided to join them for the night, so we pulled up a couple of chairs and got ready for the interrogation from Brian and Dave, right on time he said, "And what have you two been up to?"

Susan quickly said we'd been round the shops and that was it, we got away with it, because Brian certainly didn't want to talk about the shops. I whispered 'nice one' to Susan.

We said to the girls that we were going to miss Singapore and their company for sure but we would be back as soon as we got some more leave. Tony and Robert said they would not mind going to Aussie on the next leave, little did we know that our next training session was going to be in Australia.

We all had a good night together then said our goodbyes as we had to be up early, so there was to be no going round the town tonight and there was no way that the girls could stop with us tonight as we had to pack our kit bags and get a good nights rest for our early start in the morning, it was back to the discipline for us and to get focused again.

# Chapter 6

The night seemed to fly by as the alarm went off at five am for us to get down to the airport, we could not grumble we'd had a great time on our leave. We chatted about it on the way to the airport where a RAF Hercules was waiting to take us to Colombo, from there we were, as we found out, to fly on to Australia to the Northern Territory for some survival training with the Aborigines, who were to show us how to blend into the countryside and other arts of survival.

We were to stay in Darwin for a few days then go to some homestead to learn how to track and survive in this desolate land with all its major cities on the coast. As we landed in Darwin they were having a plague of frogs or toads, it was so hot and humid as we stepped down from the plane and it did not look as though there was much in the place.

We were picked up and taken to a wooden colonial type of hotel/ motel which was very basic but we all had a room of our own so that was a plus for us. There were six of us who were becoming close to each other, even Dave and Brian were beginning to realise that they needed each other, so the team was me, Brian, Dave, Robert, Trevor and Tony.

This was a very lonely place but they had plenty of watering holes or bars as we know them. We were soon to find out how much these Aussie guys drank, the women were not allowed in the bars so Brian and Dave would have to look elsewhere, but there did not seem to be many women about.

The officer in charge of the groups told us to relax that night and be ready in the morning at ten, we were grateful for this as we could do with a drink so we all went down to the bar below the hotel and ordered some jugs of beer that they filled from a gun type pump, they also sold glasses of beer called Schooners and Stubbies.

We sat at the primitive wooden tables and got a few jugs, there were some Aussies betting on anything that moved, they looked us up and down and said, "Welcome, you Pommie bastards."

This was, as we found out, to be a normal type of greeting from them, so we did not raise to the bait. They seemed to want us to join in with what they was doing and invited us over for a drink with them, which we decided to do. As it turned out, we had a good night with the guys, we had a game of cards, and one man I seemed to get on with really well, as we found out later, he was the toughest guy we had ever met, his nickname was 'Tank'. He had a face like toughened leather and his main trick was, as he told me, to bet anyone to knock him down with one punch, for a straight bet of five pounds and that was a lot of money. He asked if anyone wanted to have a go and as we'd had a few drinks, there was some Dutch courage about, Trevor said he would have a go so Tank stood there with legs slightly apart and Trevor, who was nearly six foot to Tank's five feet six, placed himself in front of Tank and took one great swing at his chin. We grimaced at the thought of the connection and the crack as he hit Tank who went round the bar but he did not go down, just shook his head and said. "Who else wants a go?"

There were no more offers as all the Aussies burst out laughing and Trevor was five pounds lighter, it was worth it to see that, and we all chipped in with Trevor's bet. It turned out that we all became great friends and Tank really took to me, he was such a nice guy.

~*~

Next morning we were taken on a truck into the bush, we had driven for about two hours and arrived at an old ramshackle building with a good few Aborigines sat around. These were the men who would show us around the bush. We set off on foot with the Abo's leading the way, it was hot and humid and we were warned not to go too close to the river as the crocs would have us. The first thing that we were shown was how to cover our tracks and set others for people to follow, it was interesting how they could blend into the bush so fast, this was a skill that would be useful to us in the following years. We were to learn a lot from these very interesting people, we learnt how to find food and these great big grubs under logs and the protein in them, we were told, was good. The heat was at times unbearable, the sun was so strong and we had a job not to dehydrate in over one hundred degrees in this searing desert land, but we learnt many skills from these Aborigines.

We did not know that we were staying out that night but we were going to have to, the Aborigines made a fire and brought some strips of meat and rabbits to roast over it and in the hot ashes. As we were sat there, one of the elders started to tell us our future, he started with Brian and told him he would have many wives, we didn't think he meant get married loads of times, just women that he would go with, he also told him he would settle down with a family and that he would have to be careful as he would be close to death sometime in the near future.

Next was Trevor his was not so bad as he was told he would settle down later in life and have a family but not a lot of wives maybe one. That fitted with Trevor's personality and his attitude to women which was totally different from Dave and Brian.

"It all looks very boring for Trevor," Dave said.

Tony was next, he was to travel and go to live in a distant land, he was told that he would be very happy and have much land. After Tony came Dave, he looked at Dave and said. "You will have many problems and many women." We all burst out laughing at that and said his women bring him problems now so there was truth in that.

Next was Robert, he was to have a long and happy life and he would settle down and have children. I was to have a troubled life and many problems with the family, but I would meet someone who would love me very much. I would face death a few times in my life, but as I was strong, I would come through the crisis.

We all took this as a bit of fun as we ate roast rabbit and drank a few beers that we had brought with us. We learnt a lot of skills from the Aborigine's and were grateful for that, the time with them passed fast and we were soon on our way back to camp in Ceylon, from there we were told we were going back to England to be attached to a special unit.

~*~

So it was back to Blighty and to Malvern in the south west of the country. This was it, the real work and excitement, now all the training was over for us, it was now postings around the world, it was into the unknown and we were really looking forward to it, a little nervous, but really excited. We hoped that we would all keep together as we got on so well. We were told there would be no more leave for us for quite a while but that did not bother us, with the expectation of travel to distant lands, this was all that we wanted, we were told that we could have leave when we knew where we were going on our first posting.

We were told that we were to fly out to Habbania in Iraq, this was a Royal Air Force base about fifty miles from Baghdad, a God forsaken hole, we were to find out. We were given orders to stay in camp and leave was to be cancelled so we were not very happy about that but orders were to be observed and obeyed. Well, we were fully kitted out with weapons and survival rations so we were quite excited about this but a little scared as this was to be the real thing. We could afford no mistakes, to make one could mean your life, or the lives of others, so we had to be on our toes at all times. We were told that we would leave next morning at six for Brindisi in Italy, it seemed as though we had something to do there before going on to Iraq. We had to be in civilian clothes and would be briefed when we arrived there. We were also told to just have our pistols and stilettos, (not as people think of stilettos as in high heeled shoes, but a long slim dagger) that we kept well hidden at all times. We arrived in Brindisi and were transferred to a small hotel near to the docks, it was there that two men in civilian clothes called to see us and told us that we had to try to behave like tourists or seamen and be seen to be having a good time and mingle in the bars in the dock area. We were told that the organisation of some problems in the Middle East was done in some of the bars in the dockland area so we had to mingle and listen. Under no circumstances, were we to disclose that we had anything to do with the British forces, if we did and were caught, it would be said that they have nothing to do with us in anyway, that was made very clear to us. So we were to be alone and take care of each other for the first time in difficult circumstances. We got together in Trevor's room and he and I laid the law down to Brian and Dave about not going back to the hotel with any women as that could jeopardise what we were looking for and we could not afford that risk.

After we had dinner in the hotel, we decided to head for the various bars and see what we could pick up, we had been told it was to do with someone smuggling arms across to the Middle East, so off we went dressed like seamen out to have a good time. At the first bar we came to we ordered a drink each and sat at a table where we could observe the comings and goings of people in the bar. There were a few ladies of the night sat around the bar and we whispered to Dave and Brian to pick up all they could in conversation with them by asking if they knew anyone that would sell us some guns but to be careful. So off they went to sit and chat to the girls as the four of us kept watch on everything else in the bar.

Brian within minutes had his hands all over the woman who he had sought out, we laughed at this, 'balls before brains' we called him, this was an apt name for him, but he had a task to do and he loved it anyway. As long as he stayed clear of leaving the bar with her we were fine with it.

There were a few shady characters coming into the bar by now and immediately looking at Brian and Dave. Dave signalled us, by picking up his beer in his left hand, that he had received some information so I wandered off to the toilet to be shortly followed by Dave, who, after making sure no one else was in the toilets, told me that sometimes a couple of guys came into the bar and that the girl said, after taking them to an hotel for sex they had beaten her and some of the other girls. She told him they were very dangerous men, but if we wanted to buy guns they were the people to talk to, but she said to be careful, they did not come into this bar a lot but went into one further down the road. She said one of them had a distinct scar down his left cheek and short black hair. I said to Dave, "Thank her and give her some money," so he went out first and slipped her some money, then we all drifted out of the place and headed for the bar down the road. We decided to enter that in pairs with a few minutes between us, to try and look as though we were not together. We all had different attire on, I pulled the collar up on my donkey jacket and went in first with Trevor, Dave and Tony followed, then Brian and Robert, we all sat strategically away from each other with our backs as near to the wall as possible. This place felt bad to me I whispered to Trevor, we could see it was full of shady looking characters as we looked around, there were plenty of girls around, as you would expect in a bar as near to the docks as this one, and many visiting seamen, it was a real den of vagabonds and thieves a smoky and sinister looking place. We had arranged to do the same as we had done in the other bar, Dave to get talking to a girl then see what comes of it. He slid next to a girl who seemed to be on her own and started chatting to her, he was not as cheeky as Brian, with the touching, that's why we sent him to do it, much to Brian's regret, also Dave was not as choosy as Brian. Dave moved in on the girl and as he was talking, we were all scanning the bar slowly to see who was watching him, there were four guys who were showing a special interest. When Dave pulled out a wad of notes, we watched them mutter to each other and, reading one of their lips, it seemed as though they were looking to roll him when he went out of the bar. I told Trevor what I thought I'd seen and he said he had thought the same but was not quite sure, so we gave the signal for Brian to go to the toilets and one of us would follow. Brian got up and walked slowly to the toilets that were in a dingy corridor at the back of the bar and I followed him with Trevor, Robert and Tony keeping an eye on things. This did not look too good when we were looking for someone selling weapons, I said to Brian that we would have to allow Dave some space if we were not to blow our cover, so we agreed that just Trevor and I would follow these guys if they followed Dave to roll him of his cash. We drifted back to our seats and kept a close eye on the proceedings, just as we were giving up hope of seeing the man who sold the arms, in walked a man with a scar down his cheek, there were three others with him.

I told Trevor to send a message to him by one of the waitresses asking if he could supply us with a few guns. We gave Dave a signal to go back to his seat in the code we had arranged, that was for one of us to touch our left ear for a few seconds, so this he did, knowing something was coming off. The man with the scar looked across at Trevor and me and beckoned us to his table, we walked slowly across and knew that the guys were watching our backs, Tony had his hand on his pistol ready for anything. We sat down and the man asked us what we really wanted? I answered quite a few machine guns, rifles, grenades and ammunition he said that it would cost us in dollars, we said, no problem, we could get the cash in a couple of days so where could we pick them up from? He said that he would meet us back in this bar in a couple of days, so we left it at that, not daring to push it too far. With that we said we were going and would be back in a couple of days with the money, we said our goodbyes and walked slowly out of the bar, the others would follow us as arranged after a couple of minutes.

We waited a few buildings away as the guy came out, Dave being last because we guessed that those others would follow and try to roll him for his cash, we split up in doorways and waited for him, he was walking slowly and pretending to stagger a bit and, sure enough, following him were those four men. We picked out one each, leaving Trevor to keep a watch for anyone else that could cause us a problem. As soon as Dave got into the darkness they started to move in on him but we had the measure of them and moved in fast, they did not know what had hit them and it was a good job we'd moved fast because one of them had an ugly looking Machete type of blade. We cracked them swiftly and quietly and dumped them on to the deck of a boat that was moored up along the dock side, with that we swiftly got away from the area so we could report back on the man selling the guns.

We were on the radio as soon as we got back to the hotel and reported in describing what he looked like, the message back was that that was the man that they suspected was dealing, so we had to capture him or rub him and his friends out and leave the place as soon as possible once we had completed what we had to do. Once again we were told that we were on our own if we got caught, this was to be our first real taste of what was to come in the next few years together.

We all went back to the hotel to plan how we were going to deal with this, these were mighty dangerous people and we could not afford to make one slip between us or we would end up as fish bait in the harbour. So we arranged that we would await the call from the man with the scar and find out where we should meet him to do the exchange, so at least the man thought that just Trevor and me were wanting to buy the guns. We had to depend on the other four to cover us in case something went wrong. We had to make sure we captured him and his friends or get rid of them, but we had instructions to do our best to capture the man with the scar if possible, the others did not really matter. So we waited in the bar of our hotel but made sure that we sat apart just in case someone saw us all chatting to each other. Trevor and I sat in a corner and asked the man in the hotel to let us know if a call came for us, we had all checked into the hotel separately, hoping that no one linked us together, we did say the odd word to each other in the bar, as most guests do in hotels but not too much.

We were getting tensed up, waiting like coiled springs, it was about an hour later that we were called to the telephone by the man on the reception. True to form it was 'Scarface' he wanted to meet us at the bar we'd first met him in, then he would take us to a car where he said the goods would be. So Trevor and I set off and were followed by Dave and Tony, Brian and Robert were to go into the bar before us, just to observe the place for about fifteen minutes before we entered, this was to try and see how many they had in numbers to try and give us a chance of success in our first real task.

Together we had checked out of the hotel we were staying at and had arranged for a small fishing boat to be ready in the harbour to take 'Scarface' and his mates away from the place, so with watches set, we made for the bar at the intervals that we had arranged beforehand, this was to be a hell of a test for us. It had to go well, we were so tense but ready, as we said good luck to each other, even Dave and Brian gave each other a hug.

Brian and Robert had been gone ten minutes so Trevor and I set off with Dave and Tony not far behind, watching to see if anyone was following us. It all seemed to be going well as I said to Trevor, "Let's move as fast as we can once we have made the contact."

This was bringing our adrenalin to its peak as we approached the bar with no incidents, strolling slowly in we looked around to see where Brian and Robert were sat and sitting to their left as there was a table still empty, behind us was where, we hoped, Dave and Tony would sit and that would give us cover if anything was to break out in the bar that we did not expect, we had been trained to expect the unforeseen, but we felt relaxed and I had a good feeling about this and Trevor said he felt the same.

Just at that moment 'Scarface' and three other guys came in followed by three more and it stood out a mile that they were all together, he came straight over to us and sat down, the other three pulled up some chairs, and the three that we thought were with them sat near to the door. In walked Dave and Tony, without so much as a sideways glance they sat in the seats we'd hoped they'd use. All was going well up to now but we could feel the tension around our table. 'Scarface' asked if we had the cash and we said yes in the bag we had with us. He wanted to see a bundle so Trevor reached into the bag and pulled out a bundle of dollar bills to satisfy them. 'Scarface' flicked the bills and seemed to be happy with the situation, I asked if the weapons were all there he said, "Yes, you will have to go to the dockside to collect them."

"That's fine," we said, it would suit us. We decided to stay in the bar and have a drink and the arrangement was to leave just after each other, so we sat chatting to 'Scarface' as Brian and Robert left the bar without turning a hair of suspicion in the place. It was going okay for now as Dave and Tony then walked out with two women that they had been chatting to as a means to distract anyone from being in the least bothered about them. 'Scarface's men were watching all the movements in and out of the bar and it did not seem to bother them, looking at their faces, mainly their eyes.

We started to feel that 'Scarface' was getting to be a bit more relaxed with us, but we still had to be really alert to things, we could not afford to relax for a second. After a couple of drinks we decided to go do the pickup, 'Scarface' said that we were to follow him and his three men out of the bar, so we said okay, knowing that the other three would follow us out, we hoped that Dave, Brian, Robert and Tony were set to cover us in case anything went wrong, we were quietly confident that everything would be covered.

As we followed them out of the bar to the dock side where their car was parked, I don't know about the others, but my adrenalin was flying, I was getting a real buzz out of this. We walked behind them towards the car, just in a doorway was Dave and Tony with the women, that was a natural thing round there so no one took any notice of them. We just hoped that Brian and Robert had the other three covered, just in case, when we moved on 'Scarface' and the three men with him.

This was a real test for us after all the training we had gone through it should be a piece of cake to us as a team of super fit, disciplined guys. I became known as Mr Cool, also sometimes known as 'ice' by Dave because of my steely eyes. He once said, "I worry when I look into your eyes, they are so clinically focused on the task in hand and show no emotion."

Just as we reached the car we heard three splashes in the dock further behind us. We knew it was 'Scarface's other companions, having a forced swim, that was the signal, as I hit 'Scarface across the throat he gurgled and sank to his knees. At the same time Dave, Trevor and Tony were attending to the others, and Brian and Robert were soon on the scene to give cover after dealing with their men. It had gone well as we bundled all four of them into the car to move them just a bit further up to where the boat was waiting for us. We transferred them, and the guns out of the trunk of the car and onto the boat, it was all over in minutes, our first success together and we felt really good about it. We then pushed the car into the dock to give us a bit of time just in case anyone saw it there and guessed that something had happened to 'Scarface' and his mates, it just bought us a bit of time that we needed. The boat slowly moved away as though it was going out fishing, not drawing attention to us. We were to meet up with another boat further out to sea and transfer 'Scarface' and his mates to it.

They were starting to come round and giving us a lot of verbal abuse, but we soon met up with the other boat and, under protest, 'Scarface' and his three mates were transferred over. We stayed on the fishing boat and were to be taken further down the coast to be dropped off well away from Brindisi. It had gone so well and we all felt the buzz from completing our first real mission together, even Dave and Brian were getting a little closer to each other as time went on. There would always be friendly rivalry between them where women were concerned, we were to find out, but when it came to doing the business they were both in their own way the type of guys that I would select because without any doubt, they would be right there with us, so we had no regrets in that quarter.

# Chapter 7

We were told that we were to leave the boat soon and be flown out by a light plane to Habbania in Iraq where there was an Air Force base. There we would be briefed on where we were to go next, we had no idea where we were dropped ashore from the boat but thanking the skipper for the safe journey, we were picked up in an old truck that did not really sound like it looked, the engine was running silent, like a Rolls Royce, so we guessed that it had been souped up to perfection for reliability.

We drove down winding roads for about an hour then were transferred to a small Dove aircraft that was waiting for us in a field which was obviously prepared for small planes to land. We were all tired so we tried to snatch a bit of sleep, it felt like no time at all when we landed, to pick up some fuel we were told. After that we slept some more and were woken by the pilot who said that we were due to land in about ten minutes.

This was a Royal Air Force base and the first thing we saw was a Vulcan bomber, it looked so threatening on the runway, but majestic in its appearance. We were billeted in tents at the camp, well away from anyone else, it was dark so we did not think it appropriate to get our bearings as we were very tired, so it was heads down to get a good night's sleep. We were assigned two to a tent so Trevor and I were in one, Dave and Robert in another and Brian and Tony in the other one. It was cold that night and, as we did not feel like talking, Trevor and I got in our sleeping bags and fell asleep. We were to awake with the sun beating down and the heat building up in the tents. As we ventured out into the daylight we saw that we were at the end of a block of tents that were used by the RAF personnel. The runway was a great length as we looked down it, the base looked well cared for and we asked the other guys if they were coming to find out where we could get some breakfast.

As we headed towards some tin huts further to the left of the tents, it was as though we smelt the food cooking as we homed in on the mess tent. An officer came towards us and said that we were to have a briefing after we had eaten, we sat down to an hearty breakfast and a few mugs of tea. There were a few guys coming in and out of the mess tent but none of them said anything to us so we guessed that they had been briefed to leave us to ourselves, we did not mind that at all as we were to find out it was about us learning to live together in all circumstances.

As we were having breakfast, we talked about how smooth everything had gone in Brindisi for us, we had a laugh about the antics of Dave and Brian. Brian chipped in and said he hoped that we would have a chance to go into Baghdad to have a look around adding there may be some women there and for once Dave agreed with him. We laughed at them both talking about finding out what was behind the veils of those well-covered women, I said to Trevor, "I have no doubt in my mind that you would do your best to score in Baghdad."

This was going to be fun, if we got the time to go there, watching Dave and Brian up to their antics. Finishing off our breakfast we decided it was time to go for our briefing so we went to the hut that the officer had shown us. In there were two men in civilian clothes waiting with the officer who outranked us, but it did not seem that way as he had a great respect for us.

One of the 'civvy' guys started off by saying that we had done a good job on the gunrunners in Brindisi, also that we were to be given a few days to ourselves before we were sent off to our next assignment. Dave and Brian, both together, asked if we could go into Baghdad and with no hesitation he said of course we could, but he warned us of the pickpockets and said we had to stay close to each other at all times, but that was a matter of course, we watched over each other anyway. We would have transport put at our disposal with an Arab driver and we would be dressed in typical Arab robes not in western style, civilian clothes. This was okay with us as it was cooler and also easier to conceal our weapons which we always had with us.

So Dave and Brian were looking forward to the visit to Baghdad, it was about fifty miles away from where we were, some people might think that they were a liability to us, but at least they told us what was going on in their minds, others would not and that could then cause danger to us all, but with those two we knew where we stood as they were so open about it. The best thing about all of us was that we would die for each other no matter what, that was the key to our friendship.

After the short briefing we went and got cleaned up and dressed in the clothes, or should I say robes that had been given to us, we had to admit they felt cool on our bodies so they were very welcome although they felt strange to us.

The journey into Baghdad was a bumpy and dusty one but we arrived there with the man who had been assigned to drive us and show us around the place. We parked up and decided to have a walk round with our guide first, he was a nice pleasant sort of man but we realised that he could look after himself, having the outline of a fine tuned body.

As we wandered down one of the streets near to a market I was interested in a man sat making things out of what I thought was a block of silver and I asked our guide, whose name was Abdul, (this seemed to be the name of most of them) if that was the case? He said it was.

We were all interested and asked Abdul what he would make and he said, 'anything at a price'. I said that I would like a ring made with a camel on the front in black.

"No problem." He said, so the rest of the guys decided to have one made also, we had our fingers measured and were told that they would be ready at the end of the day.

On we went and seconds later Brian said to Abdul, "can you tell us where we can meet some women?" He immediately said that there was a private house that we could go to and have something to drink and eat, nearby there was another place that was safe and had the sort of women that they were looking for.

He would leave those of us who wanted something to eat in the first place, and then take the others to the brothel, it was an easy decision because there were only Dave and Brian going to have a look round the brothel, the rest of us elected to have a drink and something to eat, telling them both to be careful with the women. With a wave of their hands, off they went on their travels together.

As we were eating we chatted away with each other and said that

70

we would wait while we got another leave in a better place before we got mixed up with any women. Dave and Brian used to call us the clinical four and decided that I was the worse one in the bunch, I was so cool and could go into any situation without showing any of my emotions, but that was the make up of our group.

We had a few drinks, ate some chicken and bread, which tasted very good, and talked about where we thought we would be stationed next, hoping that it would be in the Far East somewhere as we really enjoyed that area, or that we could have maybe a leave in Singapore sometime in the future. We also joked about Brian and Dave the way they always had that mutual respect for each other, but they were really jealous of each other's sexual exploits. They really were a funny pair to watch at times, the way they stayed out of each other's way but when it came to women, they would both go for it as though they were trying to out do each other. It was so funny at times when they were scurrying about, seeing who they could pick up, never treading on each other's toes.

We talked about our home situations and why we had joined the forces, we all had our problems, one way or another, and had joined up to get away from it all, but mostly it was young men spreading their wings as young men should. I was sure that we would all be better for this life that we were now living as the respect it taught us and the self discipline was beyond anything we would have got from elsewhere.

Trevor said that he was fed up of not having a life as his parents ran a public house and did not have much time for him, also they expected him to work at night in the bar when he wanted to go out and enjoy himself.

Tony's mum and dad had split up so he wanted away from it all. Robert was the same, he wanted to get away from everything. I said I was sick of the lack of love and being the general dogs body in the house and fed up of all the good hidings that I received from my mother.

It was great as we sat there in our robes watching the world go by and observing what a different culture it was, but we felt relaxed even though it was so different to being at home.

We talked about how Tank had taken to us Pommies, and all of us to him, he was one tough hombre. I will always remember him as one of the toughest, nicest guys in this world and we all had a great respect for him. Living in the outback of Australia he needed to be tough in that barren centre where he worked on various sheep farms for many months of the year, trying to make a living for himself now that he had left the forces, we knew it was very hard for him at times.

Dave and Brian were a long time so we ordered some more drinks and chicken. While we were waiting, Tony told us about the almighty rows his mum and dad used to have and how he lay in his bed cringing and crying to himself. He said that he could not stand the constant rows in his house and when they decided to split up it broke his heart as he loved them both. He then made his mind up to leave home. So we all had our different reasons for doing this and joining the forces. All Trevor's father bothered about was making money and he ignored the needs of the family.

Robert came back with, "it was the lack of money in our house that caused all the problems." He went on to say that they had a big family and his mother worked hard to keep them together, but unfortunately, his father just wasted his money on beer. He had made an allowance out of his army pay direct to his mum to help her with the family just as most of us had, and as long as his father didn't get his hands on it, to waste on beer, he would continue to send it to her.

So that was a brief history of our home lives. We continued to wait for Dave and Brian to come back and tell us everything as usual. The bonds between us were getting very strong and my particular bond with Trevor was like a brother and he was the same with me, we felt so close it was uncanny, we also felt very responsible for each other, a little more than the rest of the guys if that was possible.

Trevor said they should be coming back soon, and if they weren't back in another thirty minutes we should go look for them. We sat drinking, eating and just chatting in general, it was very hot and dusty, but the food that we had was okay, in fact it was very tasty.

It was not too long before Dave and Brian turned up with a smile on both their faces. What a pair they were, we were prepared for the breakdown of what they had been up to, both wanting to tell us at the same time. I looked at Trevor and smiled as we sat and listened to what they had got up to, it seemed that they had both had a couple of young girls of about seventeen years old. They told us that the girls were very inexperienced, but Dave said he had enjoyed himself, Brian said it was a waste of time, "she just laid there like a wet rag."

We burst out laughing at him, what did he want? A love affair after meeting her for a couple of seconds.

We decided to go for a walk to see what we could buy, so pulling the robes around us, we set off down the street trying not to bring too much attention to ourselves. It was a very dodgy place to be, we could feel the tension and were ready for any trouble, but the day went by without any incidents and we all decided to go back to the truck, picking up the rings that we had ordered on the way back to camp.

When we arrived at the little shop the man was still sat outside carving his silver. He turned to us and said that they were ready and would we try them on? The rings were beautiful, really well made, he was a real craftsman. I just loved mine and so did the others, I kept mine on to save losing it and was so proud of my silver ring made in such a unusual place personally for me.

~*~

We arrived back at camp to be told that we were to go on a mission the next day, so after getting cleaned up, we had to go for a briefing before tea where we were told that we had to go into Iran to pick up some men who had been working out there and were in danger from some organisation in Tehran.

We were to set off in the morning in a couple of Land Rovers with a guide, it was going to be a long hot and dusty trip so that gave us the excuse to have a few beers that night in our tents.

Trevor and I were becoming close to each other, like two devoted brothers who watched out for each other all the time. As we sat drinking and checking our weapons, we chatted about home and trying to get back to Singapore for a leave sometime. After a few

73

drinks we decided to turn in to be fresh and ready for our early start in the morning.

We had not expected to have to move so soon but had been told that this was an emergency and these men were in danger if we did not get them out. They could not fly out as the air traffic was being watched closely in case they made their escape that way, so it had to be overland and back to Habbania, from there they could be flown home by the Royal Air Force.

So early in the morning, before daylight, we were awakened to go for breakfast before we set off with our guide. We got in the Land Rovers after checking that we had plenty of jerry cans of fuel strapped to the sides, plenty of water and ammunition.

Trevor and I took the first Land Rover with the guide, Dave, Brian, Tony and Robert were in the second one. They had a light machine gun mounted on theirs covered with a sheet just in case we had a lot of trouble, but the plan was for Trevor, myself and the guide to go in and try to rescue them, before anyone knew that we were in there, then get out fast with the rest giving us cover.

It was getting hot as we sped along dirt tracks leaving clouds of dust in our wake. We needed to get as near as we could to the point where we were to pick up the men before dark then make camp, eat and refresh ourselves. This was so no one could see the clouds of dust we left behind which made it easy to follow us if someone was patrolling the area, we had been told that, at times, there were heavy patrols, so we had to be ready at all times.

After driving for quite a few hours the guide told us we had gone far enough to the area where we were to meet up, all being well, saying that we should stop now and pull the sheets over the Land Rovers to give us a bit of cover. We shovelled sand on the bottom of the sheets and tossed a light covering on the camouflaged sheets, hoping that we would not be seen from the air if any small planes were passing over. We huddled under one of the sheets, two keeping watch while the others ate and drank. The light of day soon began to leave us and we had not been spotted so things were looking good for us, but we were taught never to relax no matter how good things looked.

Early in the morning while it was still dark after having an incident free evening, we removed and folded the sheets moving slowly forward to cover the last few miles that we had to go, with hearts in our mouths we were hoping everything went to plan.

I was nervous and so was Trevor, we touched each others shoulders to acknowledge our fear, the rest of the guys were in the same boat, scared but having an adrenalin rush. It was healthy to show some inner fear at times and the adrenalin was flowing fast as we started to slow down and listen for any sounds.

We had to wait for a whistle that was to be the signal when we reached our point of contact.

We stopped at the point we had arranged, being very alert and quiet, we must have been there an hour before we got the signal we were waiting for.

With that, Trevor and I moved slowly forward in the direction that we had heard the whistle, we were about twenty yards apart and both moving at the same pace just in case anyone opened fire on us, we could spread the area in front of us without the fear of hitting each other. We were reassured that the guys had us well covered also as we ventured forward with great caution.

We saw shapes in front of us, it looked as if these were the men that we had to pick up, there were three of them with two Arabs who had brought them to the rendezvous. After we had shaken hands we said goodbye to the two Arabs and set off back towards the Land Rovers. Just as we reached them we heard shots being fired, so we quickly got into the vehicles and set off, hell for leather, away from the direction that the shots had come from hoping that the two Arabs had not walked into trouble. We got a few hundred yards away when a couple of flares lit up the sky and we heard the whistle of shots going past us, so it was top speed ahead. We swung in front of the other land rover as they dropped back and uncovered the machine gun and returned the fire, the vehicles were bouncing all over as we held on for dear life, the sound of gun fire was deafening in the still of the desert.

We seemed to draw away from the flares and shooting but kept going at a fast speed until we were sure that we were clear of any danger. After about half an hour we heard no more but we decided to keep going and take turns at driving, this was so we did not have to drive in daylight in hostile territory when a plane would easily spot us.

We each drove for a few hours as it was hard driving in the sand dunes and the heat was becoming unbearable, when we approached what we would expect to be a safe area, we decided to slow down and relax a little as we could see the camp in the distance. We were safe and had an easy run back, the three men thanked us as we went for a debriefing, then we were going to get some sleep, hopefully in one of the huts and not the tents, as they got really hot. We were only too pleased to turn in as we were dead beat and needed a few hours sleep at least.

We awoke to the blazing heat and we went for breakfast. After we had eaten we were told that we were to leave that evening for a base in the Far East somewhere and that an RAF plane was going to take us to our destination. What a surprise was in store for us when we were told that we were going to be based at Changi in Singapore for a short while, this was great as we all smiled and laughed together.

Dave and Brian of course looking forward to the bounty of women that were there at their disposal, that's all those two talked about all day until we were ready to go but we were all very happy to be going back so soon.

~*~


We had a couple of refuel stops to make we were told in India and Ceylon before reaching Singapore, but we were used to stopping over at different places so it did not cause us a problem. It was a good flight and we were not held up too long, but what a sight for sore eyes when we drove in to the base, it felt so good. We were told which quarters we were to have, and we knew that they were some of the best on the camp and away from the main barrack rooms, at least we would have some privacy for ourselves. We dumped our kit bags and made our way to the bar for some food and drink, everyone of us decided not to go into the town that night as it was too late, we would rest tonight so we just sat chatting away and laughing amongst ourselves.

Brian said, "I wonder if the girls are still here? I hope that they are."

Robert replied, "I don't think it will bother you, Brian, if they are not."

We picked up our post from home and I had a letter from Ann and another one from her friend, Elsie Wright, the girl I went to school with. She wanted me to start writing to her. When I told Trevor he asked if I was going to, but I said no, I didn't have the time and didn't want to get too deeply involved.

Trevor asked me if I would write to her and ask if he could keep in touch with her and write the odd letter? I said that I would and told him that she was a real nice girl. He insisted that I did it there and then and, knowing that I'd get no peace until I did, I asked him to get a pad and pen from the bar. I wrote the letter asking Elsie to write to Trevor and told her he would send a picture to her and would she send him one back, he was very happy with that. I said that was my good deed for the day, wondering what Elsie would say.

Tony and Robert were having a few friendly words with Dave and Brian telling them to keep out of trouble, the banter went back and forth as Trevor and I watched them, grinning at the performance, as it was getting late we decided to go to bed and made our way back to the rooms, I must have fallen asleep as soon as my head hit the pillow.

~*~

The morning came too soon for me as I heard a loud banging on my door, it was Trevor and Dave to see if I was going to breakfast, so I pulled some shorts on and decided to get a shower afterwards. As we headed for the mess the other guys were just coming for us, one of the chefs who was there before said hello to us welcoming us back and asked how long we would be there this time? We said we did not know for sure but hoped it would be for a good while, we collected our breakfasts and decided to have a good natter to each other about the time we would be here and what we would do.

Trevor and I were going to explore the island fully this time and go over to Sentosa. Dave and Brian said they were going to explore the women but what else could you expect from them. Everyone of us, including the chef, burst out laughing at them but as always they took it in good spirit.

Robert and Tony said they wanted to come with us so we would go to the car pool and draw out a land rover or an Austin Champ to tour the island. Saying that we'd leave Dave and Brian to their own devices, we all went back for a shower and arranged to meet at the vehicle pound. When we got there, we were told it was no problem and that we could have one anytime, so we fuelled up and set off around the island. There was a beehive of shops as we drove down some dusty streets, some of the keepers were asleep outside, others just opening up as we sped into the countryside.

It was very dense in vegetation with very pretty birds flitting about the undergrowth, we decided to take turns in driving and stopped to have a beer when we came across anywhere that we could get a drink.

We had a water bag on the front of the land rover just in case we did not find anywhere, as we were not too familiar with this area. It was not long before we came to a thatched type of bar so we stopped to have a drink, asking the Singaporean who was the owner where we could go next? He told us to drive through the plantations and round the coast, he said some of the tracks were a bit rough but would be no problem for the land rover, so saying our farewells we set off again. It was pretty hot and humid with steam coming off the undergrowth, the island was very pretty and the wild life was in abundance it was a real pleasure and so peaceful. We drove past some colonial houses in their splendour and wondered how the other half lived.

By the time we got to a small beach we were all getting hot and uncomfortable so we decided to have a swim, but to keep near to the shore, this was just in case there were any sharks around as we did not know what was out there so caution was the order of the day. The water looked so warm and inviting and it would be a pleasure to get the dust off us as we all ran towards the sea shouting at each other to see who would be first in, I think we all made it at the same time. Desperate to get the dust off us, we splashed about in the shallow water watching for danger all the time.

We stayed there for about an hour, content to just lay in the shallows of the warm sea, it was so peaceful. Eventually we decided to get a move on and get back to Changi and leave the land rover at the vehicle park so that we could go out on the town. We arrived back still hot and dusty after racing down dusty tracks hell for leather, but we all had really enjoyed our day together. It was straight into the shower, except for me, it was the bath, full to the top, for me.

That night we went to Happy World, this was a place where most of the Yanks went and we got on well with them. Brian and I decided to call to see if Susan and Mary were still here with their parents, so after the shower I called Susan's house and her mother answered the phone, she called for Susan who picked up the phone saying hello in her posh voice.

I said hello and she asked, "Where are you?"

I told her we were back at Changi, she seemed excited and said she would call Mary, if that was okay, and meet us later?

I said that was fine and told her to meet us at the camp, then we could go into town. I went to Brian's room and told him that they were coming and he was happy with that.

We decided to eat in town, at one of the stalls in the hawker centre because we knew it was good food, it was a couple of hours before we all met up in the bar. I was not in love with Susan but liked her a lot and I had made it clear to her.

Brian said to me, "You are a fool to yourself being so straight with them and telling them how you feel. Tell them all you love them as Dave and I do."

But I had made my mind up to enjoy my army life and not get tied up with a woman, as that would complicate things for me, also I was not the sort of person to deceive and hurt anyone that I liked. I could not be like Dave or Brian, my family values were a bit prudish I think, but that was the way I was and I could not change.

Trevor was as near to me as anyone could get and he was the only one that I would confide personnel issues to, we were like brothers and looked out for each other. I was a bit rougher than Trevor but we complimented each other in the way we both thought.

We decided to have a drink while waiting for the girls, about an hour later Susan and Mary walked into the bar. Susan ran straight up to me and kissed me on the lips, saying she had missed me, I said, "that is nice of you, I'm pleased to see you too." Mary had done the same to Brian and they were in a gridlock, to all our amusement.

Susan pulled a chair up and wanted to know what we had been up to, I said I would tell her a bit later, with that she just smiled at me.

We bought the girls a drink and said we would go in about half an hour for something to eat in town. Susan then told us that four of their mates were coming to the bar so maybe they could come with us into town, we said they'd be welcome, so we sat chatting, waiting for their friends to come, the guys were quite pleased as now there would be six men and six women, after all, it was only a bit of fun together. After about five minutes four girls walked in the bar, they were real stunners, the gasp that came from the guys told you that.

Trevor leaned over and said to Susan, "You have done us proud." and smiled at me. Brian's face was a picture as he scanned the talent thinking that the grass was greener on the other side, all of a sudden Mary gave him a dig in the ribs, much to our amusement, but it would not be Brian if he failed to scan the girls.

Introductions were made as we sat around getting to know one another, it seemed as though we were going to have a good night with all of us going on the town together. The girls and guys soon paired off and we decided to get three cabs to take us to the waterfront. When they arrived we all piled in, Trevor and his girl, Susan and me in one, Brian and Mary with Tony and his girl for the night, and the same for Dave, Robert and their girls. It was strange how Dave and Brian always managed to keep apart in certain circumstances.

It was hot and very humid as we set off for the front but it was nice when we got there with the breeze off the sea. Deciding to sit outside, at least it was pleasant looking out at the ships at anchor in the bay, we pulled some tables together just about taking over all the seats outside. We ordered some Tiger ales, pretty strong stuff as we knew from our last visit. I was looking at Brian and Dave as their eyes were everywhere watching the girls. Brian caught my glance and winked at me.

We all ordered our food, most of us were having lobster and fish, and we decided to go to a disco or local dance place that the girls knew after the meal instead of Happy World.

Paired off, we walked down the road to the dance place chatting as we went and half way there we were heckled by some sailors, one of them was out of order with his chosen words, the others then took courage and started shouting to the girls which we thought was unacceptable behaviour, so we told the girls to walk on and we waited for these guys to come up to us. There were about nine of them to the six of us, which we thought were good odds so we looked at each other and said, name your guy. Trevor and I said we would take the three on the inside, the other guys were to take three between the two of them. They stood off us a bit at first, looking and wondering what to do, they had not expected that we would face up to them, their being quite a few more than we were, but we have never ducked a fight in our lives so little did they know we were up for at least a good scrap.

Hoping to teach them some manners, which they lacked, we were up for it, I think that they sensed it and that was the reason for the delay in them coming forward but they dare not back away and lose face after mouthing off at the girls. So we were about twenty feet apart and looking at each other they realised that they out numbered us and suddenly deciding to go for it, coming towards us as we took our stance and got balanced on our feet.

Trevor and I were going to take one each as fast as we could, we knew exactly what each other was going to do. I saw Trevor out of the corner of my eye crack this guy who was in front, so hard he just slumped to the floor. One down, the next one in was mine, in a split second I ducked under his fist and came up and under and felt his nose give under the force of my blow, my fist slipped off his jaw and connected with his nose the blood was everywhere, it was only a split second again before the others came in. I brought my elbow round on one guy and caught him just at the back of the ear with a crack that sent him to the ground. Then I felt a blow to the back it was one of the sailors who had got away from Brian and Tony because they were slugging it out with the other two. I then felt a blow catch me above the eye and could feel the blood running down my face, I swung round and hit him hard, but not hard enough, because he just stood there looking at me and gave me one back.

Meanwhile Trevor was helping the other guys out, the sailor and I stood face to face now exchanging punches, he was a tough guy and was holding his own, so I thought I needed to take him out before he gave me a good hiding, I stepped to one side and let him have one straight in the throat and there was a gasp as he sank to the floor.

I wiped the blood off my face as it was running into my eye and all over my shirt and looked round to see Dave slugging it out with a guy, he seemed to be enjoying himself. Trevor had just put another one down, and stood watching the rest of us. Brian and Robert were still at it but they looked as though they had it under control, Tony was just about to put his guy down with blood pouring down his face. I think, looking at us, there was only Trevor unmarked, the rest of us were bleeding from our mouths and busted noses, so the three of us stood and watched the others finish the job ready to give a hand if needed.

With that the sailors who could get to their feet took to their heels, wishing, I bet, that they had not taken us up on the challenge, and maybe they would have better manners in the future.

We all looked at each other as we walked away to meet the girls leaving some of the sailors still on the ground moaning, we all burst out laughing as we looked a sorry sight indeed, with swollen eyes and blood all over our white shirts. As we approached the girls they looked at us and their first words were, we would not get in the club with us looking like that, so we went into a shop and bought some shirts then went in the next bar to get cleaned up and have a beer, it is surprising what you can do with water and a few sticking plasters provided by the bar owner. He knew us and knew that we were not ones to cause trouble so he wasn't bothered about the way we looked.

All cleaned up, plasters over the cuts, a few swollen bumps, but otherwise in one piece, we sat down to our beers. Trevor looking great not a bump or cut on him, It was great to relax with a beer after that skirmish, and the girls thanked us for looking after them.

We had the beer and set off for the dance place, hoping that we would get in, but Susan and her mates said it would be okay as they knew the owner. It was dark in the club with tables all around the floor and music playing loudly, the night went by quickly and we all enjoyed ourselves. It was about two in the morning, as we made our way back to the camp, it seemed as if all the guys would score tonight, the girls seemed up for it as they all wanted to stay in the barracks tonight. It was a good job that we had preferential treatment and had special rooms to keep us away from the other guys.

Arriving back at the camp we split off in our pairs, Brian was still with Mary so that was a first for him, Susan laughed and said Mary was more than a match for him with a smile on her face. So saying goodnight to each other we all went to get our heads down, well some of us. Susan and I chatted for a bit then fell asleep both tired from the night's activities, it did not seem long before we woke again. After a shower we decided to have breakfast and meet up with the others to decide what to do that day. As the girl's fathers worked for the forces it was okay for them to have breakfast in the NAFFI with us, Susan and I drifted down to find Tony, Brian and Robert already sat in there with their girls. Trevor followed us in and we all sat together waiting for David and his girl.

There were a few sore heads but we did not look too bad after the skirmish last night. We tucked into a good breakfast chatted about what we were going to do that day. It was decided that we'd go down to the beach and laze about for the day.

David arrived and with his young lady, yawning as she came through the door, and did he look rough? We told him that we were going to have a lazy day on the beach with the girls, so after breakfast we collected our swimming gear and some beers and walked down to the beach near to the camp. It was a beautiful day, the sea looked great and was so clear, we spread ourselves far and wide as though we owned the whole beach. We were chatting and swimming and having loads of fun together in general. Then we sat in a big circle drinking beer talking about what we were going to do that night, we came to the conclusion that we would go down town again rather than stay in the NAAFI.

The day passed quickly and we were looking a bit sunburnt, so we packed up and went back to have a sleep and a shower as we were to meet at eight that night to hit the town again. We drifted into our respective rooms, it was nice to get out of the heat and the humidity. The girls had all gone home to get changed before coming back to go into the town. After having a shower I daydreamed on the bed.

Eight o'clock came round too soon for me so I got dressed and knocked on Trevor's door as I was passing, he was ready and came straight out and we walked to the NAAFI together, knocking on the doors as we passed just in case anyone had fallen asleep. Most of them were already waiting, all done up looking good, ready to make our descent on the town. Brian and Mary looked as though they had been having words, but that was on the cards as Brian could not stay with one woman for very long, but they had calmed down a little as we ordered the cabs, so we were all happy little bunny's again, we left hoping that we did not have any trouble that night.

The cabs arrived and we all got in and set off for the front again to have a meal and in general just have a bit of fun together, as we paid off the cabs and walked towards the bars, Brian and Mary were making up, kissing as they walked. I smiled at Susan and she smiled back and held my hand tightly as we walked, it was such a nice night as we sat down taking over most of the tables again. The girls asked how long before we had to go again, we did not know but replied by saying we were to be based at Changi for a few months. So that settled, the girls knowing that we were to stay a bit in Singapore in between jobs, as we liked the place and the company that we had here.

Most of the girls were from wealthy parents but we knew that by the houses that they lived in and the jobs that their fathers had. We were just normal guys from a working class background who had joined the forces for an adventure and we were to get that for sure, but the girls were good fun to be with and did not show their airs and graces. I thought that Susan was hoping for more from our friendship and I was going to have to be careful, not wanting to get involved. I just wanted to enjoy my army life and my view was it would not be right to get to involved with someone with the risk that this job had for us. Also it could cloud your judgement in a crisis and we were to have a good few of those in the time that we were to spend together. So I had to make it quite clear to Susan that I was in no way going to get attached to someone, when I told her she said that she understood but there was sadness in her voice as she asked if we could be good friends. I said, "Yes, of course we can be good friends," she was a beautiful girl and great company. I did say to her that I would not think her parents would approve of me anyway with the money that they had, they would want someone better for her. Her reply was, "Money does not and cannot buy happiness."

But I could not detract from the reason that I joined the forces, the home life that I had was bad, but here I had mates that would die for me, and me for them, so I had to be strong where women were concerned. Little did I know that was going to be the story of my life, shrugging off women when they got too close, this was to become my problem, I would never get too close to a woman for fear of losing her. I also had a problem getting close to anyone except Trevor, Brian, Robert, Tony and Dave, this was because we all knew that we were in such a dangerous job that any one of us could be killed at anytime.

Well we were having a great time with the girls in Singapore enjoying every minute that we were together, a bit later we left the restaurant, saying to the girls that we would drop them off at their houses, this we did, saying goodbye to them all before going back to camp.

When we got back someone told us that we had to report to Captain Rennie as soon as we arrived back in the camp. He told us it was unfortunate but something has cropped up of great importance, and that we had to go on standby and get ready at short notice, we were told not to leave the camp for the next two days because they did not know when we would be needed. We had no idea where we were going, but it had to be somewhere in the Far East we guessed because otherwise they would send someone else.

# Chapter 8

We hung about the camp in the bars, when the girls called, we told them that we could not leave the camp for a few days, they understood as most of their parents worked for, or in, the forces in some way. We finally got our orders that we were to leave the next day so it was to be no drink that night, fruit juice only. Later that night we were to fly to and be dropped into Cambodia, our mission would be to destroy a drug cartel there, and the place where it was all stored, just on the border near to Phnom Penh. We were told that this was to be no easy task, so eight other men were to come with us, mainly to give us more cover if we needed it, as we went in to sort the problems out.

It was to be our worst operation yet because we had to stay at a small village for a good while observing the comings and goings from the place where the drugs were kept and the deals done. There were some people in the village that we were to stay in who were paid by the British, we were told that they were loyal because of the misery that they and their families had to endure at times, also we were told that it was secure, up to a point, but to trust no one, but that was part of the game, we would watch everything with caution.

That night we told the girls, as we drank fruit juice and they drank beer, that we were to leave early in the morning, saying that we would likely be away for a couple of weeks or more, we were all sorry that we were leaving, that proved my point of not getting too attached because the girls were all upset at our going so soon, but we made the most of the evening. Susan sat close to me all night, same with Mary and the others, when it was time to say goodnight we were all a bit down with ourselves and even Dave and Brian realised that there were to be no girls in the rooms that night because next day it could mean life or death and we all had to have rest and have our wits about us. It was goodnight kisses and straight to our rooms, as I kissed Susan she said, "Come back safe my dear friend, if that's all we can be."

I said, "we will be fine, we'll look after each other so please try not to worry too much."

After breakfast the next morning, we were sent to the airstrip, nerves were slightly on edge and the adrenalin was running high in anticipation of what was to come for us, this is always the case when going into the unknown. The other eight guys that were to go with us were the same, not doing much talking either.

We were to be dropped as close to the village as possible, without drawing too much attention to ourselves, as we boarded the plane we wished each other good luck and shook hands. We all had different tasks to do yet relied on each other's skills to survive, Trevor and I, as always, grasped each other's hand and said good luck, Trevor was the one person that I loved like a brother and he told me he thought of me the same way, in a totally different way than Brian and me, who had grown up together as real good friends. Trevor and I had this special bond between us, we nearly knew each other's thoughts at times. Just as the plane started down the runway for take off we wished the guys with us all the best and hoped that they'd come back safely.

It was quiet on the plane at first as we all gathered our thoughts, some of us would be thinking of home, others of their girls. I was just, as I knew Trevor was, preparing myself mentally for the task ahead of us hoping that God was with us and we would come back safe and sound together. After about an hour we started to chat and we talked about anything and everything, Trevor told me that he and Elsie were getting close with the letter writing, so I said good luck to you both. I told him I did not want to get close to anyone really. Brian and Dave said they were going to get all the women that they could and that was to be an understatement from them two as we all burst out laughing, they took it in good humour as they always did.

The time passed quickly and it was not long before we were warned to prepare to leave the aircraft as we were approaching the drop zone. We wished each other a safe descent, and with that we checked our equipment and made sure we had quick access to our weapons just in case anyone was waiting for us.

You never knew in this type of terrain what to expect but we were ready for the unexpected and, most of all, knew that we could rely on each other in a crisis, there had to be strength in any team and we knew that we had each other.

Trevor and I grasped hands and wished each other a special good luck as the lights went on to get ready to jump, this was again a stressful time, hoping that you got down safe. Out we went, one by one, the buzz you got was always the same, a great feeling as we all floated down watching the terrain beneath us, hoping that we would all get down safe without any broken bones. Everything went well with no accidents so that was a plus as we buried our chutes, then we waited to be met by one of the villagers who was to take us to his village where we was going to stay.

We positioned ourselves around so we had everything covered and waited for someone to come. It was nerve racking as we waited and the adrenalin was pumping round our bodies, not knowing what to expect. It was so strange, we were all like tense steel, waiting for the unexpected in this bloody hot and humid place. We were all being silent using our hands to send messages to each other as the time passed by, when suddenly we heard a slight rustle and with rifle safety catches off, ready for the unexpected, we waited until we could identify the noise, wondering if it could be a wild animal as we lay so still with just the sounds of the jungle around us. We heard the call that we had been waiting for, a short whistle followed by another one, so, with a sigh of relief, we answered the call and still did not reveal ourselves.

Trevor and I came out and stood apart with rifles ready while the rest of them covered us just in case we were shot at. We made sure we were far enough apart to cause problems if it was a trap and then we could make sure that we did not die in vain, but it was fine as the guide came out with hands in the air. Trevor and I kept him covered and the rest did not reveal themselves just then until we were sure.

I went up to the guy and asked him if he had something to drink and he answered with the code; "Yes a cup of tea." typical of the English to think of that, so satisfied that we were clear, we asked him how long to the village that we were to stay in, he said about two hours through the jungle and warned us that the rebels had people all around so we would have to be really careful.

Picking up our gear we decided to set off with Trevor and I taking up the front with the guide and the rest flanking us to give us maximum cover as we proceeded to the village. We were glad to see that the guide was a very confidant man who knew every inch of the jungle, it all looked the same to us, so dense and humid we were wet through after travelling a few hundred yards.

He told us that the drug and arms dealers had shot and tortured some of his villagers after raping their young women, he also said they were installing fear into all the villages around the area, this made us all the more determined to either capture or kill them all.

I saw red when we were told that young children had been raped and killed, I said to Trevor and the rest how can we rest until every last one is killed? How can another human kill young children who have never harmed anyone in their short lives?

We were making good time when suddenly the guide raised his hand to stop us dead in our tracks, we melted into the undergrowth and waited. About five minutes had passed before we really heard anything ourselves but the guide was used to the jungle sounds. Then three well armed men came by, smoking, not really bothered about keeping quiet, pretty confident that they were in charge of the area. They were moving very slowly unconcerned with anything around them. I signalled to Brian and Tony that we three would take them out as the others kept us covered. Signalling that it had to be silent by drawing my hand across my throat, we all went together, after leaving our packs on the floor to give us more freedom of movement, to take them out without too much fuss.

It was to be a testing time for us to get all three of them before they could squeeze the trigger and get off a warning shot that would blow our cover and bring others to the area, then we would have real problems. As we drew close to them we all had our razor sharp hunting knifes out ready, the guys seemed relaxed as they continued on their way unaware of the danger creeping up on them. We were within ten feet of them and I signalled go, it was all over in a split second as all three of us cut their throats with precision timing. This we did knowing that at all times our guys had each of us well covered, also with the added satisfaction that the other men that were with us had us covered as well.

The guys then came in and dragged the bodies into deep undergrowth, covering the tracks as they did so, with Trevor and me keeping watch along with some of the others just in case there were anymore rebels following on behind. The guide was shocked at the speed we had carried out the exercise, but he had a smile on his face to see some of the rebels that have raped and pillaged his village dead.

Checking that all signs of a struggle was cleared from the scene, we set off once again for the village where a hiding place had been arranged for us. It had been set up so that we could hit where we wanted and then disappear into the jungle with the rebels not knowing who it was and where they had come from. It was going to be a tough assignment because we would have to do the job fully to save any repercussions on the villages in the area.

~*~

The guide told us that there was about thirty five of the well armed rebels at their main base and were split into two camps, this did not help at all not knowing how many were in each camp. This made us realise that it was not going to be an easy task at all for the six of us to deal with, but we did have the other guys as a back up.

We arrived at the village with caution and the guide took us to a compound where they had some chickens, he lifted a cover under the straw and revealed a ladder down into a room that they had carefully dug out for us, it was a good size, they used it to hide the women sometimes. He then said he would bring us some food and the village elders wanted to talk to us. It must have taken them weeks to dig this out, it was quite a feat, besides, thankfully, it was a lot cooler down in our little pit beneath the ground. We all picked our spots to get our heads down, sort of claiming a patch. The guide came back with a young woman and some fresh food for us, fruit and chicken.

Dave and Brian were weighing up the young woman and wondering how many of them they could add to their conquest list, as more women were made available for them, they would take full advantage of them no matter what. One thing you could guarantee was that they would waste no time between them, the pair of them were like rabbits on heat, Tony remarked with a chuckle.

We all got stuck into the food, the chicken always tasted better to us when it had been running around at will, we gratefully drank the coconut milk and ate the chicken and fresh fruit that they had kindly brought for us. After about an hour the guy came back and said we were to follow him to one of the huts to see the elders, we insisted that four of our guys kept a watch just outside the village along with their people. They had no problem with that but we could not trust anyone fully in situations like this it was life and death for us.

We sat down in the hut with the satisfaction that some of our guys were outside, and the elders started by telling us how grateful they were for us coming to help them with the very difficult situation that they were in with these drug dealers. They said they would help us all they could and told us if we wanted some company we just had to ask, meaning of the female kind, as Dave and Brian's eyes sparkled at the thought.

Brian said, "this is going ok after all."

I said to them, "You had both better keep you weapons to yourselves," as the others laughed at my remark.

The elders told us that the rebels had two camps of about sixteen men in each, but that there may be more than that, they were not too sure about the numbers, so we had to anticipate that there could be many more and prepare for that outcome. We decided to go out in a couple of small groups and reconnoitre the area around the village.

Dave said he could not wait to find a nice young woman tonight to which Brian agreed without hesitation at all, these two were to cause us some problems for sure with their brains between their legs, but to be fair they both were good mates and good soldiers, we all had our faults, none of us was expected to be perfect, but some of us had a little bit more commonsense than others. We were to rest up for the remainder of the day and carry out a full surveillance of the area in the morning to familiarize ourselves with the landmarks around us.

That night the elders had guards around the village and the guys that were with us had two on at a time to give us time to rest and we were grateful for that. We sat around the fire, just back in the shadows of the flames but close enough to smell the food and feel the heat, they had cooked fresh food for themselves and us. A good few of the village people joined us and as usual Brian and Dave were weighing up the women, one of the elders saw them and told them that they could take their pick then asked us all if we wanted women? We all declined except a couple of the other guys so we did not feel too bad about Dave and Brian.

The evening passed without any incidents, Dave and Brian were getting on well with the two very pretty young women as were the two other guys, we had a couple of beers but not enough to dim our senses.

After a couple of hours the guys with the girls drifted off to the huts, the rest of us stayed near to the fire and decided to sleep outside that night, it was a pleasant night and the sweet smell of the jungle was very refreshing for us.

The elders were telling us how cruel the rebels were, taking the women and young girls from different villages, and killing the young boys. We were determined to sort this problem out to stop the rape and pillaging of these very friendly people. The more we heard of what was going on, we knew it had to stop, not just for the villager's sake but for the drugs that were being moved around the world. We talked into the night and dozed off to sleep, we were quite relaxed knowing that we had the villagers, and our back up guys were keeping a look out for us, we were grateful to be able to partly wind-down for the night.

Next morning we were awake early, the other guys along with Brian and Dave joined us with smiles on their faces, and we guessed that we would get the full details later on the performance of the women.

We decided to split up into two groups to reconnoitre the area, we had a guide with each group as we set off into the thick undergrowth which was very hot and humid. The six of us were together as we knew how each other worked and thought, just the same as the other guys, it was a fact that we had two very good teams to deal with this situation.

We made slow but steady progress as the adrenalin was running once again, after about two miles we heard some movement to our right so we all froze in our tracks. The noise was staying put and we heard voices as we lay very still, so we decided to creep up on them, Trevor, myself and Dave went to the right, Brian, Tony and Robert went to the left. As we came near to where the voices were coming from, we could see through the undergrowth a clearing and about ten dirty, evil looking, hombres and there were three young women and two men tied up. We decided to observe for a few minutes just to make sure that there were no more of them around, we did not want to jeopardise what we had come to do and that was to destroy the drugs. These guys were so into what they was doing that it looked as though they did not feel threatened by anything at all around them. They were beginning to make moves on the young women who looked frightened to death, we guessed that these were part of the people that we had been sent in to dispose of.

Knowing that we were in sight of Brian, Tony and Rob, we signalled for them to pick some of the guys nearest to them and we would take the others, we were going to manoeuvre ourselves so that most of the rebels had their backs to us watching the women, four of them were touching the women on the breasts and beginning to tear their clothes off so we gave the signal before it was too late.

Slowly moving towards them, hoping not to have to shoot any of them because it would be heard for miles, all we wanted was to get the women and two men back to the safety of the village. We crept up and they were unaware that anyone was watching them as they proceeded to tear the clothes off the young women leaving the two men who were tied to a tree facing us.

One of them saw us and we signalled for him to keep quiet as we approached the clearing, he saw the guide we had with us and realized that we were there to try and help them. All the rebels were concentrating on the sex they were going to have with the young women and not feeling threatened or worried about anything around them. Trevor, Dave and I decided to hit the three guys that were watching and waiting for their turn with the women, from behind. Brian, Tony and Robert would be doing the same, the other guys would sweep up the rest for us, we made signs to them which three we were going to take out first.

Their weapons were on the ground quite a few feet away as they were concentrating on other things at the moment, so we were confident that we could, hopefully, pull this off with no shooting. We waited until the three guys had dropped their pants then we all moved together hitting them at the same time with arms around their throats and snapping their necks with one hard sharp twist.

The men with the girls turned round but it was too late as we had pulled our knives and were on top of them slitting their throats before they knew what had hit them. The rest were taken out by the guys in the same manner, the girls screamed as the blood ran from the rebels bodies. Brian had been cut but it was not too bad, it was over in seconds, we were thankful for that as we cut free the two men and the guide made a fuss of them.

The girls, sobbing to themselves, retrieved their clothes thankful that they had not been raped then killed by the rebels. We decided to bury the bodies as fast as we could and head back to the village. After we had finally buried them we brushed the area clean as best we could, to hide the fact anyone had been there.

Looking back I said to Brian, "It looks like a good job, my mate, how are you?"

It was just a small cut that would need a few stitches, he said. I told him that I would stitch it as soon as we got away from the area.

Moving away, while keeping the girls and men in the middle of us, we had gone about a mile when we stopped so I could stitch Brian as he was bleeding quite badly.

I put some antiseptic powder on the wound and got a sterilized needle and gut out of my pack I stitched it up with five stitches, then sprinkled powder on it again and bound it to keep it clean. Brian thanked me and said that it felt a lot better.

We then set off for the village once again, on arriving there the other guys were not back yet but they had kept quite wide of us on the way to the village so it would have taken them a bit longer than us to get back. We decided to be careful and keep out of sight until they arrived back. We took up positions around the village after handing over the girls and the men to their friends and waited for the other guys to come back safe.

The villagers fetched us some food and they could not do enough for us but we had to keep focussed, one slip and we could be dead meat. So we concentrated on keeping a look out for the others hoping that they all came back safe.

A couple of hours had gone by and we had eaten the chicken and some sort of bread that had been brought to us and washed it down with coconut milk when we heard a slight movement in the jungle and hoped it was them. Sure enough the guide came into the village to make sure all was okay, he then signalled to the others to come in, we were glad to see them and broke our cover.

The villagers then put some of their people to watch, this gave us a chance to brief each other on what we found, they had not encountered any problems but had found out that there was a camp of about thirty at least that they had spotted when they went wide of us on the way back. It was about five miles away from the village and they had observed from a distance and said it looked as though they were well armed and had lookouts around the camp. This looked as though it was the main camp and our mission was to wipe it out altogether and destroy the weapons and drugs. We decided to spend a few days watching the camp by sending a couple of guys with a guide each day to observe them. This was to track their movements to see if they had some sort of pattern to them. Trevor and I were to go in the morning leaving everyone back at the camp to relax as best they could.

That night the villagers made us join them in eating roast wild pig and offered us their thanks. Trevor and I went to bed as we had an early start in the morning leaving the others to enjoy themselves, the night passed quickly and we awoke to rain the like of which we had not seen for a very long while, it was coming down in torrents.

We still decided to go, the jungle was steaming as we set off with some food the guide had sorted out for us, they were such friendly people, how could someone abuse them they did not want to hurt anyone but this is what money does for you and the ruthless people that were doing it did not value anybody's life at all. "It is a sad world," I thought to myself as I said to Trevor, "how can anyone hurt these friendly people?"

But as Trevor said, this is a cruel world at times and we can only do what we can to stop these people being abused by the rebels. I prayed to God to help us as we were making our way to the camp through the torrential rain, the jungle was becoming soggy underfoot but the guide said it would soon clear up. It took us about two and half hours to get into a position where we could observe the rebels, there did not seem to be very much movement in the camp at all, so we settled down in the heavy growth and were ready to shoot our way out if we were spotted.

The morning was not too bad with very little movement except for the fact we saw some prisoners, they were being kept in a compound that the rebels had built in the middle of the camp. There were about seven young women and five young men as far as we could make out through the binoculars.

I said to Trevor that we could not risk freeing up the prisoners until we have decided how we were going to wipe out the camp for good, we guessed that they were there for the pleasure of the rebels because during the day someone came in and took some of the women away and then after an hour they brought them back and locked them in again.

Just after we had eaten, a truck came into the camp and they started to unload some boxes that looked like ammunition and arms. We observed where they took the arms as that would be a useful piece of information when we came to attack the camp, it had not been a wasted day and the rest of the afternoon passed without much going on.

The time came for us to set off back to the village, we made good time and were back inside two hours ready for a wash down, the other guys said that they had a good day around the camp in general.

Dave and Brian told us that they and some of the other guys that were there had spent the day having fun with some of the women, this was with the blessing of the elders of course. Brian was telling me that they knew how to please a guy, saying that we should take them up on the offer. We said 'no thanks' but there were some very beautiful young women and it was tempting, but we were to decline the offer along with Tony and Robert. Some of the other guys were taking up the offer but not all of them.

We then proceeded to get washed down and have something to eat, it was our turn to relax tomorrow, Dave and Tony were going out to observe the camp so Trevor and I briefed them both on what we had seen.

We had some beer that night as we sat eating the roast pig, we talked about Singapore and Trevor said he had written a few letters to Elsie and asked Janet in the NAAFI to post them every two days. I said I think you are falling in love with her and promised him he could come and stay with me if we ever got back to Blighty. He asked me what I was going to do?

I said I cared about a woman but could not fall in love yet as I was not sure but I was to find that out later in my life. I, of course, wanted someone to love me, I said to him, but who and when, I didn't know. He asked about Susan but I just said, "God will tell me when the right person comes along I hope, but sometimes you can live a lifetime and be alone. I just want to help people after seeing the misery that is caused for the people in the third world countries."

Trevor said that Brian and me were two different creatures but we got on so well, then he turned to me and said, "You are like a brother to me and I hope that I am to you."

It turned out that we were to become the best of friends for the rest of our lives. We talked late into the night and enjoyed our beers together feeling secure with the guys on four hour watch.

We talked about our home life, Trevor told me again that he had been brought up in a pub in Leicester in the Midlands. I told him my home life was not happy and my mother used me as a skivvy and I was beaten at times with a shoe or whatever she could put her hands on. I passed my eleven plus to go on to college but she would not let me, so Brian and I decided to join the army once we were old enough. I told him my father was a kind and careful man with a talent for being able to play any musical instrument and that he used to compare at the clubs around the city. I also told him that a girl called Ann was my friend, along with Elsie and a few others, telling him that Ann's father and mother liked me a lot. Ann's father had his own building business and Ann was the only child. She and I were excellent friends and cared for each other very much as did Elsie and I.

Trevor told me that he used to help in his father's pub and had loads of women friends who came into the pub but he said that he wanted some excitement and not to be stuck behind the bar all the time, so that was the reason he decided to join the forces. He also told me that his family did not have much time for him with having the pub to run. I carried on telling him how Brian and I had grown up with each other and looked out for each other on the streets. It was the early hours when we decided to turn in for the night knowing that we did not have to rush in the morning and looking forward to a day of rest with us all taking turns on watching the drug dealers camp.

When we woke next day Dave and Tony had already gone out to observe the rebels. We ate and then went down to a stream, stripped off and lay in the refreshing water with a couple of the others keeping watch for us, it was so peaceful just laid there relaxing.

We chatted about the cruelty that these rebels were inflicting on these very gentle people, asking ourselves why and how could another human hurt young children and the helpless?

Realising that we had to do our bit and try to wipe out as much of the misery that these barons caused. We had been there about two hours, the time had flown by as we had laid there in the running water, finally pulling ourselves out we decided to head back to the village where we sat in the shade of a tree and drank some coconut milk that was brought to us. The rest of the guys were spread around the village just lazing around.

We had been sat there about an hour when we heard a rustling noise, we melted into the undergrowth with our weapons ready, wondering why the guys keeping watch had not raised the alarm, but it turned out to be Tony and the guide. Dave wasn't with them so we asked where he was. Tony said that they had come across some girls washing in a stream, Dave had gone up to them as Tony and the guide stayed out of sight, Dave caught one of them by the hand and led her into the undergrowth. Tony didn't shout out to Dave as that could have given them away, so they just sat quietly there waiting for him to come back. There was a scuffle in the undergrowth, then within a minute out came Dave and the girl with their hands tied behind their backs and five rebels surrounding them, the other girls had melted into the undergrowth.

Tony decided to follow and see where they took Dave and the girl who was sobbing her eyes out, finally they ended up at a small camp, but not the one that we had observed the day before, that was fortunate because we could have fallen foul of the drug dealers in that camp when we decided to raid the main one. The guide said that there were about ten rebels in this camp and Dave and the girl were put into a hut and one of the rebels was watching them.

Tony said that they could just see, with the help of the binoculars, that they were being tied to a stake in the hut so that was a small plus for us. He then thought it would be best to make his way back to the village to let us know.

I said to Trevor, "Bloody balls before brains again, not happy with having the girls here in safety," good job we were not in uniform or anything that would link us with the forces.

We were scruffy looking guys so we hoped that they thought that Dave was just a Brit living out here as many did. We decided that we would go out straight away and try to get him back, and the girl of course, before they did any damage to them or killed them, also, we could not afford to leave it in case they moved them elsewhere.

Trevor and I were cursing Dave, even Brian said, "the bloody fool, there was plenty of talent here for him."

So we decided that Trevor, Brian, Tony and I would go and try to bring them back. We took plenty of ammunition and checked our weapons and such. As we set off, Tony said it would take us well over an hour to get there at a fair pace, we decided that we would have to move fast after we had watched the movement within the camp for a little while.

We made good time even though we were very cautious because we could not afford to be picked up or heard by anyone, the adrenalin was pumping round our bodies for sure as we neared the camp. I could feel my heart beating so smoothly and I felt like a piece of tempered steel. The whole mission was at stake here, we had to get David before they could make him talk and spill the beans on what we were here for. We reached the camp and Tony showed us through the binoculars the hut that Dave and the girl were being kept in, the only one with a guard on the door.

So we decided to observe for a few hours until darkness started to pull in, ready in case we saw anything else happening, then we would have to act quickly but hoped that we had the element of surprise on our side as we lay watching the camp.

We all agreed that it wasn't going to be easy, Brian then surprised me by saying, "In case we don't come out of this okay, I just want to say I love you, we have been pals now since school."

I said to Brian, "you too, my mate, we have had some tough and trying times together."

Turning to Trevor I told him that that included him because he had become like a brother to me.

We had observed the camp and saw that the men were drinking so that would make it a bit better for us maybe? There were about ten of them around the camp as was first reported to us, so we decided to give it another half hour to double check the numbers.

The plan was for me to go into the hut and cut Dave and the girl free after dealing with the man on the door. Trevor and Brian were to cover me and watch for anyone else going to the hut once I was inside. We crept nearer to the edge of the camp so we could go in as soon as the light dimmed, I said to the others that I felt uneasy and a little scared, but this was a natural feeling when you know that you could lose your life.

"We are here for you," Trevor said.

God, was our adrenalin running high I was like a spring waiting to go and the other three were the same. The time was here so I made my way slowly round to the hut with Brian, Tony and Trevor watching me, the guide hung back, ready to take us out of here when the job was done. We were hoping to do this without firing a shot as before and they would think that some village people had sprung Dave and the girl if anyone outside this camp knew about them, then it would not jeopardise the mission that we were here to do.

I withdrew my knife and crept slowly towards the guard, eyes everywhere. He had a rifle and a pistol in his belt, I also spotted a knife stuck in the belt. I put my knife in my belt, knowing the guy was mine as I grabbed him with both arms and snapped his neck, letting him drop to the floor. I dragged him into the hut then realised that was a mistake as there was a guy inside the hut who had been ravaging the girl, lucky for me he had put his pistol down on the floor but he drew a knife from his partly undone trousers and dived at me thrusting with it.

I felt a warm feeling on my arms and in my stomach as he caught me with the knife two or three times, but then I had my knife out and blocked his next stab at me and ducked under his guard, thrusting my knife up into his chest he gurgled and dropped like a stone at my feet with blood spurting everywhere.

I quickly cut Dave and the girl free and told them to follow me, I could see the relief on their faces as I told them to keep quiet, we had lady luck on our side for sure and I wanted to keep it that way. Trevor and Brian were waiting for us and we moved away from the camp following the guide into the darkness hoping that what we had done was not discovered too soon. Trevor brought up the rear and I told him I was bleeding, he had a quick look at it and said I'd need stitches when we got back to the village.

My shirt was wringing with blood and I felt wet through, Trevor wrapped a dressing round my waist tightly to slow the blood down and my arms were not too bad.

We travelled back on the main track as we had the cover of darkness with us, after about an hour we had to leave the track to head to the village that was hidden away. By this time I was feeling a bit weak and sick due to the loss of blood which was pumping with the exertion we were putting in to getting back. I was very relieved when we arrived at the village.

"Sorry, my mate, and thanks to you all," Dave said.

I just said, "balls, David." He knew I was mad with him when I called him David.

Trevor asked for some hot water from the fire to clean up my wounds as I undressed to the waist to weigh up the damage, I had been cut twice on the arms and in the stomach and my clothes were soaked in blood as I took them all off. A young girl came and cleaned my wounds while Trevor got some antiseptic out and sprinkled it on them, he passed me a needle and some gut and I began to stitch my stomach, telling Trevor he would have to stitch my arm. I put about five stitches in my stomach and it looked okay.

Trevor then passed the needle to the girl and said to me she would make a better job than him, we laughed because he really did not like blood or the sight of it on me.

The girl did a neat job then I cleaned it down with boiled water and put some antiseptic on, the last thing I wanted was to get an infection. We then went for something to eat and drink, I decided to have a few beers as did Tony, Trevor and Brian as the rest kept watch. We would have to lay low for a few more days so that the rebels thought it was the villagers from somewhere around that had sprung Dave and the girl. Dave was keeping clear of Trevor and me, he had got the message from the way we called him David and the strong words Trevor used on him. We said how lucky we had been, we were fortunate that I came away with just a few cuts. We were looking forward to getting this over with and getting back to Singapore.

We talked together and decided not to report the incident with Dave as we would gain nothing for the mistake he had made. It could have been very costly but we put it down to experience, we all had our faults and we were a good mix together and we had also been through a lot with each other. We were confident that we could pull off the mission okay in a few days time when things had settled down at the rebels camp.

We ended by having a good old natter together while eating the roast pig that was so very tasty.

~*~

Trevor and myself were just like a couple of devoted brothers watching out for each other and he was so grateful to me for putting him in touch with Elsie. I knew that they would get on well together and maybe get married one day and I said this to him, he just smiled at me and said, "My mate, you will be the best man if we do."

"It will be my pleasure to do that for two very special people in my life." I said.

The night was so peaceful sitting there in the warmth of the jungle with my special friends who would die for me and I for them, it was a great feeling.

We decided to say goodnight and made our way to the hut we were sleeping in ready to go to ground if the rebels came to take some revenge. The villagers were very friendly and could not do enough for us, it was a pleasure to be there with them. I thought to myself 'I hope we can pull this off and help them have some peace in their primitive lives, for a little while anyway.' They were so happy without the material things of the life that we had in the UK.

As I drifted off to sleep I thought of the abuse that these people, and their children, were taking from these barons of misery and it made me more determined to overcome the problems that they were having just now.

These people, who had put no value on a person's life, and were making so much money at the expense of others who could not retaliate, needed no mercy at all in my eyes.

The next day I was determined to tell Dave what I really thought of him and how he could have given us a big problem with the mission that we had to carry out. It would have to be delayed a few days and we would have to come up with an excuse when we reported in tonight. Trevor and I decided to say that we were having a few problems with the comings and goings of the drug barons because we did not think all the rebels were at the main camp so we would have to wait a few days to make sure that we got them all.

We all met for breakfast that morning and I laid the law down to Dave and to the rest of them. Dave was real sheepish about it and said sorry to me in the best way that he could.

Trevor laid into him saying you could have got us all killed not just one of us injured, I said once again, "David, you think the grass is greener on the other side and it has caused us all problems."

Tony and Robert echoed all our thoughts on the issue and Brian just kept quiet about the whole thing.

My stomach was very sore but my arm was okay, the natives made some compound up and covered the wound with it and bound it to hold it in place saying that it would draw any poison out of the wounds.

We decided to just have another look round the area to see if any of the rebels were roaming around, I set off with Trevor and Brian, Dave, Robert and Tony went in another direction the others, and the men from the village, split into two groups and also took a good look round the whole area.

As we went in different directions to approach from different angles we wished each other good luck. We travelled for about half an hour and found that there was a good lookout spot at the top of a stream with loads of cover for us, also it was quite pleasant sat near to the water just listening to it cascading down. If was peaceful up there and we realised how the tranquil surroundings gave a sense of peace to our minds, it was so relaxing. The morning went by and we saw nothing so we guessed they thought some of the natives had freed Dave and the girl. We were lucky that they had not seen us when we freed them because that would have caused us a problem and lost us the element of surprise.

We decided to stay until late afternoon just to be sure. Everything was quiet and we had enjoyed the day just chatting to each other, the noise was drowned by the sound of the water.

Dusk was coming so we decided to set off back to the village satisfied with what we had seen, when we arrived back the other groups were there and they said it had been quiet also.

Anyway at least things did not look too bad for us as we sat down to eat the food the villagers had prepared for us once more.

We had a meeting that night and decided to go in tomorrow and clean up the rebel camp, we thought it was the best thing to do before they started to retaliate against the village people. We decided to take out the main camp first early in the morning when we guessed that they would all be a bit sleepy.

We all agreed to set off about three in the morning with the guides leading us through the jungle to the camp. Our intention was to creep up on them and take as many as possible without a sound as they slept, but we knew that we could not afford to show any mercy to them, because they did not value life anyway so we had to think and act like them: kill or be killed.

We could not show any feelings and we thought of what they had done to the young girls of the villages, that alone gave our adrenalin an added dose. We decided to have a bit of sleep before we set off, but first checked our weapons.

I thought as I dozed off to sleep how easy it would be to live here in this peaceful place without the drug barons that were raping the people and taking their young women away to be sold into a world of misery. The time passed and soon Trevor was shaking me saying it was time to go. I quickly washed my face in a pitcher of water to waken me up.

We had decided to go in two groups and enter the camp from two different directions as that would give us a vice like grip if anyone tried to get away. We all mustered together and wished each other luck and a safe passage back, Trevor hugged me and said, "Take care my brother."

I said, "You too Trevor."

We set off with the guides taking us through the dark and eerie night, guessing it would take us about two hours to reach the camp. Silently we passed through the thick undergrowth on a track that was okay to use, it being dark. You could feel the tension and the guys were sure up for this after seeing the misery that had been caused.

As we neared the camp we decided to stop and watch for a while to observe any movement that there was in the camp at that time of the morning. It all seemed quiet and there was four guards just sat at each end of the camp, they were not really taking notice, they were a bit complacent to say the least, so that was to our advantage and we would not complain about that. We were to take the guards silently as we entered the camp.

We crept up to our two and Brian and Tony were going to take them out as I covered them.

They had the weapons which were a piece of wire with a dowel like piece of stick at each end, it was very effective and fast, but not very nice if you were on the receiving end.

We watched as they both approached the guards, we were expecting Trevor, Dave and Robert to be doing the same at the other end of the camp.

In seconds they both struck, there was only slight gasps from the two guards as they slid to the floor, we were ready to kill anyone that moved. With that over we all moved towards the main part of the camp hoping that we could do this and complete our mission without too many casualties, this was going to be all down to the speed that we carried it out once we had struck.

We were very lucky, as we had taken them totally by surprise, so far a few shots had been fired at us as we took what cover we could, the fire that we were under seemed to be coming from all over as the drug barons heard the shots. Unfortunately, one of the guides had been shot but he was the only one hurt as we quickly moved in sending an hail of bullets into the camp sparing no one as we advanced forward shooting everything in our sights that moved.

Taking no chances we rained hand grenades at the various huts that were around while spraying them with lead, suddenly it went quiet from their side so we proceeded with great caution as we moved across the camp ready to shoot anyone that got in our way.

After we had checked the huts to find not one of the rebels left alive, we decided to pull out after setting some prisoners free that were in a compound at the side of the clearing. On our way out we set some short fuse plastic explosive around the huts to blow up the camp and the drugs that were stored there, we paid special attention to making sure it was all blown to smithereens.

Then we were out of there as fast as we possibly could, heading to the point where we were to be picked up by helicopters watched by some of the village people, who could not thank us enough for our help. It would not stop the rebels, we just hoped that it would slow them down a bit and give the villagers some respite for a short time. We left them some weapons that we had collected in the rebel's camp, these would at least help them defend themselves a little.

With that the helicopters came into sight and saying our last goodbyes we boarded and waved to them until we were out of sight.

Looking down on the jungle as we passed over it, we wondered how anyone found their way in the thick undergrowth below us. We were taken to a small camp that no one would even think was there, to have a night's rest and to be briefed on another band of bandits near to one of the rivers that ran right through the area.

After being de briefed, fed and watered we settled down for some sleep before setting off again in the morning, which came too soon for us as we started taking on our rations and ammunition, thinking 'here we go again' but this time we were to be on our own, the other men were to go somewhere else.

# Chapter 9

The helicopters were going to drop us as near as possible to the area without drawing attention to us, all this had been checked out before, to make sure that it was the right, and a relatively safe, area to drop us.

We boarded the helicopter after being told that it was a fairly short flight to our destination, and sat watching the passing dense jungle as we were flying at a low altitude. After about forty five minutes we were told to prepare to disembark making sure that we had everything we wanted with us, before we were five yards away from the helicopter, the pilot whisked it up and away from us, we then took cover waiting to see if we had been spotted from the ground.

Although we did not expect any trouble as the drop zone had been picked out for us as a safe place to start the mission from, we stayed under cover for about thirty minutes then decided to make a move after Trevor had taken map references and compass readings.

Proceeding with great caution we spread out in a 'V' shape, the adrenalin was running high once again, it felt really good to be able to help the vulnerable by getting to these drug barons. We knew that we could never stop it, but at least we must help some unfortunate people, by taking some of these evil people from society.

We were silent each with our own thoughts as we proceeded through the thick undergrowth, Trevor and I looked at each other and raised our thumbs acknowledging that we were both okay with a smile. My thoughts drifted to home, thinking of Ann and Elsie and wondering how my sisters and my younger brother were keeping, it was very strange as I never ever got home sick, I guessed I was going to be someone who could live anywhere in the world and adapt to the country that I was in.

I think that it was the unhappy home life that I'd had that helped me not to get homesick, my father was a good man who never raised his hand to us at any time, it was my mother who used to beat me and use me as a servant at her beck and call.

My Auntie Joan and Uncle Bob were good to me so I used to spend a lot of time round at their house to try to get away from the drudgery of having to do all the work. They both knew how I was treated and an uncle in Canada had wanted to take me back with him one time when I was younger. My thoughts drifted back to getting on the train with not a penny in my pocket when I first joined the army, it was a strange feeling of relief now, as though I had grown into a man overnight and I am sure that was the case, having to look after myself along with my mates. I did think it would have been nice to have been loved by the family and not used so much, my little brother and my sister loved me to bits and I loved them. My other sister was my mum's favourite along with my brother, as he was the youngest it was to be expected, we all loved him.

As I mentioned my father was a good and very clever man but my mother made the rules. He was quiet and softly spoken and he deserved better. He was hard working and would have gone a long way if it had not been for my mother. I just wanted to please him the best way I could and I think he was proud of me in his own way. If he'd had more money I am sure that he would have let me go to college to achieve what he had missed, but I would get there later in my life I told myself - if I came out of this alive.

Back from my thoughts and concentrating on the mission in front of us, I sometimes used to dream as we pushed our way through the undergrowth but my mind was focussed on the job we had to do it. It became second nature for my mind to drift now and again yet I could keep focussed on the task ahead. Nowadays I watch people and seem to be able to focus sometimes on their thinking, always alert, it never leaves you.

We had been going for a few hours now and we decided to make a camp for the night in a nice thick piece of undergrowth we had come across, there was a clear view all around from the area we had chosen so we decided that this was the ideal place to spend the night. It was too risky to light a fire so it would be cold beef and water tonight with some beans.

We tried not to mess up the undergrowth too much putting what we had taken from the middle, where we were going to spend the night, over the edges making the middle clear where we could bed down. With the undergrowth being freshly cut it would look as if it was just a mass of brush that had become vastly overgrown. We made it so dense around the perimeter you could not see into the clearing we had made in the centre. This made it more secure for us in case anyone came by, we hoped that they would not give it a second glance. After checking it from all the angles and filling in any gaps that we could see, it finally looked good to us. So, feeling safe for the night, we decided to split the watch into three with two being on watch at the same time, this would give us all a decent amount of sleep each. Trevor and I decided to take the first spell, then Tony and Brian, followed by Dave and Robert. We all quickly ate our food and we took up our positions as the others got their heads down. The silence was soon to be broken by the noises of the night, as it got dark we looked across at each other, but said nothing each of us with our own thoughts.

~*~

The night soon passed and before we knew it we were waking up Brian and Tony for their shift, I knew no more because as soon my head hit the ground I was fast asleep, I must have needed it.

Morning soon came round with no problems for us, as we prepared to leave the area we buried all the rubbish that we had, then dragged a branch over the whole area as we left, to conceal where we had been. It was starting to rain so that would help wash away any evidence that we had been there just in case.

As we proceeded through the undergrowth the rain was driving down but it was quite refreshing, we estimated that we had about twelve more miles to go before we encountered the people that we were to meet, and they then would show us the way to the drug barons. We did not anticipate an easy run this time, this sort of drug production was a big and dangerous situation to get yourself involved in, at times these people killed their own when they got greedy, this was when someone was trying to take an extra cut of the money, the problem was that they were never satisfied with the amount that they received.

It is an unfortunate situation now in the world that we live in that there are people who will exploit the vulnerable of this beautiful world of ours and turn their lives into a nightmare for them. This was what drove us forward, thinking of all the youngsters who had become victims of these drug barons who do not value life at all.

It certainly got my adrenalin flowing, they were the scum of the earth, and when they targeted young children and abused them in many ways it made our blood boil, so we had no mercy or compassion for these sort of people, I for one would not blink when rubbing any of these sick barons out of existence. We had a mission to do and that was to help vulnerable people by taking out as many groups of drug dealers as we possibly could. My mind would think of someone hurting my young brother and what it would do to me and my family, so I could see what it would do to most other families out here who could do nothing about it.

It was to kill or be killed for us so we had to show no mercy at all to these evil predators of life because they would not hesitate to torture us to death if we were caught. We were all very focussed on doing our bit to rid the world of the thousands of 'Mister Bigs' in this evil money making business.

We were following some signs that had been left for us and getting near to the spot where someone was to meet us, we proceeded until we heard a sharp whistle to our left, three of us went that way and the other three covered us, but it was a genuine as we approached the three men who were waiting for us.

They thanked us for coming to help them and began to tell us about the death and destruction that these evil barons were causing for their people, it made us feel sick inside to think of the abuse that was going on. We were to go to the village on the bank of the river and stay there to rest up and plan what we were going to do.

We were to radio in for any materials we needed to be dropped, the village people then would pick them up for us so that would be a blessing. As we settled down to talk to the head of the village they fetched us some food, as usual it was chicken but it always tasted better than anything back home. We were so grateful for the hospitality shown to us by these very friendly people in all the countries that we have been to. They deserve better than they were getting and needed to live in peace with their families in their simple but happy lifestyle without the threat coming from the drug barons of this world. We talked about the place that the drug barons used, it was in a small township on the edge of a river that ran through the area, they used a large building there to control the packaging of the drugs, the peasants were being used to bring them in from the fields for processing, while others were used to deliver them to various locations for pick up. So we said that we would want to observe the movements of the bosses to make the mission worthwhile and then it would be safer for the village people if we could destroy the whole operation in the area.

Our camp, by the way, was near to the Mekong River and that was about eight miles wide in places, there were thousands of islands there, the largest of which was called Don Khong, so we were pretty confident that we had a safe haven to return to. We were lucky as we had managed to have a couple of fast boats put at our disposal, but the insects were a real nuisance to us at times but the natives gave us some sort of leaf to rub on our skin and that seemed to help us a little, the fresh fish and mangos that were given to us were a very welcome supplement to our diet.

Around the area were very beautiful temples and golden Buddhas. The temple of Wat Phou was one that we visited very close to the Cambodian border and we believed it to be one of the oldest in the area. The butterflies were a sight to see, their beauty was breath taking. It was very hot and humid but we were becoming accustomed to the temperatures and the humidity, which was just as well as we suspected that we were to spend a long time in these countries.

We were told that the drug barons were very relaxed with their operations and not too worried about anyone coming in to disturb them. We thought that they had become complacent but still they were very dangerous people to deal with and they ruled by fear. They put no value on life at all, but we were trained to deal with such situations and we could be just as dangerous as they were, also our super fitness would far exceed theirs. We warned Dave and Brian to stay out of trouble and leave the women alone as our lives were at stake, we told them to wait until we got back to

Singapore. Trevor said to them both, "brains before balls" and everyone started to laugh which added a little humour to the situation as they both nodded their heads in understanding.

We decided that in a couple of days we would go down to the riverside where the barons had their headquarters and observe their movements and count how many were likely to be in the area when we moved in. It was very crucial for the exercise if we were going to be a hundred percent successful and that is what we were aiming for, total wipe out of this operation. The guys were really fired up for this and total concentration was the order for this mission, one mistake from any of us could be fatal for us all.

~*~

We enjoyed the next couple of days looking at the many waterfalls in the area, peeling off our clothes and cooling off in the crystal clear water. We laughed about the times we had gone through together, already the bond between us was stronger as we spent more time getting to know each other's strengths and weaknesses. It was a good combination and we had a team of very committed guys. We were also discussing the many things that we could do to make the world a safer place in our small humble way as we lay in the running stream. We talked about the women that Dave and Brian had entertained themselves with, and had a few good laughs, even about getting captured, we could see the funny side of it now.

It was decided that we would go out in pairs to reconnoitre the surrounding area, Dave and I would take to a boat and check the riverside, then Trevor and Brian would go one way up the river in the centre and Tony and Robert the other way as we skirted near to the banks. Because of the many boats that sailed up and down the river we decided that if we dressed as the locals did and camouflaged the boats, we would not bring any attention to ourselves.

So with fishing nets on board we looked the part, and maybe we'd bring some fresh fish back for our dinners. Dave and I set off first going up river then planning the next day to go down it. We had to act casual, as though our purpose was to fish, it was good because we could take it easy dragging the nets slowly and that allowed us to observe the bank of the river better. It was agreed to be back in six hours and we hid our rifles under some nets in the boat, just in case we ran into any trouble on the way.

As we set off I said to Dave that I was quite looking forward to the fishing because it was a passion of mine and Brians. He agreed that it would be an experience for him. So it was the usual good luck to everyone as we set off up river and decided to go a couple of miles before starting to drag the nets. We proceeded with caution, observing the banks with care, all we saw were peasants going about their business. After about two miles we put a net over the side and started to drag it along behind us we had no idea how long to leave it in the water, so after about twenty minutes, we pulled it in to see what we had caught.

Chugging along slowly and observing everything that was going on we must have travelled about four miles, pulling the net in every fifteen minutes with just a few small fish which we threw back into the river. We had just put the net back into the river when we spotted ten men who did not fit the scenery around us, we decided to go further out and drag the net so we could observe them. They had some of the local people with them that they were mistreating by pushing them in the back as they went along, this raised our suspicions that we had come across some of the drug dealers. We slowed the boat to a drifting pace and kept our heads down watching the nets while, at the same time, we glanced at what was going on at the bank of the river. Dave said to me that we had struck here, they were defiantly some of the guys that we were looking for so we decided to stop the boat and pull the net in so as not to draw attention to ourselves.

We had struck lucky, there were a couple of good sized fish in the net that we kept, hoping to enjoy them later as we threw them into a bin on the boat. The guys on the shore glanced out at us but did not seem bothered thinking that we were just a couple of local fishermen going about our business, so we continued by dropping our nets into the river again and moving the boat around the area while observing their movements.

They looked to be moderately armed as far as we could see, they also seemed to be getting very annoyed with the local people for some reason because they were now hitting them across the face, we could do nothing to help them because we wanted to get to know more about the numbers in the gangs, where they hung out and what sort of arms they had at their disposal.

We could not afford to blow our cover now even though we were incensed by the treatment that they were dishing out to these helpless human beings but Dave and I said that hopefully, and with God's help, we would soon be able to give them some satisfaction of being free from the drug barons for a while.

We were watching them as they approached a large building on the side of the river, a very convenient spot for bringing drugs up and down, they entered, pushing the natives aggressively into the building before them.

We thought it would be a good idea to drag the nets a little further out so that we could use the binoculars to watch the building that they had gone into in more detail. When we had got a good way out, so as not to raise any suspicions, we raised the nets and drifted. We had struck again with four good sized fish as we pulled in our nets. We decided to gut and clean them leaving their inners for the other fish to enjoy as we tossed them overboard, we filleted them and got rid of the bones, I cannot stand finding a bone in a cooked fish. They were meaty fish and I said to Dave, "One more haul like this and we'll have food for us all, including the natives that were staying with us."

We observed the hut through binoculars as we dropped the nets for the last time before we headed back. The time had flown by and we had found one of the places where the barons and their people had some dealings, with no movement coming from the building we decided to head back. Halfway back we raised the nets and low and behold we had our best catch yet, seven large fish, one of them weighing a few pounds I would say, we gutted them and put them with the others looking forward to our evening meal.

We arrived back at our billet just before the other two groups, we were very proud of the fish that we had caught for the dinner and were hoping that the natives would cook the fish for us. One of the women played up with us for gutting the fish saying it is better cooked whole but she agreed to cook it after we said they could have a couple of them which had not been filleted.

The rest of the guys got back okay saying they had found nothing unusual on their travels, we told them about the large building where we thought the drugs were being brought for distribution, then we told them about the fish we had caught.

Trevor said, "Great, fish for tea and I know who insisted on filleting some of them," looking at me.

We got cleaned up a bit, the fish was smelling good as it had been wrapped in leaves and herbs had been added, it looked great and the aroma from it made our mouth's water. We sat down to eat this wonderfully cooked fish with some fresh flat bread that had also been prepared for us. The natives had made some sort of homemade drink and we all remarked how wonderful the meal was, joking at such a bargain price.

After eating we decided to give it another go tomorrow while observing both banks. We would cover more of the area by all going out in boats in the direction where we found the large hut as the others had found nothing the other way. It was decided by us all that when we saw anyone leaving the building, two of us would follow them as far as we could, keeping a good way out into the river.

After making our plans for tomorrow we turned in for the night as the drink that they had given us was going to our heads for sure.

Next day we were up at first light, we had some fresh fruit for breakfast along with some coffee, then, complete with nets, and hiding our rifles in the bottom of the boats we set off. This was just a precaution in case we encountered any trouble, we had to be prepared at all times for any eventuality that occurred until we were sure of the strength of the opposition. We wanted the element of surprise on our side and the least mess, just a nice clean clear up of these evil people.

We realised that we could not stem the tide of drug dealers all together, but at least we could slow it down and make it harder for these evil people to make vast amounts of money from the natives that they exploited. It really was a very dangerous business to be in. They were making so much money, and put no value on life, in their quest to achieve the fortunes they reaped from this evil trade.

We set off up the river to see what we could find, having a bet with each other on who would catch the most fish which added a little bit of spice to the day we thought and was excellent cover for us. It was very slow going because we had dropped the nets and they pulled on the boats slowing them down, but we were content because we had to look the part as we chugged up the river keeping about fifty yards apart from each other.

We had gone about a mile or more when we decided to pull the nets, there was a look of glee on Trevor's face as he and Brian pulled in their net, he smiled and signalled to me that they had five fish of a decent size. Tony and Robert signalled that they had two decent ones, Dave and I only had some small ones but we made the excuse, as we threw them back into the river, that it was because we were nearer to the shore than anyone else. That was our story and we were sticking to it even though the guys were laughing at us. We could see the grins on their faces but we still hoped that we would have the last laugh on them at the end of the day.

We all dropped the nets again and chugged up the river, as we were approaching the area where we had seen the drug barons the day before, we decided to get further away from the bank and go in a circular motion with the boats so that we could observe better. There was a bit of movement in and out of the building so it looked as though this was the main place where the drugs were processed and distributed. After about an hour a couple of cars drove up and eight guys got out, we were convinced that they were part of the wider gang as they went into the building to join the others, we decided to draw the nets once more, this was so if anyone was watching us they would see us pulling the fish into the boats and we hoped that they would not suspect anything was going on.

After that we decided to stay another couple of hours and then head back, it looked as though we had found out where the drugs were processed. From what we had observed, we guessed that there was about twenty five men in the building, we just wanted to give it another couple of hours to be sure that we knew what we were dealing with. We wanted to make a good job of it and take out as many, if not all, that we could and maybe capture a couple to interrogate and find out if there were any other gangs in the area, if so we may as well take care of them also while we were there.

We once again pulled the nets and to our surprise we had at least a dozen large fish and we waved to the others to let them know, they waved back to acknowledge that they also had a good few fish. Dropping the nets again we went further out to give the impression that we were not observing the buildings, there was little movement, just two guys going in to the building with a couple of the native girls.

Just then a couple of fishing boats pulled in at the landing and ten men got out and walked into the building, so it looked as if there was maybe more than we had anticipated. As it was just beginning to get dark we decided to go back and, after a discussion, make up our minds and report in when we were going to take out the building and as many of the drug barons as we could with it.

We arrived back and had something to eat, going through what we were going to do and how to approach which would do most damage and take out the building and the barons. We all decided it would be best to hit them from the river and also have a couple of light machine guns on the two fast boats that we had at our disposal. Trevor, Brian, Dave and myself would go into the building leaving Tony and Robert to give us cover from the two boats and to be ready to get us out of there as soon as we wanted to be away, if we hit any trouble that we could not handle. They would also make sure no one came in after us to take us by surprise when we stormed the place. We guessed that we had a good chance of pulling it off if everything went to plan for us.

We had a couple of beers each while chatting about the evil in the world today, Dave and Brian were getting hungry for some women they said, and we all laughed and said we would have to get them castrated if they carried on like they did and we did not know who to do first, it was all in good fun and they took it in good part as we ribbed them.

Trevor said to me he would be glad to get back to Singapore to collect his mail from Elsie, he asked if Ann was still writing to me? I said yes she was and I wrote to her when I could, which was not as often as she would like, he then said she really loves you. Brian was listening and he said he agreed with Trevor, "I have watched her with us while we were all growing up together, her eyes used to shine when she was near to him, but he did not recognise it or did not want to I should say."

I replied by saying, "I don't want to get tied down as I have told you before and I wished that you two would stop trying to get me to."

I could not detach myself from this life that I was now living and really enjoying, it was the most rewarding and satisfying feeling that I had ever felt in my life, and I was reluctant to lose it through getting too emotional with a woman. Some people could handle it but not me, when I did get tied up with a woman I would want to give her my everything.

Trevor said he understood how I felt as he came from a home where his parents really looked after him, even though he was tied to the business that they ran and wanted some freedom, they had quite a lot of money and he was the only one, so it was obvious that he got what he wanted on the money side of things anyway. He told me I would have to go home with him sometime when we got back to Blighty to stay with them for a few days.

We got back to discussing how we were going to handle the mission tomorrow, the adrenalin was flowing fast as we looked at all the possible things that could go wrong and we checked our weapons and the boats, making sure that they were well fuelled up and running smoothly.

We decided to go in at noon when they were dealing and packing for export, we thought this would be the best time as we did not fancy racing down the river in the darkness. They would have had a morning of relaxation and would not suspect a hit on them as they thought they had everything well under control, with the fear that they had spread around the area.

Trevor and I honed our knives to a razor sharp edge, Dave and Brian had acquired themselves a stiletto type each and Tony and Robert had standard hunting knives, it was what everyone was happiest with that counted.

We double checked that all the guns were well oiled and cleaned, we could not afford for anything go wrong as none of us wanted to end up dead meat. The light machine guns were checked and anchored securely in the boats to give us cover if we needed it, and so we were as ready as we ever could be and would re check everything in the morning before setting off. This time we were going fishing for bigger fish.

Dave made us laugh saying he would sacrifice two weeks wages for a woman at this time, Brian said, "Don't worry Dave, soon we will have all we want for free if we pull this off, the native's will be all over us and the restrictions will be lifted and the ball will start."

Dave's reply was; "I hope so, my balls ache for action."

I said to him, "the only action you will get this time is the chance to stay alive, so you need to concentrate on what we have to do and not your sex life."

He just smiled back at me with a great understanding as my eyes pierced into him, Brian said nothing as he saw me stare at Dave.

That night I prayed to God to help us rid the country of these evil people that killed to enrich their own lifestyles. I also asked for us all to come back safely and with no injuries and thanked him for his guidance and help for us so far.

We were all soon asleep and the natives were keeping watch for us as we slept with our pistols by our sides. It was an uneventful night and we woke to rain but we were told that it would soon clear up and would not affect our plans for today at all.

We ate then double checked all the equipment for the last time, we were all on a high, eager to set off and do the business, knowing that everything was as ready as it could be.

Pushing the boats out before we started the engines and headed out into the river, you could feel the power in the engines which was very reassuring to us. Hopefully we would not need to abort the mission for any reason as we were ready for anything.

As we headed up the river we stayed right at the opposite side to where we would come in to attack the building and would then come straight in towards the bank jetty. As predicted the rain stopped so that was a blessing for us. We were all tense like sprung steel once more waiting to get in there and deal with the situation as only we knew how, hard, fast and no mercy as that could lead to our own deaths.

We were about a mile away and could see the building looming up on our left, Tony and Robert took over the steering of the boats as we were to run close to the shore and storm the building rather than use the jetty. As we approached we checked our weapons and got ready to jump onto the bank and straight into the building, hoping that not too many natives would be killed in the conflict that was about to happen.

We shot over the side of the boats as they came close to the bank before they swung out again away from the shore to take up a position where they could cover us with the light machine guns. It was so fast the element of surprise was on our side, thank God, as no one knew what was going on as we stormed into the building. Inside there were, as we suspected, about twenty eight men watching some natives packing the drugs.

We had taken them by complete surprise, they pulled their pistols, but it was too late as we all opened fire taking most of them in the first round. We must have taken out about ten of them in that first confrontation, but a couple of them took cover and started to fire back at us with automatic rifles, the rest were too slow to act but were soon pulling themselves together to counter our attack.

As we returned the fire we signalled to Brian and Dave to work round the side of them as Trevor and I stayed in front and kept our heads down. While they went to the sides to give us some cover, we moved in on them slowly and with great care. They were putting up quite a good bit of resistance to us now but we were confident that we would soon have it all under control. Trevor said to me he was going to take the two guys who were directly in front of us, if I took the guy to our left who seemed to have given us a bit of a problem when we first moved in on them. I was out of his view as Dave and Brian fired a few shots his way therefore keeping his head down.

So I crawled slowly towards where he was hiding behind a large drum and I drew my knife and headed towards a large crate that was just to his left. As I reached the crate I balanced myself and slowly reached out and grasped him round the throat with my left arm and let him feel the razor sharp edge of my knife on his neck.

I could feel the shiver from him as I told him he could live or die; it was his choice. He said he would like to live and was trembling as I said, "one move and I will cut your wind pipe."

I told him to put his hands behind him and I quickly bound some of my thin wire round his wrists, I made this just tight enough to cut his wrists if he tried to struggle out of it, then I hit him in the jaw hard to keep him silent for a little while, then deal with the rest of them hopefully quickly.

Trevor had shot the two guys in front of him with no problem at all, we guessed that there was at least another seven or eight men apart from the natives left in the building, all of them determined to kill us. It was a bit dark in the building in the area that they were hiding from us all we could see was the flash from their weapons as they took pot shots at us, so we decided to go round as far as we could to get behind them and leave Dave and Brian to cover any movement at all from the front while we made our way round.

They started to fire on Dave and Brian not knowing that we were coming up on them from the rear, we could see the fire from their guns as they fired on our mates so it helped us pinpoint where they were. We decided to pick them off as soon as we could get a straight shot at them as it was too dangerous to go and mix it with hand to hand combat there were too many for us just now, maybe if we could get right behind them we would have a bit of a better chance.

As we got further round I got my sights on two of them, Trevor put four fingers up and signalled that he had four of them in sight, so at a given moment we just let them have it and we killed five of them and wounded another. The wounded man and the one I had trussed up earlier would do as captives to find out if there were any other drug barons in the immediate area. It was with great caution that we then crawled to the very rear of the building so that we had Dave and Brian at one end and us at the other. Just then Trevor pointed to my left where there was a man who was laid waiting for us to get complacent then, possibly, he'd be able to kill some of us. He could not see me unless he turned round and as I was nearest it would be up to me to take him out. I could not get a clear shot at him and, just in case there were anymore laid in wait, I thought I would take him out quietly with my wire. He was only about ten feet away from where I was so I laid down my rifle and crawled towards him under the cover of some benches. Just as I got near to him I gathered the ends of the wire in each hand and very swiftly reached over his head and pulled the wire very taut, cutting into his throat.

He did not make a sound but the blood spurted all over my arms as I took the last breath from him, I then crawled back to recover my rifle. Trevor gave me the thumbs up, he was busy setting charges of plastic explosive as would Brian and Dave be at the other end.

Looking towards the natives they all had their hands in the air as we crawled towards the middle of the building to set some more charges before we made our way out of there.

With caution we told them we had them covered and to head towards the front of the warehouse, we then gathered the two prisoners and headed out of the building. Once we were sure it was safe to do so, we told the natives to follow us out. Robert and Tony were waiting and brought the boats to the riverbank and before we climbed aboard we lit the fuses and ran towards the waiting boats.

As soon as we were aboard Trevor and I took control of the light machine gun on each boat to cover our escape, as Tony and Robert gave the boats full throttle and sped down river as fast as they would go. This had been too easy we thought or was it because they had become too complacent about their operation or was it because they ruled the whole area by fear and did not expect anyone to challenge them.

Anyway we were pleased that everything had gone so well and we had two prisoners for our people to interrogate and find out more about this massive organisation that we had only scraped the surface of. But we did feel that we were doing our bit in not allowing them to have such an easy time dealing in drugs, causing so much misery and death among the young people and the natives of the countries. We arrived back safely and to our surprise we had come away without anyone getting hurt, thanks to God guiding us through our task. That had to be a plus because we had to expect to have a difficult time and that some of us may get hurt or even killed but that was our job and we accepted that.

The prisoners were fed and then locked up secure, we decided to leave them while the next day to see if we could find out what else was in the area. That night we had a few beers and as you may guess, Dave and Brian wanted their usual. There was no shortage of young women for them said one of the guides to us, "You can all have as many as you want."

We said just look after Dave and Brian and we will drink your beer and eat your food that you have kindly prepared for us.

After we had washed up we then sat round the open fire eating and drinking. Once Dave and Brian had eaten their fill and had a couple of beers, they said. "Time for our fun guys eat your hearts out." and off they went with one of the guides to find the women, with the blessing of the natives who were so very grateful for what we had done. Dave and Brian went with our voices ringing in their ears saying, "be careful guys, scrub up first and take your time."

Tony shouted, "see who can last longer than two minutes." And everyone burst out laughing, we all knew they were both thinking of themselves and how many women they could have in the time that they had, they were both so selfish and clinical when it came down to women.

We sat then talking about home and what we would like to do on our next leave and where we would take it. Trevor and I both said we would like to go to Adelaide in Australia and Tony and Robert said they would like to join us.

It was a beautiful night as we sat there thinking out loud how far we had come together up to now, we also wondered how far we had to go into the unknown, but that is what made it so exciting for us - going into the unknown, it drew the adrenalin from our bodies.

Robert said that he would like to go to the opal mines in Australia and we agreed that we could hire a couple of land rovers in Adelaide and drive there pleasing ourselves what we did. So it was decided that, if we got the chance to go there for a leave, and could get the travel warrants, we would do just that. We never drew any pay and it was all credited and put into the bank for us and we were very rarely near a bank - only riverbanks!

Even though it was now getting really dark we decided to go and have a shower under a little waterfall that was about hundred yards away from us, we all grabbed a towel each and set off to cool and refresh ourselves under the cascading water. We all stripped off and sat under the streams of water, it was magical just sat in the moonlight thinking our own thoughts. We must have been sat there for a good hour in silence, enjoying the peace and quiet and the wonderful warm falling water. It was Tony who broke the spell saying we should head back and it was with reluctance we agreed to go and get some sleep. We dried off and walked back with just our towels round our waists ready to go straight to bed. Dave and Brian were not back yet but we knew they would be O.K. as the guide would not leave them alone.

The night was so wonderful as we looked up at the stars, I just loved this very dangerous life that we had chosen to live. Shortly after that Dave and Brian came into the camp with smiles on their faces, as usual we would have to listen to what they had got up to right to the very last detail, so we decided to give them a couple of our beers and let them bend our ears for the rest of the evening. When we had heard enough we split off to bed saying our goodnights to each other, and taking a quick look in on the prisoners to make sure that they were secure, the natives were to keep watch on them during the night for us.

Next morning with the steam coming from the ground, the humidity was very high, we ate breakfast together and then decided to radio in and find out what we had to do with the prisoners. The message came back to us that a couple of helicopters would come in for us as dusk fell.

The fact that we were all going out of there for the time being was good, we may get some leave after all, so we prepared all our equipment and made sure that we had everything. We did not want the villagers to have any problems if anyone came through the village.

It was a precaution that we took to make sure, better safe than sorry as the saying goes.

We spent a long time checking to make sure that not one scrap of evidence was left in the surrounding area, when we were satisfied that all was clear, we relaxed and waited for the helicopters to come in and pick us up.

Just as the light was going two helicopters came in low and landed on the outside of the camp. We were waiting and were onboard within a few seconds with the prisoners boarding first and then it was up and away, with the villagers brushing the downdraught marks of the helicopters away.

It felt good to be on the move again as we flew to a small airfield and handed over the prisoners. We then boarded a light aircraft and were told we were going to Singapore for a few days then we could have a break, which we were looking forward to, after our de briefing had been taken care of at Changi. We all felt ready for a bit of peace, quiet, fun together and to feel free to drop the serious part of our lives for a few days and gather our thoughts and rest up our bodies in a different way.

# Chapter 10

It felt good as we landed at the airfield and made our way to a truck waiting to take us to Changi. The way we got on together was good for the tasks that we had to carry out and the reliance that we had to have in each other, also the comradeship that we had even though we all had different values, we respected them and looked out for each other.

We arrived at the camp and went straight for our de briefing where we were told that we had done a good job and deserved a few days freedom before we went on to another.

I turned to Trevor and Dave saying that I was ready for a break to recharge the batteries, Tony, Brian and Robert echoed my comment as we left the debriefing to go have a shower, something to eat and a few beers together. I must admit it was nice to be able to relax without looking over our shoulders and the feeling of safety was good. It was a very pleasant night as we went down to the bars, deciding that was all we would do today, we'd look for the girls tomorrow, even Brian and Dave agreed to that.

The Tiger Ales were going down a treat and we started to feel hungry so we decided to go to the open air centre for some food. Here the food was cooked as you wanted it while you shopped around the stalls and then brought to you. We all wanted some grilled prawns followed by lobster, washed down with Tiger Ale. We laughed and joked with each other feeling very smug and safe for a change.

Talk about the beer flowing freely? We were all staggering, unsteady on our feet, as we ventured back to camp walking and cursing on the dirt tracks going from one side to the other, how we arrived back in one piece I don't know but we did with just a few minor cuts and bruises after falling on the way. The guards at the camp fell about laughing at the sorry state we were in but knew it had been a long time since we had let our hair down, we all went straight to bed after saying goodnight in slurred speech.

All I can say is, as I closed my eyes, the bed started to spin round and I felt very sick so had to open my eyes and rush to the john and throw up. What a waste, paying our hard earned cash to feel like that, but we all do it during our lives and say never again, some of us never learn from the experience. As I staggered back to bed I passed Dave and Trevor also heading for the john and not looking too good. Just as I was going in my hut, out came Brian being sick all over the place, that started me off again and I cursed him.

I woke with a storming headache and headed to the showers to see if that would help me a little. The heat hit me as I stepped outside into the humidity with my towel over my arm, Dave shouted 'wait for me', he looked okay as I stopped to wait for him. He said that he had not slept much and had been sick quite a bit during the night, so with that I felt a little better to know that he had felt bad also, it's always a lift for the ego to find out you was not alone in feeling the effects of a good night on the beer. Well we stepped into the showers and, boy, did it feel good, the water rushing over our heads and cascading down the gully in a froth of suds, we were there for about ten minutes when the rest of the guys came in, all worse for wear, but we laughed and joked at the pantomime of us all, apart from Tony and Robert.

The showers made us feel a little better so we decided to go and get a few mugs of tea down us and some toast or something. At breakfast we talked about what we would like to do that day, we wanted to visit some of the old haunts and maybe go on the causeway, we also decided to see if the girls were still here on the island. We were all going together so we agreed to meet up in about an hour in the mess and get someone to drop us at the waterfront.

An hour later saw us ready and waiting and we managed to get a lift on a truck into the centre near to the Raffles Hotel. We could have a drink in there and also ask if the girls were still around. The barman said that they had gone to Bali for a couple of weeks with their parents, so that put a stop to us all going out together.

Dave and Brian said. "Don't worry guys, there are hundreds more local girls only too eager to have a few nights out with us all."

Trevor replied, "yes, we know what your nights out are, all in the sack with anyone that you can get."

We stayed in Raffles for about thirty minutes then, as one of the drivers came in, we asked him to take us down to the waterfront. We sat at a bar just staring out on to the causeway towards the sea watching the ships making their way to be unloaded. The shipping lanes were always very busy in the Straits, the turnover of goods must have been of a great tonnage, no wonder this country was prosperous and getting more so all the time. The people all worked so hard and would reap the benefits in the future with full employment.

We were happy just to sit there and have a steady drink together and eat on the waterfront as we had done many times before and watch the world go by. It was great to relax and talk through the last few weeks together and wonder what was next for us, we really were living on a knife edge but all of us knew what to expect. The good thing was that we would look after each other and also had confidence and trust in the thought that we would be prepared to die for each other.

We decided to order some food as Dave and Brian started to chat up a couple of the local girls asking them to pull up a chair each and join us for lunch, the rest of us smiled at each other as the girls who joined us were quite pretty young things, definitely attractive to Dave as he moved and sat next to one of them. We ordered some food and watched Brian and Dave get to work on the young ladies, that was an entertainment in itself, watching those two set about getting these two girls in bed and that for sure was their only motive.

Trevor and I had made our minds up to go to Australia for our week's leave, Adelaide in particular. Dave and Brian wanted to stay in Singapore but Robert and Tony said that they would like to come with us. We knew that we would all have a good time together it was so easy to relax in each other's company.

Dave and Brian said that they were taking the girls for a ride in a cab to one of the small beaches, so we said farewell to them as they climbed in the cab with the girls.

We were having a lazy day and a walk round Chinatown, going into the fish markets, which is the most amazing sight, all the fresh fish, prawns, lobsters and a lot of it in tanks still alive waiting for people to buy them, it had to be seen to be believed.

Then we walked through to the clothes and other stalls that sold everything you could think of, the atmosphere was great as we wandered from stall to stall admiring all the different things that they had on sale from gold to silver. All the tailors saying that they would make us shirts and suits in twenty four hours, as they unfolded rolls of different cloths for us to choose from, but we knew a suit would be no good to us for the next few years, then who knows, we could be anywhere, maybe have been killed or living life anywhere in the world. We did not know our destiny, that was for God alone to decide our future wherever that may be, and for us to do our duty to help the people of these countries who were being killed and used by the evil people of this world. Those sadistic evil scum that have no feelings or morals for anyone young and old alike other than exploiting them for their own means. People like that do not deserve to live in the world today.

I came out of my thoughts and we sat and had a coffee at one of the food stalls in the market, everything was fresh and clean in these places as we discussed what we would do in Australia if we were able to go for a few days leave. We guessed that we would soon find out if we had time before we went on another mission. We enjoyed our day looking round the stalls and having fun with the traders, then we decided to go back to camp and find out if it was okay for us to go to Adelaide. We went to see Captain Rennie who dealt with all our leave and also told us where we were to go next. He was great when we saw him saying; "It's O.K. you guys, you can fly out on the next Hastings aircraft and that comes in first thing in the morning."

He said that we could have six days only because we had something to do when we came back, he would not tell us what it was and just said, "have a good time guys and look after yourselves."

~*~

So we all went for a shower and arranged to meet in the NAFFI bar for some drinks that night ready to fly to Aussie in the morning. We guessed Dave and Brian would go to the bar to seek us out if they came back tonight, if not they had said that they were staying in Singapore and not coming with us but you never knew with those two, they may change their minds at the last minute.

Trevor said he had picked a good few letters up from the camp post office from Elsie and she had sent me her love and best wishes. He had picked up my mail and I had a letter from Ann saying she missed me so very much and hoped to see me soon. I also had a letter from my small brother which was very nice to receive.

Tony said he had one from a girl he used to go out with and he seemed very happy with that after the last disaster he had, all Robert's letters were from his family.

Trevor then said in one of Elsie's letters she had said 'look after my friend for me' he told me she cared about me. I told him that he and Elsie were good for each other and he agreed with me on that point. She was a very nice girl and good looking but most of all she had a great personality.

Well it was out of the showers chatting away to each other as we dried off, laughing at the thought of Dave and Brian with the girls that they had met. We dispersed to our rooms to pack for Adelaide and arranged to meet up in the bar afterwards. I put my gear together on the bed ready to put into my holdall in the morning then decided to call on Trevor and see how he was doing, as I knocked on his door it opened and he said he was just on his way to see me, so we headed to the NAFFI to meet up with the rest of the guys for something to eat and drink.

As we went through the doors there was Dave and Brian with the two girls looking a bit worse for wear, we went over to them and pulled up some chairs. Dave was very slurred in his speech and Brian looked as if he was going to fall asleep, the two girls looked dishevelled in their appearance.

Trevor said to me, loud enough for them to hear, "they look as if they have had a wild time together."

Dave looked at me and slurred, "you bet, do you want to try some?"

We both declined the offer, then in came Robert and Tony, they took one look at the four of them and burst out laughing, pulling their chairs up and proceeded to order some drinks.

We told Brian and Dave that we were going to Aussie in the

morning, they said they were staying here as the women were easier and there were more of them. We could not disagree with that statement as it was true, we just told them to be careful.

Before going into town we carried Brian to his room because he was in a real state with himself. We laid him on his bed and, as the girl had followed us, we guessed she would keep an eye on him and be able to go and get Dave if she needed help.

We got a taxi for the four of us to the waterfront and went to a nice fish bar to have prawns and lobster with a couple of Tiger Ales it seemed as though that was all we ate at times, but we all liked sea food and thought that it was good for you.

Tony said that we could hire a car when we got to Adelaide and go sightseeing around the place, in fact we were quite looking forward to it.

It was a wonderful night as we sat there enjoying our food and drink, a few girls were trying to home in on us but we were not ready to talk to them, we wanted to be alone that night to chat. We thought about where we would be sent next and had a bet on where it would be, the nearest one would get a free meal off the rest. I picked Vietnam, Trevor picked Borneo, Robert, Cambodia and Tony picked Jakarta, and we all shook hands on it.

Just talking about it gave us a buzz, one of fear and one of 'go do it' guys.

Trevor said we needed to have fear in our minds, although he said to me, "I do not see much fear in your eyes." But I told him I did get scared at times.

The night was soon over and it was time to head back and make sure that Dave and Brian were O.K. so we called a cab and said goodbye to our host. It was not long before we were at Changi and we paid the cab and went to Brian's room, opening the door, he was fast asleep with the girl at his side. So then we went to check on Dave, as we approached his room we could hear him and the girl so we gave it a miss and decided to turn in and meet up in the morning to go to the airstrip.

~*~

Next morning I went for a shower and found Tony was in there, he said Trevor and Robert had been and gone but he had not seen Dave or Brian at all. The shower was always so refreshing in this humidity. Finishing our shower we went to the NAFFI to join Trevor and Robert for breakfast.

After we had all eaten we went to pack our clothes ready to go to the airfield, and gave a shout of goodbye and banged on the doors of Dave and Brian's room as we passed. Dave answered with a bit of verbal followed by, 'have a good time' but there was nothing from Brian. We knew that Dave would look in on him so we did not worry about it, best to let him sleep it off because he had taken a good skinfull judging by the way he looked last night in the NAFFI.

We soon found a truck that was going to the airstrip and dived in the back of it. We were all quite excited about going back to Aussie, we hoped that we would see some of our old friends and have a few beers with them.

We arrived at the airfield and went over to the Comet aircraft that was waiting there, this was the plane that would drop us off in Adelaide. To be honest we were like little kids been given an ice cream, we were all talking about the leave and what fun we would have together.

We hoped to see Robin Dewer, Tank Martin and Snowy, a few of our mates from Aussie. We boarded the plane and spread ourselves across a few seats near to each other. We were to land in Darwin to re fuel and pick up some stuff there, but we were just happy to be going back to Aussie for a change of scenery.

We talked about Dave and Brian and the state that they were in, they had become a main topic of conversation for us. We landed in Darwin and decided to leave the plane and go into the terminal where we found out that they were having a problem with large frogs all over the place. We went into the terminal shop and bought a few things then went in the bar for a drink and had a couple of Schooners of beer. It was not long before we were told that we were due to take off for Adelaide.

Heading across Australia, it looked so barren Trevor commented on how red it looked. It was such a large country with different time changes across the mass of landscape and very different climates, hot and humid in the north, dry in the middle and south, and the west was like the Mediterranean. The east changed as you went down the coast to Canberra, so many different places on one continent and some beautiful ones at that.

Trevor said to me, "you either love it or hate it." and we all had fallen in love with this wild and wonderful country. There was a German village near the city called Hahndorf, it had one main street and it was such a beautiful place which went back to the time when it was founded by settlers in the country. The old buildings and shops had remained in a time warp. We said how we would recommend anyone to visit the place and go back in time, it was a wonderful tourist attraction.

Adelaide to us had something for everyone with the sea one way, the hills another and the Barossa wine valleys all within easy reach of each other. We had met a family there and we were going to stay with them, they lived in Hillcrest on Douglas Avenue, they had emigrated from Britain in the late fifties, and had settled well, apart from one of the daughters, Margaret who wanted to go back to Britain. Before we had chance to reminisce again we were told that we would soon be landing in Adelaide, it was great to be back in a country that we felt safe in, not having to watch our backs all the time. We all commented how this was a country where we could settle with no problem at all, the rest of the guys said they just loved the lifestyle and, of course, the weather. Robert said he would like to settle down in Aussie when he came out of the forces. Trevor was in love and said it would be up to Elsie, I told him that she would not want to live so far from England and laughed as I said he was under the thumb.

Tony and I said we would rather live in the States, even though we had never been but I said one day I would go and see the country. We talked to a lot of American service personnel, on our travels who were from different parts of the country and it seemed to vary a lot.

As we disembarked from the plane we were picked up and taken to a hotel in the town centre that had been arranged for us, this was right in the centre in Rundle Street.

After settling in the hotel we went to hire a car and decided to go for a short drive to the Barossa Valley wine producing centre, then call on the way back at the Mount Lofty Ranges. We made sure that we registered both Trevor and I as drivers so that we could relieve each other, the good thing was that they drove on the same side of the road!

The Barossa Valley was made up of different vineyards that people had set up, but there was not much there for Trevor and me as we could not sample the wine, to Robert and Tony's delight. We stayed a couple of hours with those two tasting the wines then Trevor said, "shall we go into the Adelaide hills?"

We all agreed and set off to sample the hills and on the way there we stopped at a cafe for something to eat. While we sat there drinking and eating, we talked about what we would do for the rest of the week. We wanted to go to Hahndorf, the German settlement, then drive on from there up the Great Ocean Road to a place that we had always wanted to visit, a small place called Port Fairy. This would be a full two days there and back but it would be a nice experience for us to see a bit more of Australia than we would normally see.

We had a lazy day in the hills walking about, it was so peaceful, the stillness and the sounds of the wild were great, it was a change for us to be able to relax for once. It soon passed as we made our way back to the car and then headed down to Adelaide again. We decided to stay in the hotel and relax with something to eat and a couple of beers, wondering where our next mission would take us, it was always on our minds even when we were supposed to be switched off.

Tony and Robert were well cut with the wine and beer, they had a start on myself and Trevor, as we downed another schooner of beer each. We ate then we decide to turn in for the night, arranging to meet up in the morning at around nine.

I lay awake for about an hour thinking of my life and how happy I was, what more could I ask for, doing a good, though dangerous, job which did some good for the people of the free world and also having some great mates who would die for each other, but most of all; the chance to visit so many countries, although in very difficult times on some occasions, but well worth it. The fear of death was always on our minds but so it would be, with the job that we had chosen as ours. I fell asleep with those thoughts on my mind and before I knew it, I was woken up by Trevor knocking on my door for breakfast.

I quickly got a shower while he waited in my room and then we made our way down. Trevor said that Tony and Robert were already down there. After breakfast we set off to Hahndorf to have a look round, it was only about fifty minutes drive, and it was on the way to Port Fairy.

We stayed there about an hour walking up the main street, it was as though time had stood still in this quaint little place, anyone visiting Australia should always take time to visit. We then set off to go down the Great Ocean Road.

This road went all the way round to Melbourne but we were not going quite as far as that. It was wonderful as we went through great forests which hugged the coast line seeing the magnificent trees that were so old and the wood mills where the logs were cut for building houses.

The light was pulling in as we approached Port Fairy, the name was believed to have come from a Captain James Wishart, who sailed into the place in search of fresh water in about 1810 in a cutter called *Fairy*.

We decided to rent a cabin for the night at a motel where we had spotted a vacancy sign. The cabins were for two people so Robert and Tony shared one, Trevor and I were in another.

We decided to go down to one of the bars, while we were chatting to some people there we found out that a base whaling station was set up in 1835. The place had history stamped all over it as we looked out at the lighthouse flashing out to sea warning ships of the dangerous coast.

It was very laid back in the bar but we were made welcome by the men in there, no women were in the bar at all. They asked what we were doing so we said just touring around the world for a few years. We stayed and chatted eating some fresh fish that was cooked for us by the owner's wife. We then decided to turn in for the night, saying our goodnights to the people in the bar and thanking them for their hospitality.

As we made our way back to the cabins the night was very warm and, as we looked into the beautiful clear sky full of stars, we all remarked on how, what we were doing, was allowing other people and children to enjoy the simple things of life, without the threat and fear that they had been going through. No human being deserved to be used and abused by others making profit from their downfall. We all said that every life that we saved from the evil of this world was worth the dangerous times we went through to help them in our small and simple way.

Saying our goodnights to each other we then went to our respective cabins, Trevor and I sat up in bed after having a shower and talked about our friendship and how far we had come together knowing that we would die for each other without a second thought. He thanked me for putting him in touch with Elsie he was so happy to have found her he said and one day, he hoped, I would find true love. I said, "Trevor, I will know when that day comes into my life, God will tell me that, it will be beyond my control."

Trevor smiled and said, "I hope so," as we both turned over and went to sleep.

I dreamt of someone watching over me, it was a strange dream but so real, it was as though I had an angel on my shoulder watching over me and it just faded away into the distance with a calming light. It was strange because Trevor had said to me once, "you have someone watching over you I'm sure of it."

I believed what he said to me as sometimes I felt someone by my side looking after and guiding me.

Morning soon came round and we were woken by a possum on the cabin roof making a hell of a noise. We decided to have breakfast before we set off down the Ocean Road again, and what a good breakfast we had, home cured ham and fresh eggs.

After we had given our thanks to the owner we then set off, pulling in at a gas station to fill the car up with fuel we asked how long it would take us to get to Melbourne, we had decided to call in and see some friends who lived there. We were told that it would take us about five hours so we set off with the intention of staying the night in Melbourne before driving back to Adelaide the next day, we had allowed ourselves a few days to travel around so that was fine.

We started to see a few more cars on the road as we got nearer to the city though not too many in these great open spaces in this changing country. We made good time and called our friends on the phone from a gas station to tell them we were nearly there, they said that they would come to meet us and show us the way to their home.

It was great to see them again after training with them in the outback, we were in for a hell of a boozy night that was for sure. Robin and Tank were their names, Tank was the hard man as you will remember from before, they both now lived in the town of Geelong but Tank spent most of his time working in the bush. We went home with them, two of us were to stay in one house and two in the other and we all agreed to meet up later and go into Melbourne for a beer, we had a lot to talk about that night before we got too plastered.

We were made very welcome by their parents, Robin had a very nice sister so it was a good job Dave and Brian weren't with us! I politely asked if I could have a bath and ventured to the bathroom for a good relaxing soak. I enjoyed it, letting my mind wonder back over the last few years. Thinking about the good and the bad, the good definitely outweighed the bad for me because it had given me a great deal of self satisfaction as we had given a lot of happiness to some people and mainly the children who deserved to grow up without being abused. I said to myself when I leave the forces and if I come out alive that's what I wanted to do; help the children at home who didn't have much at all.

Just as I was dreaming Trevor came through and said, "God how long are you going to be there? Give us a break and let me get a bath."

I apologised and said, "Give me five minutes then it is all yours, my mate."

As I was getting dry I realised how close Trevor and I had become once again.

I then went into the kitchen and Robin said his mum was cooking dinner for us and it would be ready in about an hour, then we could go into Melbourne.

So we sat down and talked about how we missed the company and the good times we'd had together. Robin said Trevor had told him how close we had come to death because of Dave and Brian.

With that Robin said, "Those two could get you killed one day," and told me to promise never to put my life in danger again because they had made a foolish mistake. He said he was going to write a letter to them both telling them how stupid they were, endangering the rest with an act of stupidity that was totally out of order. Anyway once he had got that off his chest we talked about how Tank stood there and made money out of letting guys take a crack at his jaw, and how he would bet money on just about anything at all, he just loved to gamble.

At that point Trevor came into the kitchen and Robin's mum started cooking the dinner and told us to go into the garden with a few cans from the fridge, 'tinnys' she called them.

So into the garden we went and lounged about drinking in the sunshine. We talked about driving to Ballarat, an old place called The Sovereign Hill Gold Mining Township. Gold had been discovered there in 1851 and it was well worth a visit, although it was about two and a half hours from Melbourne. Robin said that gold was still being found by individual diggers with metal detectors and you could still pan for gold yourself.

We were then called into the kitchen for dinner, Robin's mum had done us proud, a great piece of ham and eggs with chips just the sort of thing we missed on missions. There was also fresh home made bread. We soon demolished that and thanked Mrs Dewer and told her we would do the dishes while she got her feet up and had a rest before we set off into town. While we were washing the dishes Tank, Tony and Robert arrived to see if we were nearly ready to go, so they ended up with a beer each while we finished the washing up.

Tank said we would go to Elizabeth Street and start drinking down there, Trevor smiled at me with a knowing look that said we were in for a rough night. Robin said to Tank, "let's have peace tonight, Tank."

His reply was if he was left alone it will be fine, no problem at all. We hoped that no one got him going and they left him alone, then we would avoid any trouble. Anyway we would have a good time with the guys once again it was great to see them.

So saying goodbye to Robin's mum and thanking her once more for her hospitality, we decided to go in one car with Robin driving, it was a fair sized Holden with plenty of space for us, and if we had too much to drink we'd crash in a hotel for the night or get a cab back.

Telling Robin and Tank about Dave and Brian's antics, Tank said, "if anything happens to anyone of you through their stupidity tell them I will come looking for them."

And you could bet your life he meant it.

We were all in stitches laughing about Dave getting caught with his pants down, it was good that we were looking at the funny side of his antics. We also laughed about the competition between the two of them and their having a little bit of mutual respect for each other, but apart from that, they were both very brave Squaddies and in a tight corner they were good to have on your side.

Before we knew it Robin was parking up near to the Flinders Street railway station, and it was into the first bar we came to and we all ordered a schooner of beer. It was pretty empty as we sat in one corner of the bar, it was strange, here in Aussie, there were hardly ever any women in the bars. It was as though they had their place in the home and the guys were macho and went to the bars where they would bet and curse with their mates, they certainly did plenty of that.

Well we had a couple more and all was well, Tank was getting fidgety he got up and said, "let's move on guys and see if we can get any betting done."

The guy was possessed with gambling on absolutely anything that he could raise a bet on.

So with that we left the bar and knew we were in for a bit of fun anyway as we made our way to the next hotel that had a bar attached. Tank thought that there would be plenty of guys with a bit of money to spare in there so in we went and ordered some beer, it was quite full so things were looking up.

Tank told us to start a little bet ourselves and get others interested in watching us for a little while, then hopefully they'd take part. So we started to bet on who could get the most darts into the treble six with six throws, which created a bit of interest as the six of us started the game for a pound each, winner takes all.

Tony won the first round, Tank didn't get one in the treble, we thought that was funny because he had a good throwing hand, not realising he was playing a game. We soon attracted attention to ourselves as a few guys started to watch us with interest. A couple of them said could they join in on the next round, so we said okay. Tank did not throw well again and in the end Trevor picked up the money because if you missed with all your six darts you dropped out of the next round and he was consistent in getting at least one dart in the treble each time. So the other guys joined in and asked if we would raise the stakes? We said not just now, maybe next time round. This went on for a couple more rounds and one of the men won the kitty, then it was Tony's turn, followed by my winning a round, but Tank still went out in the early rounds. We thought that he was just having a bad time, then suddenly realised what he was up to. After a few more rounds one of these guys asked to raise the stakes to a fiver we all said okay, there was now about ten people wanting to play so it was becoming worthwhile at fifty pounds a win.

The first round at the raised stakes was won by Robert, the next one by Robin, then one of the guys playing won two on the trot. With that Tank said, "Let's raise the stakes to a tenner, everyone agreed to this with a couple of them saying that they could only go four or five games. So at over a hundred pounds a win it was getting exciting, we were all getting the darts in the treble, but the first game at the raised stakes was won by Tank, "surprise, surprise". Then the next game was also won by Tank with a remarkable recovery, a couple of the guys dropped out, but now the stakes were high there were another three wanting to join in. It was getting really tense as one by one we were dropping out, I managed to win one and the next game was won by Tank again.

A couple more dropped out so we decide it was time to move on, saying that we were going to make this the last game, we asked if anyone wanted to raise the stakes? One guy said twenty for the last game, three said they had finished at those stakes, but the rest of us agreed to raise them for the last game it was a case of everyone hoping that they could get their money back. To make it more interesting we agreed that you dropped out if you did not get two of the darts in the treble each round. Well a few of us went out quickly leaving Tank, Robert and two other guys. In the next round Robert and one of the other guys dropped out leaving Tank and this guy left in. They went on for about three rounds, and this other guy said why not go for three in the treble? Tank said okay if you make it worthwhile, this guy had plenty of cash as he had been prospecting and had struck lucky, so he said what about another hundred pounds each, that was a lot of cash in anyone's terms. Tank agreed to that and the whole of the bar was watching now as they spun for who went first. The other guy won the toss and said that Tank should go first, Tank placed three darts in the treble. The guy then had his turn and did the same getting three in the treble, so it went to another round. Everyone watched in silence as Tank, once more, put three darts in the treble. The other guy then had his throw and missed with the first two darts he then put two in, you could see he was sweating with the tension. He then missed with the next two, he cursed and then said that he had enjoyed the game and shook hands with Tank and the rest of us.

Tank said, "let's go now," with a few hundred pounds profit in his pocket, so saying thanks to the guys that we had been playing with, everyone parted on good terms, that's the thing with the Aussies, they loved a good bet.

We decided to go for a meal on Tank's winnings, so we headed down the street to find a decent place to eat. We found a place that looked pretty good to us so we went in and found a table that was set for eight and sat down. We all ordered a sirloin steak each and some beers, it turned out that the place had very high quality food so that was a real plus for us. We all ate our meal but we had problems getting the steak really well done for Trevor and myself, the rest had it bloody, saying we spoilt the steak by having it cremated nearly like burnt toast, but that was the way that we liked it, besides, it gave them a laugh at our expense. It just meant that they had to wait longer for their steaks.

Tank said after the meal he knew a place that we could go to for the night and play cards, having had so many beers, we decided that we would stay in Melbourne and finish the night off by having a few hands of cards in the bar of the hotel we were to stay at. Tank paid the bill and we headed down the road to book in the hotel for the night, it was an old place with a sort of character to it, anyway we booked in and proceeded to the bar having no luggage to check in other than ourselves.

We must have had another five or six beers and we were not really getting into the cards at all just sort of lying around and going through the motions. We decided, after about another hour, to turn in for the night all feeling worse for the long night drinking it was about two in the morning as we drifted off to bed saying our goodnights as we went.


Next morning after a great big breakfast we headed towards the shops to have a look around and maybe buy a few things. The trams in Melbourne were a great attraction to us, so too were the wide roads as we went in a few stores and bought a few toiletries and a couple of tee shirts each. We then made our way to the car to head back to Tank and Robin's homes, saying that we had really enjoyed the relaxation and time that we had spent with them. We all said how good it felt to be yourself and feel safe, not always on edge wondering what was coming next, but this was the life we had chosen and we really did love the challenge and the excitement of what that life brought to us.

We had to set off back to Adelaide the next day so we decided to all go out for a nice meal together that night after we had cleaned up at our respective hosts. Robin was going to take us to a nice steak restaurant nearby where you had to bring your own booze so we went to the shop for the drink. We got a case of Stubbies and a couple of bottles of red wine to have with the steak. The place was a bit rough on decorations but the steaks were laid out in the chiller to enable the punters to pick the one that they wanted, there was sirloins, rump, T bone and fillet. Trevor, Robert and I picked out a couple of thick fillets each with baked potatoes, the rest ordered a massive T bone each that must have been about an inch thick.

We then sat down and started to open the drinks getting into a conversation of how we would miss each other's company. Tank and Robin wished us all the best in our future endeavours and told us to take care and be there for each other and always come back safe. They both then asked us to remember them to Dave and Brian.

The steaks arrived so we opened the wine and got stuck in, they were exactly like we wanted them, it was plain but a good restaurant, the sort of place that you could relax in and we did just that, although we felt sad that we were saying our goodbyes to Tank and Robin once again.

The night went by fast with the chatter between us all, Robert was more determined than ever to live in Australia when he came out of the forces, he made that quite clear to us but we all loved the country anyway, it was so big with so much space, no congestion at all and so many different climates and different time zones, from one extreme to the other it was an exciting country for sure.

We left the restaurant full and very content as we headed back to go to bed and start the journey back in the morning hoping to do it in one day back to Adelaide. We would take turns in driving so that it gave us a chance of doing it in one day. The ocean road was great to drive on with the views out to sea, and the massive forests as you went inland in parts.

Morning was soon on us and we had breakfast saying our goodbyes and thanks again we set off with Trevor driving for the first leg of the journey.

We were all such good friends, that we all commented on how we were missing Dave and Brian and that we would all be so pleased to see them when we arrived back in Singapore, hoping that they had not got themselves into any trouble. We drove about a hundred miles then decided to stop for a drink and something to eat, and for me to take over from Trevor, there had not been much traffic on the road at all but the beautiful countryside and the ocean gave us plenty to look at as well as the multi coloured parrots and many other types of birds.

We stopped at a small roadside inn, the guys ordered beers and I had a soft drink as it was my turn to drive, we ordered fresh snapper as they really looked good with some home made bread.

We stayed there about thirty minutes then we decided to carry on as we wanted to get back to Adelaide sometime in the evening, this was because we had stayed in Melbourne longer than we had intended. So we hit the road again and, fed and watered, we were ready to roll. I stepped on the gas to make good time so we were really clocking the miles, I just loved driving fast, it was a good job Dave was not with us as he did not like going fast at all, but the rest of the guys were fine with it as we sped along the highway.

It was looking good we had been driving for about four hours when Robert said that he would take over for a while so I pulled in and he drove on from there. A few hours later we arrived in Adelaide pulled in at a motel to stay the night before we confirmed a flight back to Singapore to see the guys and get our instructions for our next assignment. That night we went into the city for some beers together, not knowing if we would be coming back to Aussie, mind you Robert said he would be back. We did the city that night and really had plenty to drink as we went from bar to bar and into some of the hotels, there was not much talent about but we enjoyed ourselves until the early hours. We ended up drinking in the motel we had stopped at, having a game of cards and darts together before retiring to bed at about two in the morning.

Determined that we would call the airline to see if the flights were okay.

Next morning I had a shocking headache and so did everyone else but we all made it to breakfast, after we had filled ourselves with eggs and bacon and plenty of tea we decided to check the flights, they were okay and we were booked on one at two o'clock that afternoon, which would get us to Singapore late in the evening that was great for us.

We were all well rested and ready for work once again, and wondering how Dave and Brian had been while having total freedom without us looking over their shoulders. Trevor said, "don't know about them being rested, they will both be skint and tired out."

With that we all burst out laughing, our imaginations running away with us. Leaving the motel we headed to the airport all ready for some more adventure, as we arrived at the airport we decided to buy ourselves an Aussie bush hat. We finally checked in and then went through the customs to the gate and waited for our flight to be called, it was not a very busy place like Singapore or some of the other airports that we had been to.

Trevor said he was looking forward to a pile of mail from Elsie. Robert and Tony were also looking forward to whatever mail they had. Trevor said to me, "Do you expect Ann will have written to you again?"

I said, "I guess so, she always does."

"Why don't you write back more often to her?" He asked.

"Now and again is enough as a friend, because I don't want to get tied down with anyone at all just now and Ann would take advantage if I started to change my ways and wrote to her more often," I replied.

They all laughed at that and I said to Trevor, "I introduced you to Elsie and that was your choice so don't worry about me."

Then Trevor told the other guys that Ann's father had pots of money and he would be made up if Ann and I were to get engaged or something.

Robert and Tony said, "you are a fool, get stuck in there you will be made for life."

That comment made my stubborn streak come to the fore and I dug in my heels and said no way would I marry for money. Trevor said, "you better leave him guys because he will throw a benny, look at his eyes changing, I can read him like a book at times."

"Give me her address I will write to her," Tony said.

Trevor asked him, "how long is your life span expected to be, because you are certainly going the right way to shorten it."

Trevor said that I had protected Ann and Elsie for years, "so don't think you can move in for her money if she would let you."

With that there was a silence which was broken by the flight being called to the gate, that defused what could have been a situation that we did not often have. I admitted that I was very protective of my friends and would not stand by and see them used. Tony said he was only joking as we headed to the gate and that was the end of the matter as far as I was concerned.

The flight was not full so we spread ourselves out on the seats claiming a bit more room for ourselves for the journey back to Singapore, looking forward to seeing Dave and Brian don't know why but we all said it would be a good laugh to find out what they had been up to.

The trip was not too good as we hit a lot of turbulence and the plane was dropping and bumping along, we had a few drinks that we had taken with us so we decided to have them and a game of brag until it passed.

The plane eventually settled down and we decided to get some sleep. I thought of the people back home as I was trying to go to sleep, thinking of Ann, wondering what would become of us. Then there was Elsie writing to Trevor, I wondered what would happen between them. I thought about how I was enjoying this army life, helping the disadvantaged and poor of the world, it was tough and rough at times but overall the life was great and I was very happy. I must have fallen asleep because the captain had announced that we were approaching Singapore and prepare for landing.

We stepped out of the aircraft into the humidity that wet you through but it felt good to be back in Singapore as we had some good memories there. Walking to the terminal we decided to get a couple of cabs back to the Changi base. Arriving at the base we went straight to our huts for a shower and arranged to meet up in the NAFFI in an hour to have some Tigers ales, and to listen to what Dave and Brian had been up to, if they were around. It was great to get in the shower and wash the tiredness from the travelling away.

# Chapter 11

Feeling very refreshed and ready for a good nights drinking I was looking forward to seeing Brian and Dave as I missed them in my own way, in particular Brian who had been part of my life for so very long.

Putting a light shirt and shorts on I went to knock on Trevor's door to see if he was ready to go, just as I was approaching his billet he came out with a big grin on his face, I asked him what was funny? He said, "those two! I was thinking of what they have been up to while we've been away."

We walked to the NAFFI and decided to stay there for the night as we had done enough travelling that day and it was very late. As we walked in everyone said 'hi, how did your trip go?' We said it was good and we had really enjoyed the change and seeing Tank and Robin was a real bonus for us. Ordering our beers, which were nice and cold, we sat at a table in the corner where we could chat to Dave and Brian if they came in for a drink or something to eat.

Tony and Robert joined us and we had drunk a couple of bottles then in came Dave and Brian, both pleased to see us. Brian gave me a hug and asked how it had been I told him Tank and Robin send their best wishes to you both.

We ordered more beers and food and settled down to a good night of chatting about what we all had been up to. We started telling them both that we had been on Tank's territory, and about the set ups with the gambling and that we all had a great time together. We said it had been nice to see them both again and their families were good to us, making us feel at home.

Then we sat back to listen to what they had been up to in our absence, we were very surprised when Brian said that they had both gone out together all the time. This proved a point that, when they were on their own, they could tolerate each other, also that they had a mutual respect and would look after each other when we were not around. Brian said that they had hit the town and had a different woman every night, well what did we really expect from those two?

Dave wanted to tell us about one girl in particular and kept interrupting Brian, so we were back to normal with them. Brian said that they had nearly been arrested by the shore patrol, because Dave had caused a fight over a girl and then started smashing tables up.

When asked what regiment Dave told them and they just told us to clear out of there and arrested the other guys, taking them to the brig to cool off for the night. Not content with that warning, Dave, much the worse for wear, wanted to go in a few more bars to find a woman for the night, according to Brian he was on a high and determined to go, so he had to tag along to keep an eye on him, even though he was exhausted and wanted to go back to bed because they'd had too much to drink.

Brian said that the next bar was full of beautiful girls so he was pleased that they would not have to go too far to satisfy Dave's need. He picked one of the girls saying to Brian, "what about you?" Brian said, "not tonight Dave, too much to drink," so they called a cab and Dave took the girl back to camp. Saying goodnight to Brian who went straight to bed, Dave and the girl went into the NAFFI to buy some drinks for his room. The laugh was at breakfast next morning Brian asked how it had gone and Dave answered; "She was great but I was unable to perform and it cost me a good bit of cash on food, drink and a cab to take her home. So for once the laugh was on him, Brian said he was like a pig with a sore ear the rest of the day. All in all they had a great time together but did say that they missed us and we had to admit we missed them also.

We then got on to the question of where we were to go next, it was down to the serious stuff again we could feel the adrenalin building up in our bodies when Brian said that we were to report in the morning for instructions.

Knowing that we had a bet on the outcome, we asked Dave and Brian if they wanted to join the bet and have a guess, they both said they did and we raised the stakes. Dave picked the drug fields in Afghanistan and Brian picked the Philippines. So bets made, we had a drink on it and we would find out in the morning what our fate was to be.

We had a great night together, glad to be a team again, after finishing our drinks we decided to turn in and meet at breakfast before we went for our briefing the following morning. Walking to our billets in the humidity I said that I was going to have a shower before turning in for the night, Trevor said he was going to write a letter to Elsie and said to me "isn't it time for you to write home to Ann?"

I told Trevor I would see how I felt when I get out of the shower, see if I was in the writing mood.

I got in and stripped off for a shower knowing very well I was not going to write that night, there was no way I wanted to get emotional just before we started another mission together.

I could not get involved at all with any woman, I just could not handle it at the present time, I just got sick of repeating it to everyone. I was very happy for the first time in a long while and so in love with the life that I was now living. Helping the disadvantaged of this world was so very rewarding for me, I had plenty of time to settle down if I came out of this alive, I felt no fear at times it was frightening the way I felt.

I suspected Ann loved me but there was no way that I could get involved with her. She was a good looking young woman and a very dear friend, like Elsie and the guys. Elsie told me that Ann's father had told her to keep writing, "because you will then be there when he is ready to commit himself." Her father liked me very much.

Maybe I was an odd bod but I did not want the responsibility of a relationship at this time in my life, the company was nice when on leave but that was as far as I was prepared to go.

Before I knew it, it was morning and Trevor was knocking me up and, after a quick shower and pulling on a pair of slacks and a top, off we went to breakfast, meeting the rest of the guys in there. We were looking forward to our next destination and the job in hand as we chatted and ate our breakfast. We were all a little apprehensive of our next journey into the unknown as we ate up and went to the briefing room to find out our fate and of course who had won the bet.

We all sat down and Captain Rennie came in and the first thing that he asked was had we enjoyed our leave? This was before going on to the real point of the briefing. He then said that we had the job of destroying some drug fields on the mountainsides in Afghanistan. He said that we would be alone and it would be very dangerous but they could not take any responsibility if we were captured, the land was very volatile and the terrain difficult, with very narrow paths on the mountainsides, we were to be dropped near to the targets by parachute. So Dave had won the bet, "born lucky, that guy," Trevor said.

Captain Rennie said that we were to get kitted out today and would be flown out in the morning, and we were told that drinks were off limits that night. We knew that we had to be very disciplined about our fitness and ability to react to any situation that was thrust upon us.

We were to have soft drinks that night and Dave and Brian were told to stay in camp, we could not have any mishaps before tomorrow.

Captain Rennie then said that they had some maps of the terrain, positions of the poppy fields and a couple of camps where the drugs were processed. We were to study them now as we would not have the time to plan in the morning, all plans and details had to be decided today so that we knew what we were going to hit first. This was also so plans could be made to pick us all up if successful. You see there were a few flat openings where they could send in a small aircraft at night, this had been arranged by the contacts on the ground in Afghanistan.

It was clear that there was a massive trade in hard drugs and millions to be made by these evil people who did not care about life at all, just using children and the poor people to their own ends, this made my blood boil and I know it was the same for the others.

Captain Rennie finished briefing us and we then went through the fine details with him, marking the map up with alternative plans in case anything went wrong. We were to destroy the poppy fields first then hit the two compounds where the stuff was stored. We were going in because the contacts on the ground had said that there were huge stockpiles waiting to be sold, and also it was the best time to hit them before they started to move the drugs out of there because it would then be difficult for us to destroy it all.

Captain Rennie bid us good luck and said God be with you all and return safely. He was a good guy and really cared about us. We gathered from the maps that there was a river called Helmand which ran across the country so that was useful to know as a guide to us if we got lost we may end up near to the river and then could follow it out of there. Unsure about the terrain and the near impossible passes through the mountains, it was going to be very rough for us. We realised we were in for a very tough time as bandits flourished in the mountains on the border of Pakistan, we were going to enter from the Pakistan side after stopping in Karachi.

This was for final instructions and to pick up a guide who knew the mountains and all the caves that ran through them. We were pleased to have someone coming with us who knew a bit about the area as we knew that this was going to be very difficult for us with the mountain passes, and the many, very aggressive, bandits in the area. For most people it was a no go area but this was what we had been given to do and we would give it our best shot as we always did, after all this was our job.

We all sat talking about the task in hand and the dangers that were in front of us in this unknown territory and we were very nervous as we had heard a lot about the area as a whole.

We all knew that we would die for each other no matter what and we were in this together, as far as I was concerned I could not have a better bunch of mates around me and I'm sure we all felt the same.

The day passed by slowly, just passing time having a game of darts in the NAFFI observing the no drink rule. Dave said that he wished they could go into the centre and pick up a couple of women and bring them back for the night, I told him no way was he going out of the camp that night, if he did, he would not be going with us tomorrow. Brian was not a problem, he understood the danger of something going wrong by going into the centre of Singapore, it was sod's law something would happen when you did not want it to, and he said to Dave, "we will have a great time when we get back."

He soon came out of his sulk and continued to play darts with us, we played for a few hours to pass the time, then went down to the stores to renew our equipment and prepare for the morning and also pick up our weapons: a hand gun and a telescopic sight each for our 142 rifles. We already had our own knives and other bits of equipment that we used.

Satisfied that we had all we needed and checking the rest of the stuff that was going to be dropped with us, most of it we would use as back up just in case we encountered any problems. After double checking everything, each one of us cross checking what the others had drawn out of the stores, we then signed for them and went to the NAFFI for a snack and a glass of warm milk each before turning in for the night. We were in there about half an hour then we bid each other goodnight and headed for our billets to try and get a good night's sleep.

I lay in bed thinking of my life wondering where it would take me to and where I would end up, 'dead in an unknown grave?' Or would I finish in the forces and go home and settle down with someone that I loved and have a family of my own. I was unsure, all I knew was that I loved life and was determined to continue to enjoy my new found freedom. I thought of the great mates that I had met and how we all helped and supported each other. I could handle this, the adventure and travel was in my blood for sure. In a way, my life was complete and I was very happy doing what I was now committed to do. Still it takes all sorts to make a world I suppose, at least it taught us to respect people and property so that was a plus for us.

I must have fallen asleep because I woke with a start when Trevor and Brian started banging on my door to see if I was coming to breakfast. Telling them I would catch them up after I had been for a quick shower, I shot out of bed and dived under the shower to wake myself up, then headed to the canteen to meet the guys and have breakfast.

As we ate Brian said, "I wonder when we will get another breakfast like this?"

Trevor said he had no idea how long we would be away and I and the others agreed with him, we were once again in the hands of

God, only he could decide when we came back, if we came back at all. But this was our job so we just got on with the forward thinking of keeping each other alive as best we could under the circumstances.

We were to leave the camp at Changi about ten in the morning heading out to Karachi first before being taken into Afghanistan. The old adrenalin was starting to flow through us all once again as we began the build up to the task in front of us. We went back to gather our kit and check everything for the last time, everyone was ready on time as we were used to being clinical in whatever we had to do. The land rovers came to pick us up and take us to the airfield and we all dived in, our hearts pounding, the adrenalin flowing, the heat was more humid than normal as we sped towards the airfield, we were sweating pretty bad but we were used to this and there would be no shower for quite a while.

We arrived and boarded the plane, it was an RAF Hastings fitted out for carrying troops and gear which would take us to Brindisi. We all got comfortable on the plane and within twenty minutes we were taking off down the runway into the unknown but we were very sure that we would all be okay, everyone of us positive in what we did for a living. The discipline was there and we could not afford to be any other way as the slightest lapse of discipline could be the downfall of us all.

We arrived in Karachi very relaxed and were told that we were to stay about two hours before we set out to be dropped over the border in Afghanistan with our guide that we had to pick up there in Karachi. After being told that we were allowed one beer each but that was all, anything else had to be water or soft drink, the beer was great, ice cold and went down a treat.

We were soon ready to go, the two hours had flown by so now it was all systems go for us as we all wished each other safe return and clasping hands said we would look after each other as we began to taxi down the runway once again going into the unknown, but we were ready to help get rid of some of the drugs that are spread around the world causing distress, death and misery throughout the free world. The children had to be protected from these profit taking barons who exploited them, this is why we all thought it was worthwhile doing what we did after all the children are our future. We saw it as our duty to, at least try, to stem this evil trade in human misery and to give the children a chance, they would otherwise get dragged into this abuse of their innocence.

We were to be dropped in a region that had been well checked out so we could get to know the land around us, at least we had a guide who knew the area and would direct us to the drugs and the fields of misery. We all looked at each other and Trevor said, "Here we go guys stick like glue and protect each other."

Brian said he could not wait to get on the ground, it was strange Brian never really had liked flying at all but had shown courage because he would not be with us if he did not fly. We all understood he would rather have his feet on the ground where he had control.

We all fell into our own thoughts as we went towards our destination, I was thinking of people back home, of my friends and my dear young brother who I loved so very much, also my two sisters. I was pleased that my brother was getting treated well, not abused as I was, so that made me happy to know that he was okay. *Little did I know that he would die in my arms from a brain tumour at the age of forty-four, that broke my heart. I loved him so much and he was one of the world's gentlemen who would not hurt anyone and cared about the environment that we lived in. He left a wife and one daughter and I have still not got over it to this day, I would have given my life for him to live longer, but I guess it was God's wish, even though it was not the wish of any of us. I do ask myself why at times when I am alone.*

We were soon over the drop zone and it was just pulling in dusk as we got ready to jump, the equipment was to go first so that we could direct our chutes towards where it was going to drop to the ground. All in a line waiting, David first, then Trevor, Brian, Robert, Tony and then me as the guide was to go in tandem with me. Out went the equipment chutes then one by one we followed. The evening was warm as we looked down at the terrain beneath us it looked so pretty from up above, but we knew that it was very wild, dangerous and desolate in many areas. We drifted down to the ground in the moderate breeze hoping that no one had a bad landing as could happen sometimes, we prayed it was not this time. We were all okay and had a safe landing as we hit the ground, no one hurt and pretty near to the equipment which was a relief to all of us as we all put our thumbs up to signal all was well.

After I had released our guide he then led us to a small cave in the side of the mountain that had been prepared for us, this was after we had gathered all the equipment that we could carry, the rest we would come back for as soon as we had left the heavy stuff in the cave.

It was about thirty minutes to the cave and, once we had dumped the equipment that we had brought, Trevor and I were to stay there, with the two of us keeping our eyes on the surrounding area and with rifles ready after we had taken good positions a bit higher up from the cave so we'd have a good view of anything that moved and could give covering fire to the rest of the men and the guide as they brought the rest of the gear into the cave.

It was about two hours before all the equipment was brought and stored. We noticed that in a big cave next to ours about eight horses were tethered for us to use up and down the mountain side. It was then coming in pretty dark so it was fortunate that the guide had picked a cave with a ledge where we could light a fire without the flames being seen, but we had also, as a further precaution, dragged a small broken down tree to the front of the cave, and, to make double sure, we draped a groundsheet on the inside. We were to stagger the watch through the night to make sure we all got a good bit of sleep after we had eaten. All of us were to do a four hour shift with two on each shift, we had night sights and did not expect anything to move but we were prepared for the worse. So we all ate with the guide giving us half an hour on watch, then Trevor and I would do the first shift and let the guide eat, he was to do no more watching, he could sleep all night, lucky guy.

After eating we took up our positions, as we scanned the terrain in front of us we talked softly to each other reminiscing about our short lives, we also talked about how we were going to destroy some of the poppy fields and how we would do it, both of us agreeing that we hit the fields furthest away so that we could take out a lot before they were harvested if we were careful. We decided that we could get rid of most of them in the immediate area. The night was warm and the days were very hot just now, we hoped that it would stay dry so that it would be easy to set the fields of death alight and help stop more human misery in the world.

We talked about our friends at home, and Trevor thanked me for introducing him to Elsie.

Then he said, "Ann has feelings for you, don't you have any for her?"

My reply was that we had known each other for a long while since school days, but I did not want to get tied down, that is why I refused to write to Elsie when she asked me. "We go over this time and time again."

We were not tired so we decided to let the others sleep a bit longer as we continued the watch, it was a nice night so we did not mind, and we were enjoying the chance to talk to each other about personnel issues without others putting in their two pennies worth.

We spoke about our families and what we were going to do on our next leave whenever that came, Trevor wanted to fly home if it were possible but we did not think that it would be allowed. We then decided to wake up two of the others to give us a break as our eyes were getting tired scanning the terrain, this we did saying everything was quiet with no movement at all. Taking to our sleeping bags we whispered goodnight and before I knew it I was fast asleep.

~*~

Morning arrived quickly and we all ate our breakfast that had been prepared by the guide in the cave to hide any smoke, we all welcomed a pot of tea before we were to set off on a 'recce' of the area with the guide. We dressed in well worn head gear and robes with our weapons hidden beneath them, we really looked the part and blended in well said the guide.

It was the individual groups of bandits that we thought would cause us more problems than anyone, because they were opportunist groups, afraid of nothing, living off others. But we were more than ready for them and would be alert all the time, having the guide that knew the area well was a huge bonus to us.

156

Brian and Tony were going to stay at the base to look after things as Trevor, Dave, Robert and I went out to look at the area around us, working out the best way to start destroying the fields of poppies. We mounted the horses that the guide had arranged for us as the paths we were to travel down were very steep and dangerous and we would make better time with the horses.

I felt a little uneasy, feeling like a sitting duck, but Trevor reassured me that we would be okay, it was the first time that I had felt uneasy about anything we were doing, the feeling left me after we had been travelling about two hours.

We soon came to fields of poppies and passed by them with the people in the fields not taking a second look at us, but we had our hand on our rifles ready to open fire at the first sign of trouble, but nothing came as we passed field after field of misery to the world. My heart went out to the people who suffered from the sale of these drugs manufactured from the poppies.

We mapped out and counted the fields as we travelled along, deciding that we would go on for a few more hours and stay out that night to really see the extent of the poppy fields.

We would then decide how we were going to work our way back after setting them alight, it was very dry so that job would be easy once we started. We rode down some desolate tracks but there were still fields of poppies everywhere we went. This was not going to be so easy, to set alight that many fields and get away, because of the nature of the terrain that we had to travel on, as we ventured further we talked about how we could do it. I suggested that we may be able to destroy some of the fields that were furthest away by setting up some magnifying lenses that we always carried with us in case we needed to start a fire and had run out of matches. So with that in mind we decided that before we set off back to base we would give that one a try on one field. We would set a lens up the night before, then we could get clear and not be suspected because by the time the field caught alight we would be back at our base camp miles away so anyone seeing us would not put it down to us.

We travelled for about another three hours then decided to set up the lens, the sun was low so it would not start the fire until late the next morning. We just hoped that the rain stayed away because this would put paid to our trial.

We set it up at the side of a field of cultivated poppies where it was nice and dry and hoped for the best as we set off back to get clear of the area before it got really dark, we wanted to avoid travelling at night for safety reasons. We found a small clearing and decided to bed ourselves down and get up at the break of dawn to get back to base, we hoped that we could observe and at least see the plume of smoke when the field caught alight because of the height of our base camp. Our guide said that we should at least see the smoke and maybe much more as we were well up the mountain, we just hoped that this would work for us.

We ate some cold food that we had brought with us, we did not want to bring attention to ourselves by lighting our own fire, so we had to make do with water and some cold chicken and bread. We did not have a watch on that night because the guide told us that no one would be down these small tracks at night, as long as we were away by the break of dawn it would be alright. We were still a little bothered about not having a watch so we set up some trip wires on the path just in case, at least that would cause a noise if anyone came our way.

Morning came around fast or so it seemed when Dave woke me up, he was always up early. Trevor had joked that it was because he was used to doing a runner before any husbands came home!

We came to our senses and set off without eating, we could eat when we got back to base camp. We all said we would welcome a mug of hot tea, surprising how good a mug of tea was when you were deprived of it. Well the sun was rising as we set off back so that was a plus for us we just hoped that our little test worked, we guessed it would take a couple of hours before it caught alight. With this in mind we hoped to make good time going back up the mountain tracks with the horses slipping and sliding as we progressed towards our base.

We were all pretty well rested and in good humour with each other, saying thank God for the horses because it would be hard going up these tracks without them. We were making good time according to the guide and should be back at camp in about an hour and forty minutes, we guessed that we were in the sight of Brian and Tony by now, feeling sure that they would observe our safe return to base.

We were about twenty minutes from base when we looked back to see a small plume of smoke in the sky which seemed to be in the right direction of where we set up the trial fire. We hoped that no one could get to it before it set the whole of the field alight.

Dismounting at the camp and tethering the horses near the entrance to the big cave near to ours, we all stood and watched the fire while Brian offered to make us a mug of tea each, which we were very thankful for.

The fire was beginning to get a good hold, we could see the flicker of light as the flames began to shoot into the air, we could not see any sign through the binoculars of anyone rushing to put it out so with luck on our side it would get a good hold and burn more than we had thought with everything being tinder dry.

With that Brian brought our tea and we settled down with a few dry biscuits to watch the events, wondering how long the fire would burn for. We could see that it was really getting a grip on the field as the flames were spreading through the dry grass thus burning the poppies.

The smoke was getting very high in the sky as Trevor pointed to a group of people heading towards the fire, but it was burning well now so we were not unduly worried about them putting it out for a good while as the wind was helping the fire spread faster. It was getting very hot so the weather was also on our side as we lay back and enjoyed our tea and biscuits.

We observed the people through the binoculars rushing towards the fire that looked as though it was getting a real hold but that was good, if it got out of control and destroyed a lot more fields than we had anticipated. It sure felt good to be doing something once more to help stop the trade in human misery from the poppy fields that were to be harvested and processed into drugs that brought in millions for the drug barons.

Looking down the mountainside the smoke and flames from the tinder dry fields was spreading more than we had hoped when we first observed it, it was really out of control.

We decided to move further along the mountain paths to hit some

159

fields in another area because it would be some time before we could move down this part of the mountain range, it also seemed that lady luck and God was on our side with the devastation that was down there now.

Next morning the area below was still burning away so we agreed to move, have a burn up in new fields, then get the hell out of there as, by then, they would be suspecting someone was setting the fields alight.

We were to go over the mountain into Pakistan to be picked up and taken back to safety but we were determined to cause real problems while we were here setting up some booby traps to get rid of some of the bandits, and also to hopefully pick a few off with our rifles as we went back up the mountainside. This was going to be quick and very clinical with what we had to do to create havoc and cause as much damage as we possibly could to these fields of death.

It was now becoming dark but the fields were still burning away, we could see the flames in the evening sky, it had gone much better than we could have imagined, watching the fires burn away as we settled down for the night ready to move next morning to another part of the mountainside, taking one last look at the fires burning away in the distance Trevor said, "let's turn in for the night as we have a long way to travel early in the morning."

So we hit the sack for the night ready for an early start tomorrow, the night passed and before we had time to blink the dawn was upon us as we made ready to move. Dressed in the robes that the guide had got for us to travel in, we mounted up and got under way, looking at the fields still smoking. With a look of satisfaction on all our faces we set off along the side of the mountain, deciding to have some breakfast in about a couple of hours once we had got clear of the cave we had stayed in. The rocky paths did not give much room for mistakes, but we were very careful and the horses were used to it, we looked like a group of natives travelling together for safety in this very volatile land. We had our weapons hidden under our cloaks ready for anything that was thrown our way. Brian said he felt good about what we were doing and so did all the other guys. We had been going about three hours and came to a big cave which the guide said would be a good place to stop and eat and also take the opportunity to check over our weapons. So we all dismounted and led the horses into the cave and gave them some food and water before feeding ourselves.

We had some corned beef, bread and a mug of tea, the bread was good, the guide had cooked it for us the night before in the cave. We checked that all our weapons were clean and in working order then had a rest while observing the paths down the mountains with our binoculars. The countryside around us was very wild looking and a tough environment to be in but we were here to destroy as many poppy fields as we could in the time that we were here, this we would do with great pleasure for the innocent children and people that are abused by the people who deal in death and make millions of dollars for themselves at the expense of other people's lives and misfortune. This really dug deep into my heart and filled it with hatred for these people, I believed that this would haunt us all for the rest of our lives.

These sorts of experiences never leave your subconscious, they would be there for the rest of our lives. How could a normal human being shut this out as though it never happened, you would not have any feelings if you could forget all this human misery brought upon people by greed.

We all got ready to depart after checking everything was in order, Trevor was in front, behind the guide, followed by Dave, Brian, Tony, Robert and me taking up the rear as we headed along these very dangerous passes it was a good job the horses were used to the terrain that we were having to travel on. It was getting hot as we proceeded, sometimes at a snail's pace, but when we could, as the paths widened, we moved a little faster.

We asked the guide how long to the next mass of poppy fields and he said about five hours, so that meant we would have travelled all day, but at least we had some sort of idea. Dave said, "my bottom is numb already." Which brought a loud chorus from the rest of the guys agreeing with him, at least that made us all laugh. We were very alert to an attack by bandits who roamed this area looking for easy pickings, having no scruples about killing people, this sort of thing goes on all the time in these perilous passes, so it was our motto this time to take no prisoners, kill or be killed.

We had travelled about another two hours when the guide stopped behind a large overhang of rock, he then bade us to dismount and take a break while we surveyed the area through our binoculars. Taking the opportunity to stretch out which was a nice feeling, Trevor went higher up, away from the path, to survey the way ahead making sure it was clear as the rest of us checked down below.

Brian suddenly said, "quick look at two o'clock, down the mountain, there's a small group of riders heading our way."

They did not look a very peaceful bunch we thought as they brandished their rifles in the air, the guide said that they were not to be trusted and they would kill us without asking questions just to get the horses. We decided that we should pick them off when they got close to the rock where we were taking cover. Counting them, we all agreed that there were ten of them. Surveying the rest of the area we could see no more, Trevor came down and said the path was clear ahead and all he could see was the group making their way up the mountain, confirming that there were ten of them in total so we agreed to pick them off when they were within range.

We had no other choice because if we tried to make a run for it they would follow us as we would be in full view once we left the cover of this rock overhang, so we had to be accurate as we did not want anyone to know that we were in the area. Identifying our targets to each other by the position that they were in coming up the mountain, we spread out waiting while they were within a no miss situation, no one had to get away as that would certainly blow our cover. We were not worried about the gun shots as they often shot aimlessly into the air, it was a way of life to them. Getting ourselves comfortable we waited, I was to give the signal to open fire, it was a tense wait as they made their way towards us slowly.

I was waiting until I could see the forehead of the guy who was mine and I had already picked another one the last in the line then intended to go for as many as I could and the other guys would do the same. As his forehead came clear I gave it a little longer as we all had different eyesight, once I could get my sight lined up between his eyes I gave the order to fire as I pulled the trigger.

Like one shot the first seven went down and I had already taken out the last man, I looked and no one was left standing, saying well done to the guys we lay and observed for about ten minutes to see if there was any movement, ready to shoot again at anything that moved. But we had done a good job and decided to move on our way, they would be found and it would look like they had been ambushed by a bunch of rebels, so it would not cause any alarm to anyone except their own people, who, we suspected, would go on a revenge trip and that would help our cause, having them fight each other.

We had about another three hours travelling before we were to make camp for the night, from where we would make ready to survey the number of poppy fields that we could take out of production this time. We were just going to use gasoline as we rode by, tossing petrol bombs into the fields so they caught alight fast as we headed up the mountain to safety, sheltered by the smoke from the fields, intending also to set some charges on the track to blow up parts of it. We hoped that the wind would be in our favour blowing down the mountain or at least across giving us some cover from anyone taking pot shots at us.

We arrived at the spot the guide wanted us to stop at, we were all sore and very dusty, no chance of a shower or anything, just glad to dismount from the horses. The guide had picked a good spot with plenty of cover for us and the horses, easy to defend against groups of bandits, while it was still light we got a fire going in a small cave determined to have a hot meal and a mug of tea, typical English - wanting tea.

We all remarked at the pleasure of getting off the back of the horses, it was such a relief to stretch our limbs after all those hours in the saddle. Trevor and I scanned the area through the binoculars while the rest of them made food and a mug of tea for us, we went up the side of the mountain a little to get a better view of the area.

Trevor remarked on the large amount of poppy fields, they went as far as we could see.

There were one or two men on horseback wandering around but not too many over the area, maybe about twenty in total spread all over and never more than three together.

We observed a little longer but there was not much change so we decided to go and eat with the rest of the guys. Brian and Robert said how good it felt to be able to lay out and stretch the spine on the ground, Tony said how small pleasures pleased you when deprived of them, adding for Dave's sake "a good woman would be better," with a laugh.

Dave's remark was, "I am too bloody tired and my backside is very sore so if there was a woman here she would be safe for at least one night."

Trevor said, "I don't think so Dave you would soon recover if it was there on a plate for you." Dave just smiled back at him.

We were all really grateful for the shelter and food as we were weary and very dirty. We started to look for a place to bed down for the night, spreading out so that we were able to watch the path below us until the darkness came, then we guessed it would be fairly safe because it would be treacherous to travel at night in a terrain like this, one slip and you would be dead. It was becoming dusk and the night was getting very cold, we crawled into our sleeping bags with the satisfaction that we would be warm for the night and we all said goodnight to each other.

After a long and weary day on the tracks it was not long before we were all fast asleep, the guide was going to keep watch for a few hours then wake Trevor or me to cover the rest of the night. I was in a really deep sleep when I was aware of being shaken by the guide, it seemed as though I had just gone to sleep but nearly four hours had passed, so I let him get his head down as I sat up snuggled with my sleeping bag around me, rifle in my arms across my chest and leaning with my back to a rock as I stared into the darkness with thoughts drifting through my mind. It was a peaceful night and all I could do was think of what we had been through together and the people back home. I thought of how we would all die for each other and the comradeship that had developed between us, the total respect that we had for each other went beyond friendship.

I thought of all the folks back home, of the girls and mates that I had grown up with, it was strange but I did not miss any of it at all, I was very happy with the company and environment that I was in and had been for the last few years. It would not be everyone's idea of a good life but I was happy and very content with my lot, it was totally by choice that I was in the forces and I loved my new family, at least it taught me to respect people and property. The other guys also seemed happy with the life that we had chosen.

I thought of Ann and of my little brother, he was the one thing that used to take me home on leave sometimes. How he enjoyed the letters I'd write home to him he loved the different stamps on them, apart from that I did not miss home at all. My life was here with the adventure and the danger and also all the travelling around the world, seeing different cultures.

Daylight started to break so I boiled some water for a hot drink and was going to give the guys another hour to sleep as we had a difficult day in front of us all. I sat with my mug of coffee staring down the mountainside watching for any movement now daylight was approaching, but it seemed very still, no movement as yet but I expected there to be some soon, hoping that there would not be too many people to deal with. We would leave someone up here while we went down to the furthest poppy fields, working our way back up the mountain from there, hoping to get away with the least conflict that we could and back into the Pakistan side of the mountain range, so we could be picked up and taken to safety.

The guys started to wake, Trevor wanted to know why I hadn't woken him to relieve me. I said that I was very happy to sit there on my own, daydreaming during what had been a very pleasant night. He respected my wish and said thanks for letting us sleep, we all had some more coffee and discussed who was to stay here and watch our progress and cover us as we went down and back up the mountain.

After a discussion we all agreed to leave two up here and the five of us would go down to set the fields alight, so we decided that Brian and Tony would stay and watch our backs. The four of us, and the guide, would go down the mountain to the poppy fields to create as much damage as we could then get the hell out of there hopefully without too much trouble.

Deciding that if we went down about three hours before darkness, that would take us to the main mass of poppy fields, we would then lay up for the night and at first light we would start our mass destruction, this was because we would then be able to make our retreat back up the mountain as the fires burnt away. We were lucky as the ground was tinder dry so it would spread fast, we hoped, we had changed our plans because we were a little worried about lighting the fields during the afternoon, it was a gut feeling that some of us had that we would be better doing it at first light even though it meant staying around for another full day nearly, but there again it would give us chance to observe a little more as there was one or two rebels with rifles slung over their shoulders.

They always seemed to leave the fields late afternoon so that would give us chance to get down there unseen with luck on our side, so decision taken, we had a game of cards while a couple of us kept watch. Tony had seemed a little upset for a few days now so I said to Trevor that I would take the first watch with Tony and try to find out what was wrong. We moved to a good vantage point while the others played cards. After scanning the mountainside and beyond, I said to Tony. "what is the matter, mate? We have noticed that you seem a little upset."

He explained that the last letter from his girlfriend had said that she was going out with someone else, with him being away.

I said, "this is what happens, my mate, unfortunately not many guys in the army keep a girl for long, always being away from home and it has happened to you before. That is why I will not get too involved."

"It would not be so bad but the man she is seeing is a friend taking advantage of me being away," he said.

"Tony, it takes two to tango, if she really loved you she would not do this, I know it's hard but it's true. You can give him a good thrashing when you next get home, if that would make you feel any better, but you must remember that you have been there before."

"Maybe," he said, "but the guy has some friends who would help him."

I turned to him and said, "but you have some friends that love and care about you and we could go with you next time we're in England if you like."

He looked at me and smiled and said, "yes I have real friends here with me that I could trust with my life. You are right, if she loved me she would wait for me to come home, maybe they deserve

166

each other."

I could see the relief in his face as I told him there were plenty more fish in the sea. I said he would find someone who would respect and love him one day and he would know then it was for real.

"Look at Dave and Brian," he said, "they take women as they come and the rest of you are caring."

"That's Dave and Brian," I said, "they will never get hurt by a woman."

He then said to me, "you will only fall in love once in your life, and I am talking about real love, just look how you gave Elsie to Trevor to write to when she wanted to write to you, and you have Ann at home who loves you and you cannot give her the love that she wants back."

He said that he was feeling better now, and we laughed about Dave and Brian and the women that they had been out with, "too many to count," he said.

With that out of the way we began to scan the mountain below with the binoculars observing the rebels that we could see with rifles slung over their shoulders. In total we could see about twelve of them spread around in twos and threes, we were not unduly worried about them.

Our two hours were soon over as Trevor and Brian came to relieve us. Trevor said he had lost a few dollars to Dave laughing as we swapped over and we went to play cards. We were playing three card brag so money was changing hands fast but what else did we spend our money on? We had a fast hand each Tony and I watching Dave and Robert try to out brag each other, winning the hand again, Dave was looking very full of himself, so we decided to bluff him and teach him a lesson. We looked at each other knowing what was going to happen, dealing the cards out, hoping one of us had a good hand in case the bluff did not work, it's always a chance to take. We started out with a dollar each and all of us going round without throwing in our hand, not knowing what each other had, we were just hoping, the kitty got to about fifty dollars. Dave then decided to quit, with that Robert and I threw our hands down also, leaving Tony to pick up the fifty dollars without anyone calling his hand as we had all quit.

Tony then dealt the cards again and Dave was not so happy this time, the game was now getting serious and it was everyone for himself this time. We must have all had good cards because we all kept our hands again. I had three fours so was happy to continue, it went round the group twice before Tony threw his hand in, to be followed shortly by Robert.

Dave looked across at me and I just smiled back at him, he said to me you are bluffing me, I said, "well, it will cost you."

"No," he said. "I'm going to run with this." So we went on and raised the stakes to the amusement of the other guys. Dave was really convinced that I was kidding him, the stakes got to about one hundred dollars when Dave couldn't stand it anymore throwing in the five dollars to see my hand. Well, I threw the three fours down for him to see and a few swear words came out as he said he was convinced that I was kidding him. He had three twos and under normal circumstances it was a very good hand, his mouth was wide open as I scooped up the money saying, "Thanks Dave."

We all burst out laughing at his face it was a picture, the guys said that they did not want to play anymore as they were going to relieve Brian and Trevor, so we started to get the gear ready that we would want to take with us. Checking our rifles as Trevor and Brian came back after being relieved by Dave and Robert, Tony could not wait to tell them about Dave losing his money and they both laughed.

With that we continued to get the equipment ready that we would be taking with us, we intended to soak some dry rags in gas, we thought that this simple way would work as good as anything else as we would also spread gas around to help it spread more quickly and be difficult to control. We had four cans of gas so we reckoned that we would have plenty to get it going well as we worked our way back up the mountain to safety, also we would be setting some charges on the track as we went down the mountain ready to light in the morning. We were hoping that the wind would be helping us as it was quite windy up here, with the dry weather in our favour the fields should burn well.

So checking everything we needed to take we were ready to go when Dave and Robert came back down we would make a move leaving Brian and Tony here to watch our progress down the mountain, then the next day they would be there to give us some cover if we needed it. We decided to sleep in a field for the night once we had got down as far as possible and set our charges, so we just had to come back up the mountain lighting our fires and setting off our charges that we had set as we passed the poppy fields, leaving, we hoped, a trail of destruction in our wake. It seemed so simple after some of the things we had done but you never know what could go wrong for us. Dave and Robert came back and said that the guards on the fields down below had thinned out a bit as they went for something to eat and drink, so saddling up and having a quick check that we had everything, Brian and Tony then set themselves up to watch our descent down to the fields.

We set off with the adrenalin running once more, it was strange how the body performed when the thought of danger went through our minds. We were all ready for anything that could happen to us as we moved slowly down the mountain paths hoping that we would not be seen, so alerting people that strangers were about, but it was becoming bad light which was an advantage to us. We were making good progress as we passed all the poppy fields, deciding to settle for the night as it was now getting very dark, we believed that we had come far enough to cause havoc in the fields. So we ventured into a field away from the track to get some sleep and rise at first light to complete our task.

Light came quickly, so gathering our gear, we proceeded to light the fields while making our way up the mountain paths, the fields were very dry and so soon caught alight and began crackling away as they burnt, encouraged by the wind. We could feel the heat of the flames so we had to get a move on and not get overcome by the flames and smoke which were giving us very good cover. We all felt good at the thought of the wealth we had taken from the evil people as the fields burnt away, taking money away from the scum that dealt in the abusive drug industry exploiting innocent people who would not hurt anyone. This made our blood boil at the thought and made us more determined to help rid the world of these people, when you think of the misery it causes across the world but more so in the countries where it was grown, where people lived and worked in fear and young children abused with no feelings for their little lives.

It was a great comfort looking back and seeing a wall of flame burning away. The searing heat from the burning fields along with the smoke was becoming a real threat to us as the wind was stronger than we had anticipated, so we were having to move more quickly with the danger of having an accident while doing so, but it was the only alternative to getting caught up in the fires that were raging away. There must have been so much confusion among the rebels seeing all the millions of dollars being burnt to the ground before their very eyes. There would be some heads rolling among the rebels that were supposed to look after the crops, but that was not our problem we had done what we had been sent to do.

Suddenly we heard the crack of a rifle and Robert's horse went down. Not knowing where the shot had come from, we decided to cut through a field for a few yards giving ourselves a little cover, this was after I pulled Robert up behind me on the back of my horse, heading up the mountainside, at the same time we were looking around us for any movement, just then Trevor said, "there, they are just about five hundred yards to our left."

Trevor and I dismounted, Robert took care of my horse and Dave grabbed Trevor's reigns and they continued up the mountain. We looked through our binoculars to try to see how many rebels there were and we spotted four of them, we did not think they had seen us drop off the horses, as they were looking away from us at the other guys. That was a major plus for us as we sighted them up in our telescopic sights which gave us an advantage over them as they had older rifles.

We both picked two each, I had the two to my left and Trevor the other two to his right with that we both fired at the same time and dropped two of them quickly with a shot through the head then same for the other two, before they knew what had hit them they were falling to the ground. We turned to each other and clasped hands before we started to make our way up the mountain to the guys who were waiting for us further up. I climbed on behind Robert and Trevor mounted his horse, the others congratulated us on getting rid of the rebels. I was able to hold my rifle at the ready just in case we spotted any more bandits as we made our way further up the mountain.

We had got back onto the tracks to make better progress, Trevor said we must now be in the sight of Brian and Tony and they should be able to give us some covering fire if anything happens on the last half mile up to them.

The flames and smoke behind us filled the horizon so no one on the other side of the fires would see us, every now and again we heard a loud explosion when the fuse of one of the charges that we had set caught alight and blew up the plastic explosive causing more havoc down below us.

We were very relieved as we saw Brian and Tony waiting for us and they had everything packed up ready to move out as soon as we had eaten and had a drink.

That was a job well done and after about ten minutes break to recover and have a snack and a drink, we set off following the guide across the mountainside to the spot where we would be picked up. He told us that was about three hours away, looking down on the fields that no longer had healthy looking crops all of us felt a great satisfaction with the devastation that we had caused to all those fields of misery, that would be many million dollars gone up in smoke and would help stop a bit of misery through the world.

Keeping a sharp lookout as we travelled along the mountainside hoping that we could get back unseen, the men we had shot would be caught up soon in the raging fires so no one would know what happened to them if their remains were ever found, anyway it would be thought that they had perished in the fire.

These mountain paths were very steep, narrow and easy to defend so we hoped that we did not encounter any rebels on the way to our pick up point. Looking back at the fires that were still reaching into the sky and still raging away, the smoke could be seen for many miles around.

The amount of caves that were just off these tracks were unbelievable some that went deep into the bowels of the mountains. We thanked the guide for their people's loyalty to us and he replied with, "We thank you for risking your lives to help us destroy the poppy fields."

In turn that would help the people in the villages around for the time being, we were making good time as the guide in charge said it was about forty minutes to a small flat area where an helicopter could land to pick us up and take us into Pakistan and from there we would hopefully soon get a flight out to Singapore.

Just then there were some shots fired at us and they thudded into the mountainside, we dismounted quickly and scanned the area with our sights and binoculars looking for where the shots were coming from. More shots started to send splinters of rock flying around and were getting a bit too close for comfort. As we scanned the area Tony gave a shout that they were coming from three o'clock where there was a great big clump of boulders. We quickly put the horses into one of the many caves just off the track, then taking some cover ourselves behind a few small rocks whilst we were putting the sights on our rifles, we then waited. It wanted just a movement for us to zoom in on them, Trevor suddenly said they are waiting for us to move so that meant that they could not see us now. Robert and Tony pushed a small boulder down the mountainside and with that there was a hail of shots at the point just near to where we had pushed the boulder. We had a sight of two heads and all four of us fired at them, we knew that our volley of fire had hit them, wondering how many more were there.

Trevor and I were to crawl down on our stomachs taking any cover that we could as we proceeded down about one hundred yards, it seemed to take forever, we decided that we would get a different angle on them if there was any left behind the boulders.

The guys then started throwing small rocks away from the area that we had crawled down to divert attention away from us if anyone was still there. They must have been on edge because a stream of shots thundered into the area where the rocks had been thrown. Now knowing that some guys were left behind the boulders, we both worked our way across to where we would have sight of the other side of the boulders that they had taken as cover for themselves. We carefully crawled down enough to see if anyone was behind the main boulder where they had taken shelter. There, as we reached a spot with a little cover for us, we heard the guys firing some shots off at them to keep their attention away from us. We just could not see how many were still there from where we had taken cover so we crawled further round without much cover.

But the guys could see us and started to fire at the boulders to keep the attention of the bandits away from us. So concentrating on where the firing was coming from, we moved about another twenty five yards then we had a good view of the five bandits who were left behind the boulders.

I said to Trevor, "let's pick two out each and then both go for the other one."

This time we could not afford to miss as we did not have much cover, setting ourselves up with our targets and with the usual handshake we decided it was a go and fired at will taking four of them out with no bother. The fifth guy turned and shot at us while scrambling to get some cover from us, but exposing himself to the rest of the guys because he seemed to bounce as shots rained into his body. Breathing a sigh of relief we headed back to the others so that we could get out of there.

Mounting up we continued down the track to our pickup point hoping to get there without any more confrontations, we did not have time to get stuck on this very narrow path high up on the mountainside, also we could get trapped for days if there was a very determined group of bandits.

Looking back we could still see the fields of poppies burning away in the distance, every single one of us felt really good about the mission that we had just completed without too much bother and no casualties for us. We must have caused havoc in the rebel camps because of the huge loss of crops, guessing that they would all be blaming each other for the disaster.

Making good progress, the guide said that we would be there in about fifteen minutes as we turned round a corner further up there was a clear flat area where we would wait for the helicopters and hoped that they wouldn't be too long. When we finally arrived it was amazing how big the clearing was with caves on the mountainside.

The guide said that the rebels were using the caves at one time and had cleared the area just outside to drop supplies, but realising that the area was vulnerable to any attack with the tracks being a good bit wider, they had pulled out and gone further up where the tracks were very narrow making it easier to defend against any other rebel gangs that came their way.

There were lots of different groups competing against each other, so that was to our benefit or we would have had to cross the mountain into Pakistan, that would have taken us a very long time and we would have been very vulnerable to attacks which could have kept us holed in for days in the difficult terrain. This could have given us casualties also or even all of us could have been killed, so taking the horses into one of the large caves we sat at the mouth, from there we were just watching and waiting for our ride out of there, the guide was going to take the horses once we had gone. We made some coffee after lighting a fire deep in the cave, eating some of our rations while keeping a watch out for any rebels venturing our way. We had been waiting for about two hours when we heard the sound of the helicopter in the distance, we all came out of the mouth of the cave and scanned the whole area as the helicopter would be vulnerable to anyone that wanted to fire at it. We signalled that it was all clear to land and we were all ready to make a fast getaway and after wishing the guide the best of luck, we quickly climbed into the helicopter, then in seconds we were on our way over the mountain into Pakistan.

Looking down, the pilot said over his speaker, "you lot have caused some bloody damage down there." He had observed it on the way in to pick us up then he said, "a bloody good job guys."

He said we would be about an hour and he was under instructions to leave us at a small airfield, from where an aeroplane would be waiting for us, to take us to the base in Karachi where we had a small number of personnel stationed. From there, after having a good night's sleep and some decent food, we were going to be flown back to Singapore and our next assignment. We would have a few days back in Singapore which we would look forward to, at least that is what we hoped.

After being well fed and having a good night's sleep we caught the plane that was to take us to Singapore, we were all feeling good about ourselves and what we had achieved in the last few days.

# Chapter 12

As we approached Changi airfield we could see all the ships in the Straits that separated Singapore from Malaysia. No wonder this country was becoming very wealthy, all the activity in the Straits contributed to that. As we touched down and taxied to another part of the airfield away from the main buildings, we gathered our kit and double checked that we had left nothing behind.

Once the steps had been put up to the plane we descended and there were two land rovers waiting to take us to the base. It was a good feeling to arrive back safe and sound in Singapore once more, it seemed like a second home to us, also the good thing was that we all enjoyed being there and being able to relax without any worries at all.

Trevor said that he was looking forward to the letters that he hoped Elsie had written to him. Dave and Brian both said that they were looking forward to meeting old friends in Singapore, we all laughed and said that we knew that they could not wait to get out on the town once more.

With that we arrived at the camp and surrendered our rifles and pistols to be looked after in the quarter master's store, they would then also be checked over for us and any parts that needed it would be replaced, we kept our knives and then went to dump the rest of our kit in our quarters. After a shower I went down to the mess for dinner and a few beers, Trevor, Robert and Tony were already in there, which left Brian and Dave to follow on.

After I got my drink, Trevor told me that he had picked up his mail and said that Elsie had been asking after me and sent her love, he was pleased and his face was beaming because he had received ten letters from her. The rest of us had not picked our mail up yet. Ann had asked Elsie to tell Trevor to tell me to write to her as soon as I had time as she missed me. I said I would write to her tomorrow, with tongue in cheek as I said it. Mind you it made sense to do this while we were able to get some letters home from Singapore. Tony said that he was going to have a good drink tonight and let his hair down, we all said that we would join him as we did not get much time to relax.

In came Dave and Brian, the two that loved to hate each other. Robert said, "let's all go to Raffles for a few drinks and just sit and watch the gentry living their lives of luxury with their ladies done up to the nines in their best clothes all made here in Singapore at very little cost."

Silk was used a lot by the tailors of Singapore and it was of good quality, we all agreed to go there and observe them for a short while at least, maybe we would see the girls in there with their parents if they were around. All agreed, we called a couple of cabs to take us to Raffles, we all looked smart and very tanned in slacks and short sleeved shirts. As we entered all the eyes in the main room turned to look at us we must have looked quite a motley crew to them. We could feel the eyes of the women burning into us, I would think with quite a different feeling than their men folk!

We sat at a large table just in one corner and ordered some drinks from one of the waiters who was buzzing around. It was pretty quiet but we decided to stay a little while before going down Orchard Road to some of the clubs that were around that area.

Looking round and about Robert said, "you guys just look at the wealth that we have sat around us without a care in the world between them."

Then Dave spoke up and said to our outburst of laughter, "some of these women would give you anything to have a discreet affair with any one of us, I may just try it on to see if I am right about this."

Tony said to Dave, "I am sure that you are right because you can glance around and see the women undressing you with their eyes, then many of them looking at their rather portly husbands."

With that Robert said, "let's bet Dave that he can't take one of these women to bed in the next two hours."

We all said we would put twenty dollars each in if he pulled it off.

"That's a deal guys," he said, "what about that woman at the bar now?"

She looked okay so we all agreed.

Dave got up and made his way over to her, they were just within hearing distance of us. He pulled a stool up near to her and we watched her turn to him as he asked her if there was much to do here in Singapore? She smiled and said, "are you new here?"

"Yes, we will only be here for a few days I think," said Dave.

"You look a healthy bunch of lads," she told him.

"Where is your husband?" he asked.

She turned and said, "over in the other room playing bridge, I was bored so I came in here for a drink away from the smoke."

"What on earth is he playing bridge for when he could be with a beautiful woman like you?" Replied Dave.

She turned and kissed him on the cheek saying, "how sweet of you."

"Where are you staying in Singapore?" asked Dave.

"Here in Raffles, bored out of my tiny little mind."

"If I had a beautiful woman like you I know where I would be right now."

We could not believe our ears, straight in for the kill, that's Dave, it would either be a slapped face or he'd get the come on.

"Well," she said to him, "I know what I would like if I had one of you healthy looking guys around me for long!"

"But," said Dave, "your husband is through there, not that I am bothered but I would not like you to get into trouble for talking to me."

"That's where he will be for the next couple of hours and he would not bat an eyelid if he saw me talking to you. He would be only too pleased that you would be keeping me out of his hair for a while, so you don't have to worry about that."

"I'm not worried about him because I can look after myself, I am worried about you," said Dave.

With that she took his hand and said, "he will not even know that I've gone, so take me for a walk please."

Dave gave a sideways grin to us as they got up and strolled out of the room heading towards the lifts and we all knew where they were going. Trevor said, "looks like we have lost our money."

We sat and watched Dave and the woman go out of our sight and decided to order some more drinks. Brian called the waiter over, we knew that he was seething with Dave for having taken the well-to-do woman to her room, it showed on his face.

We just sat there talking to each other for the next three quarters of an hour, a few more people came into the place during that time and it was filling up a little but there was not much talent about. Just then in walked Dave on his own with a big smile on his face as he came and sat down again with us holding his hand out. Brian said to him, "you look as though you have had your money's worth anyway."

Dave laughed and said, "You bet I did, her old fellow does not bother with her and she was crazy in bed and I enjoyed every minute of it. She told me to get all our drinks on her room bill so we may as well stop in here tonight, not one of us complained about that, for tonight anyway. Just then, as cool as anything, she came down and walked across to us saying, "is it okay for me to join you all?"

"Sure, sit down," we said.

Then she said would we all like to have something to eat in the restaurant. We said not at these prices. "Not to worry, we will pay," she replied.

She then asked the waiter to go through and ask her husband if he wanted to join us for dinner, her husband came through and she said, "these nice soldiers have been keeping me company so can we take them to dinner?"

He said, "sure, but I want to finish my game could you go on your own with them?"

She introduced him to us all and he asked what we were doing here.

Trevor said, "we are just based at Changi until we move on."

Saying, "have a nice meal, talk to you later," he was gone, ambling back to the other room to finish his game of cards.

Dave said out loud to us, once he was out of earshot, "you bloody fool."

The woman, who was called Gwen, said, "come on then, my men, let's go to dinner."

The head waiter in the restaurant said to her, "evening madam, where do you want to sit, your usual table?"

She said, "no we are all together and the table will not be large enough for us all so could we have that large table over in the

178

corner please, then if my husband joins us there will be room."

"Certainly madam," he said leading the way and holding her chair until she sat down.

He then brought the menu himself and asked if we wanted drinks? She told us to order anything we wanted so we did, and she ordered a bottle of wine for herself. Patting the chair next to her for Dave to sit near her like a little puppy.

It was very expensive but Gwen said once again order anything that you want, don't worry about the cost, you boys deserve it, looking at Dave she said, "and you all need to keep your strength up."

We all smiled at that and it was taking us all our time not to burst out laughing at the remark.

Ordering our starters most of us having prawn cocktail and every one of us ordering fillet steak for the main course, Gwen ordered fish. Just then her husband came through to join us with two other couples and invited them to sit with us once the waiter had joined a table on to give us more room. They all seemed very nice people, they must have had plenty of money as all of them were staying at Raffles and had been here for a couple of months now.

Gwen's husband said to us thank you for entertaining my wife while I played cards, we said it was no bother, knowing that Dave had really entertained her and he had a big smile on his face.

The dinner went well and we were made very welcome and they asked us how long we were in Singapore? Trevor answered saying we did not know as we were in transit not giving anything away.

We were having a very cheap evening as they would not let us pay for anything at all, so we ate and drank as much as we wanted to. Trevor whispered to me that he thought that Brian was stroking one of the other ladies' legs under the table and she was loving it. I could not see from where I was sat but I caught Brian's eye and he knew what I was meaning as I looked at him and gestured with my eyes, he gestured back, acknowledging that I was right. With a smile on his face he saw me confirm it to Trevor who shook his head in disbelief.

Trevor whispered to me, "they will get us shot one day."

The three husbands asked us to join them in a game of cards,

179

Robert said we do not play bridge, but will play three card brag for a little while.

"Okay," they said. "Does everyone want to play?"

Brian and Dave said no but we knew what they were up to! Gwen's husband said to them, "please stay with our wives and keep them company while we go into the other room where the card tables are."

Both Dave and Brian said, 'sure'.

So we ambled off to play brag and they went into the bar to talk about other energetic games.

There were seven of us playing brag, we said that we could not play for big stakes starting off at a dollar and intending to raise it later in the game. Robert took the first game followed by me then Tony.

Gwen's husband then won a game they did not seem bothered about losing, just enjoying the game with someone other than themselves for a change. Tony got a run on as he won the next four games and pocketed a good few dollars. After playing for a couple of hours all four of us were well in front with our winnings, so we decided to call it a day, thanking them for the most enjoyable evening.

They said, "no problem, we have enjoyed the change of company, chaps. Please come and have dinner tomorrow, at least you get our wives out of our hair for a little while and that is worth it to us."

So saying goodnight we went through to the bar leaving them playing cards on their own. Dave and Brian were still with the three women, laughing and joking as we went up to disturb them and let them know that we were going and were they coming with us?

They both decided to leave with us and said that they would come back tomorrow night. Gwen said to Dave, "could you escort us round the shops tomorrow as we don't like going on our own?"

They said that their husbands did not like going round the shops at all. Dave and Brian said they would love to and the women told them to get a cab and pick them up at the hotel then we could all go into the centre together, saying they would settle the bill for the cab.

We thanked them for dinner and said goodnight as we walked out of the hotel to get a cab back to camp, as it was too late now to go into the centre of Singapore. Arriving back at camp we all went straight to bed.

Next day at breakfast there was Dave, Brian and Robert all dressed ready to go and us three in our shorts. Dave said, "We will screw them for all we can and more."

That's Dave, no scruples at all.

Brian said, with a smile on his face, "We will screw them in more ways than one."

Robert just sat there quietly wondering what he had let himself in for.

We told them we would see them tonight at Raffles for dinner as their cab arrived and the three musketeers set off for the day.

Tony asked if we fancied a lazy day round by the pool. Trevor said, "Yes it will do us good and we can write a few letters home, then get the RAF guy at the post office to send them off at intervals for us."

He reminded me to write to Ann. I said I thought it sounded like a good idea so it would be round the pool sunning and swimming in between letters today.

The morning was going well, in and out of the pool, and writing some letters home, my letters ended up being postcards which I went to the NAAFI to buy. Trevor laughed at me and said to Tony, "letter writing is not one of my dear brother's strong points." Tony agreed he was not good at writing letters so that made two of us, we decided to go to the mess and sit outside and have some sandwiches and a couple of beers before going back round the pool for the rest of the afternoon.

We walked towards the tables outside the mess and noticed that there were a group of young girls with their parents having something to eat and drink, we took up a table next to them, when we had ordered one of the girls asked us if we knew where Raffles was, as they wanted to go.

Her father said that they had arrived yesterday and had been posted to Singapore for twelve months, so they would have to find their way about. In answer to the girls we said that we were going there tonight and if they would like to join us they could, we told them that the prices were pretty high so we were having a few drinks at

Raffles then going on to the waterfront for a meal. One of the fathers' said would we mind if they all strung along with us, we said we wouldn't, and he said he would arrange transport for us.

So saying our goodbyes we arranged to meet outside the mess room at six thirty, when we would go to Raffles and see what Dave, Brian and Robert had been up to with the ladies. We remembered that we had been invited to dinner that night with Gwen and her friends, but maybe we could get out of it, if it was to our advantage.

We called in the post office and posted all our cards and letters, Trevor left some to be posted one at a time for the next week, then we headed to our rooms for a rest and a shower before the evening. We all said that we were looking forward to the night out in a big crowd as we departed into our own rooms.

We were lucky having good rooms like we had, away from the main block, the officers' married quarters were just across from us, the surroundings were very pleasant so at least it gave us some home comforts while we were there.

Tony said, I wonder how the lover boys have got on?" As we walked to our quarters.

"You don't need to worry about them they will have got all they wanted," I replied.

We then split up and went into our quarters saying see you in about two hours. At about six twenty we made our way down to the mess and NAAFI to meet up with everyone else, the driver was waiting for us. There were two couples and five girls so we climbed onto the back of the truck which had seats down each side, and headed off to Raffles for what we hoped would be a good evening out.

~*~

Everyone was getting on fine together, chatting away, so it was not going to be hard work as sometimes it can be if people do not mix very well. Arriving at Raffles the girls and their parents marvelled at the splendour of the building, one of the parents saying it was a typical British colonial hotel. We told them we called it a palace for the rich.

Walking into the bar there was not too many people about as we all sat down at a table, the waiter came over to ask what we wanted to drink, acknowledging us from the nights we had been there before. The girls all wanted a Singapore Sling saying that they wanted to try the local drink and all of us guys ordered beer. The parents of the girls marvelled at the splendour of the place and went for a look round while the drinks came.

The girls said it seemed a bit dead in here, 'a place for the retired gentry' were their words.

One of them asked if, after we had a drink, could we go into the centre of Singapore to eat and drink.

We said it was fine with us as long as their parents would let them, so when their parents came back the girls asked if they could go into the centre with us. One of the girls' fathers' said that it was okay as long as they all stayed with us and didn't wander off. He then pulled out his wallet and gave them all some money and told them to pay for our meals as well, with that we all decided to drink up and go.

Tony asked if we were waiting for Dave, Brian and Robert.

"No, we could be here all night," I said.

We left a message behind the bar to say we had gone into the centre, the girls were good fun and it was a pleasure not to have Dave and Brian with us trying it on, they would not care whose daughters they were, they would all be classed as fair game to them. So we took them to a waterfront restaurant and we all ordered drinks and asked to look at the menu. The girls thought it was better than being sat in the frumpy hotel, they asked if we would take them for a walk down the waterfront after we had eaten our meals?

We said, "sure, no problem." It was very relaxing chatting away to them and they told us that they had come from their father's last posting in the Middle East to here, then said, "from what we've seen up to now, we would like this a lot better."

We all ordered fish dishes and when it came it looked wonderful, lobster, prawns and white fish, all laid out for us to help ourselves, the lobsters were massive, the girls said they have never seen any as big as they were and we all tucked in to enjoy our food.

As we were sat eating who should walk by but Dave, Brian and Robert with the three women, the look on Dave's face when he saw us sat with five, very good looking, young women was a picture.

Gwen asked if it was okay to join us. So they all then sat at the next table and pulled it closer to ours. When they had settled down and ordered their drinks and some food, Gwen said to Dave, "show them what I have bought you David." (giving him his full title).

Dave was squirming in his seat as he showed us a beautiful gold ring that she had bought for him, Trevor whispered to me, "I can't get over his face he did not expect to see us on the waterfront, especially with five good looking girls."

We all said how nice the ring was, then we introduced the girls to them. They asked if we had been to Raffles and when we said yes, Gwen asked if we had seen their husbands there?

Trevor answered by saying, "no the place was empty but it was early and we did not go into all the rooms."

"Have you not been back there today?" I asked.

"No, we have been shopping all day," was the response.

So much to Dave's disappointment we had finished our meal and the girls wanted to go for a walk. Tony asked, "everyone ready to go?"

Without giving any of the others chance to say anything, we said that we would see them back at Raffles in about two hours, we had promised the girls' parents that we would take them back there. Dave's face was like thunder, Brian and Robert were okay as their food had just arrived, so we all got up saying, "See you later folks." And strolled away, smiling to ourselves as we left.

Once out of earshot one of the girls said, "your friend did not seem very happy with himself."

So we decided to tell them why, also telling them to beware of Dave and Brian, but we had no need as they were very street-wise girls and had weighed up the situation already.

One of the girls said, "They are bored housewives wanting some younger blood, it happens around the camps we have been at with our parents."

We told them that these were people travelling the world with plenty of money to burn, telling them how it all arose out of a bet, saying also that all their husband's did was play cards all day, drinking and smoking big cigars. One of the girls said they must be

184

very frustrated women then. We strolled along the waterfront smiling to ourselves.

The girls asked us how long we were posted here for and Trevor said, "a couple of weeks maybe, we were not sure." They asked us what we did in the forces, and I said, "we go round bases repairing things like engineers do, that is why we are not in one place for long."

That seemed to satisfy their inquisitive minds for the time being anyway.

We called a cab to take us back to Raffles and as we walked back in, the girls' parents waved us over to where they were sitting and asked us if we wanted a drink. We sat down and the girls were busy telling their parents that they'd had a great time with us and a wonderful meal on the waterfront. Their parents thanked us for looking after them and we said they were good company for us, we were only too happy to do so.

Just then in came Gwen's husband, he saw us sat there and asked if we had seen the ladies and our friends. I replied that we had left them eating on the waterfront.

With that he said, "oh good, we will go and eat ourselves." He asked if we had eaten and Trevor said we had so he and the other two husbands said join us later if you want.

"We will have a drink with you later, when the rest of them come back," I replied.

We sat chatting away with the girls and their parents and about an hour later in walked Dave, Brian and Robert with the ladies. They walked over to a table near to us and Trevor told the ladies that their husbands were in the restaurant having a meal. They said that they would leave them be to enjoy their meal as it was a big change for them to have someone attentive to their needs.

Trevor and I caught each other's eyes and smiled, we would get the full story later from the guys. Our understanding of each other was unbelievable because we could feel each other's moods at times.

Just then in came the husbands, walking across to us and asking if their wives had enjoyed themselves. They all said, "yes, thank you, darling, Dave, Brian and Robert were perfect gentlemen."

Tony whispered to me, "I bet they were."

185

Gwen's husband asked us if we wanted a drink and bought a round for us all, he then said that they were going to play cards again. It seemed as though they were all very pleased that the guys had taken their wives off their hands and escorted them out for the day.

The girl's parents asked us if we wanted a lift back to camp with them, it was rather late so we all decided to go back and have one last drink in the NAAFI. On the way back the girl's parents thanked us once more for taking care of them and the girls also gave us their thanks for a lovely evening. Trevor poked me in the side to look at Dave there he was, next to one of the girls, whispering in her ear and she was giggling to herself.

So I said out loud, "Dave, how did it go today, show the girl's the ring again that Gwen bought for you."

If looks could kill that would have been my lot, as he held his hand out with the ring on it for all to see.

Trevor said, "you must have been good company for her to buy you that Dave."

Dave responded by saying, "Brian and Robert were bought something also, it wasn't just me."

Brian said, "yes, I got a camera." And Robert chipped in with, "I had a couple of silk shirts made in the plaza."

Arriving at the NAAFI, we thanked the girl's parents for the lift, they said they were turning in for the night, the girls asked if they could stay with us but were told it was too late, time for bed. So we said goodnight, see you in the morning, as we went inside.

We went into the bar to hear the sordid details of what had gone on with the women who Dave, Brian and Robert had escorted for the day.

The first words Dave said to me were, "you had no need to highlight the ring Gwen bought me."

"I did it, Dave, to keep you out of trouble with the officer's daughter who you were ogling, and don't you think you have played with fire enough for one day?"

He then started to tell us that he and Gwen had booked into an hotel for the rest of the day after they had finished shopping, he said that she was all over him and asked him to call at the hotel tomorrow as her husband had some business to attend to.

186

Brian said he and Betty did the same and she gave him a good time. Robert said they just walked round the shops and had a few drinks together before meeting up again with the others for something to eat.

Tony said to them, "you have real nerve but one day it will land you in big trouble."

Typically Dave replied, "it will have been worth it, you lot need to loosen up a bit, you are too soft when it comes down to women." Adding, "I will use women to my advantage without any real feelings for any of them."

"One day, Dave," Trevor said, "you will fall in love and you may be hurt, just like you hurt some women with your philandering."

Dave shrugged and said, "there's plenty more fish in the sea."

Next morning at breakfast we decided to go into the old quarter of Singapore for a walk round all the quaint little shops and stalls, to pick up a few gifts to send home. Dave came with us saying he would go to Raffles later in the day. Trevor said, "what's wrong Dave, tired of her already?"

"Mind your own business," he replied.

We all said, "admit it Dave you soon get tired of one woman."

He did not answer, just shrugged his shoulders.

Just as we were leaving, in came the girls with their parents, they asked where we were going and when we told them the old part of Singapore they asked if they could come along. We said if it was okay with their parents then it was fine with us. Their parents agreed and asked what time we would be back?

We said around two o'clock, and we were told to get a couple of land rovers out of the vehicle compound, after the girls had a quick drink and a bit of breakfast we set off.

It was magical in the old part, stalls full of cloth and musical boxes and all sorts of little gifts. Most of us bought some musical boxes to send home as they were very well made and decorated in all shapes and sizes. The girls bought some silk to have made up at the tailors, and we also went into the fish market to see all the fresh fish being sold, most of it was kept alive in big tanks, massive lobsters crawling around waiting to be bought by the restaurant buyers. It was amazing to see all the different species of fish in the hustle and bustle of the fish market, I could have watched it all morning, but was hustled along by Brian and Trevor who knew how I liked to watch the different cultures at work and also being very interested in fishing.

Time passed by and after everyone had finished buying we went back to the camp, it was about two thirty as we drove into Changi base to drop the girls off and then go round the pool for the afternoon. One of the Royal Air Force guys came up to us and said that Captain Rennie was looking for us, so we went straight to the offices to see him. He told us to sit down and asked if we were enjoying our free time.

We all said, "yes, great, thanks."

He said, "sorry guys, I have to spoil your leave as there is a big job to be done. We have been told that some 'high up' Philippine man has been captured by bandits and was being held just outside Manila.

Unfortunately you have been given the job of rescuing him and bringing him back with you to Singapore."

I asked when did we have to leave?

"First light in the morning, you will be dropped at a point that has been identified by some people that we have in Manila, they will then take you to where he is being held by about twenty or more bandits. You will have to lay low for a couple of days to find out what you will be up against, the rest is up to you and if you can bring someone else back with you please do."

Dave said, "that's our plans for tonight gone out of the window, we will have to get all our gear together and check it all over so it will be a night in the NAAFI."

Tony said, "it has helped you out of the mess you could have got yourself in Dave, send a message to say you have had to leave Singapore for a few days."

"Yes," Dave said, "I will do that, I have to admit she was very possessive and I did not like that, after all, I was giving her something that she wanted with no strings attached."

Brian said, "I'm pleased that we are going away, they may have gone when we get back."

So after going over the maps with Captain Rennie who pointed out on the map where the man was being held, it was to the east of Manila in a very dense area of jungle. Captain Rennie said, "this is going to be a tough one guys, I know you can do it, that's why you are going, we believe that you are the right guys to pull this off, but come back safe and best of luck to you all."

We went straight away to draw our weapons out of the armoury and check them over cleaning and oiling them after getting all we needed to take with us, which consisted of camouflaged ground nets and plenty of ammunition, also some plastic explosive fuse wire and a few grenades. We went to pack our back packs, double checking each others, making sure that we had binoculars and telescopic night sights as well. We could not afford to slip up in what we should take with us, so until everything had been double and treble checked we stayed with it before going to the mess to eat.

The adrenalin was pumping through us all once again and we all knew that we could rely on each other no matter what we got into. We would certainly give our lives for each other without a second thought.

When we walked into the mess, the girls were sat with their parents having a drink, we sat down near them, after getting something to eat, and one of them asked if we were going to the waterfront.

"Sorry we have to be up early to help repair a bridge somewhere," we said.

They accepted that but their father's looked at us with a knowing look but said nothing and we left it at that. We were all on edge with the adrenalin taking over our bodies just the same as it always did before we went anywhere, it was the excitement and knowing that we were going into the unknown. Finishing our main course of beef, mash and vegetables, we went up for a sweet, eating more than normal for comfort.

Captain Rennie came in to see us and asked if everything was ready for the morning, we said yes but he seemed a little uneasy, it was strange how we all picked this feeling up. He said, "could you all come over here so I can talk to you away from anyone else?"

So we went over to the other end of the room, he said, "listen lads, I am worried and have to tell you this is not going to be easy at all because I have just found out that there has been two attempts to free this man and they were both unsuccessful with heavy casualties. That is why he has been moved to this new camp, making it harder for anyone to get in to him. I love you all as sons and want you back safe."

Our reply was that we never expect anything to be easy and thanked him for his concern but we had a job to do. To add a bit of humour Robert said, "you may love us as sons but if you had a daughter you would not let Dave near to her."

At that point everyone burst into laughter, even Dave so that took the tension away from things. Captain Rennie then said, "come on guys, let me buy you all a drink before I go."

This was to the surprise of the girl's fathers who were first lieutenants, who had not really been around as much as he and ourselves had, but they had an idea that Captain Rennie had a free hand here at Changi from talking to other officers on the base.

He got the drinks in and said, "Cheers lads, best of luck, see you soon, every man jack of you."

With a parting shot of 'early to bed you guys,' he said he would see us in the morning bright and early.

With that he turned and went out of the bar leaving us in peace to console each other. He was one of the best officers we had ever met.

# Chapter 13

So we played darts for a little while before the girls came into the games room and asked if they could play also. We set up two teams with one dropping out each time to mark up the scores. It was a good night and Dave and Brian behaved themselves with the girls. It got to eleven pm so we decided to say goodnight to everyone and then all disappeared to our billets for the night. The beer had helped us to relax a little but I know that I lay awake thinking about the mission and praying that we'd all come back safe, I knew the rest of the guys would be thinking the same as me.

Eventually I fell asleep and was awoken by Captain Rennie at about five am telling me to get down to breakfast then collect my kit. The others were coming out at the same time heading for breakfast as he had got them out of bed before me, we were all on edge again with the adrenalin flowing fast as we walked into the mess to stoke up our bodies with the last hot meal we'd have for awhile. We all had bacon, eggs and everything else we could get with it, washing it down with hot tea.

After breakfast we assembled with our kit and a lorry came to take us to the airport. Captain Rennie was coming with us to the airport and he said that if we let him know, when we radioed in, if we were short of anything he would get it dropped in for us straightaway. He said that some ammunition had been dropped in for us already and should have been taken by natives to the coordinate that was given to us, after all without adequate ammunition we would all be very vulnerable, we could find food in the jungle but not ammunition.

We arrived at the airport and Captain Rennie shook all our hands and said, "best of luck, God guide you all." Adding, "please come back safe you lads and look after each other, I'll talk to you on the radio soon."

With that we boarded the plane for the journey away from our favourite posting, we put our parachutes by our side ready to put on when we reached our destination. Trevor said, "I am going to have a sleep," and this was echoed by everyone else because we had all been laid awake most of the night thinking about today.

It was all heads down as the plane taxied down the runway and we were soon airborne and on our way to the unknown, unsure who would be coming back, we must have all soon fallen asleep because we were wakened by the second pilot shaking our shoulders, we were twenty minutes away from the drop zone. We were soon wide-awake, checking our kits were strapped tight and parachutes on.

We checked each other and helped tighten up then sat and waited for the signal. The lights came on and we lined up, shook hands with each other, and waited for the signal to go. We followed each other out of the plane quickly looking down at the jungle below for the clearing that we were told would be there for us, we watched the plane turn around and head back with a wave of its wings. We were in freefall for a little while then Dave pointed to the clearing, it was just to our right. We opened our chutes at different times to give us space and headed towards the clearing, they had cleared a big area so it was quite easy for us to get on target as there wasn't a strong wind to throw us away from the area.

We all landed safely, thank God, and quickly got our chutes off, there were a couple of Philippine guys there waiting for us, they were to gather the chutes and take them away. We all knew that this was going to be a very dangerous operation calling on great physical strength, nerves of steel and most of all mental stamina, but we knew that together we could survive.

The hot and steamy bed of the jungle, and the animals in it, were another thing we had to contend with along with any booby traps, but we knew that there would be small rivers and streams to refresh ourselves in. The guides who were there to meet us said that we were about ten miles from the camp where the person we had to bring back was being held, he said that it was very well guarded because of previous attempts to set him free.

They then took us to a small clearing about another mile towards the target where the undergrowth around was very dense and they had built us some cover using growing vines and tree branches. A lot of thought had gone into this and we would only have to make minor adjustments. They showed us where they had dug out a small hole and buried some of the stuff that was dropped for us.

The ammunition was raised above the ground and covered well to keep it dry because when the rains came the jungle bed got very swampy. In all they had done an excellent job for us, they were to stay with us and help in anyway that they could.

"Very useful people to have when you are stuck in this jungle." said Robert, they had even prepared some food for us.

We got rid of our kits first then settled ourselves down to tuck into the cooked chickens that they had done for us. There was a little stream about two hundred yards away, but they said that they had boiled the water for us anyway, and there was a couple of big containers full for us to be going on with. They had been preparing for our coming for a few weeks, finding the right spot for us and then preparing the hide, they'd even dug a big hole for all our rubbish just away from the camp and covered it with vines so nothing was left for us to do but find a way to free this important person and from what we have heard it would be no easy task for us to complete.

We settled in for the night after setting up some trip wires around the perimeter of our camp, and sat talking about how we were going to attack the camp where he was being held. First thing we would do was to observe the movement in the camp while setting up some plastic explosive around to help us in our retreat to our pickup point where a helicopter would come in to take us to safety if we were successful. We were to observe the place in a group of three, plus one of the guides. Taking turns and the rest staying here at the camp, we would do this for as long as it would take us to be very sure that we could get it right and get him out safely. So Trevor, Dave and Robert were to stay at camp for the first day and Brian, Tony and I would take first pop at it. The reason we were doing this was so that we would have back up at all times if anything went wrong, also we would have different eyes looking at the situation for the attack. We put our mosquito nets over us as we got our heads down for the night, at least they would stop a few of the bites from the nasty little creatures.

Next morning we went down to the small stream that had a few deep pools to freshen ourselves up before our journey through the jungle. After eating breakfast we set off, taking the radio with us to keep in touch with base camp, so they knew what was happening, we were to call in once every hour just to re-affirm that we were okay.

The going was tough in parts and very swampy, we reckoned it would take us about three hours or more to get in a position to observe the camp. In the first day or two we would plan where we would place some plastic explosive, not only to divert their attention away from where we would enter the camp, but to help in destroying it as we left. We would also map out our escape route thus setting charges to cover our retreat away from there. We radioed in on the hour with just a quick message to say we were making good progress, it was very hot and sticky as we made our way through the undergrowth. Coming to a very swampy area we had to go round because it was draining trying to plough our way through it, we were up to our waists in mud and damp, rotting undergrowth created by the vast amounts of rain that had been falling in the last few weeks. It was not the best time to travel in the jungle but we could not choose when the guy was going to be captured.

We were still making good time the guide told us as we made our next radio in to base, we guessed the next time we called in we would be able to confirm that we were nearly on site ready to observe the camp. We must have looked a sorry sight being covered in mud and sweating in the humidity. The guide said that none of the rebels who had our prisoner left the perimeter of their camp, then he told us that it consisted of a couple of large huts and ten other smaller ones which had been there for a few years, some natives had lived there before being driven out of the place.

We arrived at a point where we could see the clearing, this was quite large with the huts round the perimeter and a big clearing in the middle where they got their helicopters in and out of the place, so we sent a quick signal to say we were there.

Looking through our binoculars Brian remarked how well it was guarded with a couple of armed guards at each hut. We needed to identify the hut that contained our objective, so we were quite sure where he was when we went in to, hopefully, bring him out alive.

We lay low while watching the movement of the rebels in the camp, we reckoned that there were at least thirty of them.

The good thing about it was that all their guards were placed with their backs to the huts, that would be a bonus to us if we were careful, we would have a bit of cover from them while we were setting some charges on the jungle side of the huts. We assumed that they thought, with them all facing the jungle or the hut opposite, they would have sight of the jungle around them, but if we came in line with the huts from the undergrowth we could hopefully get right up to the rear of each hut to plant some charges. The huts were on stilts so it would be easy to plant charges directly under them.

Tony said, "I do not know where our man is just yet, there is nothing pointing to his whereabouts."

That was our first objective, to find where he was being held. We had been observing for about an hour when someone came out of one of the larger huts and went to a smaller one with what we thought looked like some food on a plate, this confirmed to us that it was the hut where our man was being held.

We watched the rebel pass the plate over to someone who came out of the hut to collect it, we did not know how many guys were in there, it would have to be a case of trying to identify them as they came in and out for any reason. We spent another couple of hours checking this and we reckoned that there were four guards in there with him. We then worked our way round the perimeter of the camp checking where we could create a diversion, away from the hut where he was held.

Brian said he could set up a big diversion of plastic explosive under the two huts furthest away from the hut, then some a bit nearer, to follow on from them. We decided to give it a try and see if Brian could get under the huts with us giving him cover in case he was discovered, so we skirted round in the undergrowth to the back of the other huts where we could observe Brian coming in from the back. He would bury the plastic with fuse intact and cover the fuse wire as he retreated back from the huts.

Once we were in to position to cover him and rifles ready, we signalled to him it was a go and he started to crawl with his plastic and fuse wire to get under the first hut, it seemed like a lifetime with the adrenalin flowing fast.

He was under the first hut setting the plastic then covering the fuse wire as he slowly scraped a small furrow with his bayonet to lay it in. He slowly retreated, being very careful with the fuse wire and covering it as he did so. One done one to go, he then started to crawl under the next one, just then he froze as one of the guards walked towards where he was laid under the hut, fortunately this was just to relieve himself.

We had both guards at that hut well in our sights ready to blow them away if they found Brian, but everything went well, the guard went back to his post and lit a cigarette. With that Brian continued to progress under the hut putting the plastic in place. He then retreated after setting the fuse wire into the undergrowth and out of sight, he crawled back round the camp taking a wide berth into the undergrowth to where we were. We covered him all the way until he was back with us before relaxing a bit.

We then pulled away from the rebel's camp to radio in and head back to our base camp for the night, we seemed to get back faster than we got there, but that always seemed to be the case, like any journey anyone makes.

When we had unloaded our small packs, our first job was to go down to the stream to relax in the water. We all stripped off and got into one of the deep pools, laying our bodies in the warm water, it was heaven as the moving water went past, sort of massaging our bodies, getting rid of the dirt and the ache in our tired limbs.

After lying there about half an hour Trevor came and said, "come on you guys, the guides have cooked us some stew." We left the pool reluctantly but our stomachs were calling, it smelt so good even with us not knowing what was in the big bubbling pot, we all got stuck into what was a very enjoyable and tasty meal not daring to ask what was in it.

After the meal we all gathered round as Tony, Brian and I outlined what we had accomplished, identifying the two huts that we had set the fuses and plastic under and explaining also the layout of the camp. We then agreed to put explosives under all the huts except the ones either side of the hut containing the guy that we had to bring home, we could take them out as we left with grenades if everything went well.

So with the drawing done with the layout of the camp and the huts identified, it was agreed that myself, Trevor, Dave, and Robert would go in the morning to take care of the rest of the huts, with Brian and Tony staying behind with one of the guides staying with them. Hopefully they would put on a feast again for us when we came back hot and stinking from the jungle, having been successful in setting the charges under the rest of the huts.

It is amazing how good food tastes and smells when you are limited in what you can have to eat, but we were used to living off the land wherever we went. So sometimes the most primitive food tastes really good and can be very nutritious with the raw ingredients that go into it, a lot better than the processed stuff we sometimes have at home. The problem with food is knowing the content and the thought of what it is that can put you off, but if you are in a life and death situation you will eat anything that you can lay your hands on. The guides had brought us plenty of coconuts so we sat around the fire that was burning brightly drinking coconut milk, we all seemed to enjoy the creamy taste of the clear milk.

We chatted away and Dave began to open up about his brief encounter with Gwen telling us that she virtually tore his clothes off him when they went into the hotel room, he admitted that her body was not the best toned he had experienced, but then said that she did put some effort into their love making, telling him that her husband never bothered with her in bed. She told him that she had got tired of trying to get him interested in having sex with her, he also told us she had given him a few hundred dollars as well as the watch and ring she had bought him. We all agreed she was a very pleasant lady. "Easy meat for Dave," said Trevor and we all agreed.

Dave said, "well I have the gifts and I enjoyed myself with no strings attached at all."

He told us that their main home was in London and they had a holiday home in Portugal, after selling their business they were travelling the world, even though her husband was still a director of the company. He said that their parents also had pots of money so why should he worry about taking a bit from them, we could not disagree with that.

Brian said he would not want to get tied in with them for too long and hoped that they had left Singapore when we got back. Robert said all he had done was go round the shops, he could not fancy the woman in the physical way but she was a very nice, sincere person and good company to be with. He showed us a gold chain that she had bought him it was very nice and quite heavy so must have set her back a little.

Tony said he did not know how Dave had the nerve, when her husband was there the first time, he could have gone up to the room at anytime. Dave laughed and said he may have paid me to look after her, if not what could he have done to me? Absolutely nothing at all, but he did say to Tony and the rest of us he was sure that her husband knew what she was up to but turned a blind eye to it, as long as he could do what he wanted to do and have peace away from her. We all laughed at that because Dave may have hit on the truth for once because, after all, Gwen's husband told the guys to take them out shopping, either way it would not have bothered Dave, if he had been caught he would have stood his ground.

After much small talk we settled down under our mosquito nets for the night, ready for a start at first light saying good night, we fell asleep to the sounds of the jungle. It was soon first light as one of the guides woke us before turning in himself for a few hours after being on watch all night, whilst his mate who had been asleep came with us.

It was the same procedure, call in on the hour, as we made our way to the rebel's camp once again in the steaming jungle. It was good to be going with Trevor as we both cared so very much about each other and if I was to die I wanted to be with him because we were more like brothers and somehow we became very attached to each other.

Making good time we checked in to say all was going well for us and we were progressing on to the camp. Brian wished us the best of luck and said they all wanted us back safe and sound tonight.

So pressing on in the swampy undergrowth, trying to speed up to get the job done, then head back to base, we called in for the last time before arriving at the rebel's camp saying that we would call in again as soon as all the charges were set.

We arrived in sight of the camp and after observing through our binoculars for about forty minutes we decided that Dave and I would set the charges. Trevor and Robert would give us the cover that we needed so filling our small rucksacks with plastic and fuse wire we set off round the camp opposite to where Trevor and Robert would cover our every movement. There were seven huts to do, as we were leaving one either side of the hut where they had their prisoner, so we decided to work in towards each other and whoever laid their charges first would get a bonus of doing the last hut.

We were both sweating and nervous with the adrenalin running freely but we were assured that Trevor and Robert had us covered in case we were spotted, and at the very first sign of that, they would kill all the guards that they could. We would then try to rescue our man, and be out of there as fast as we possibly could, but we were not looking at failure as Dave and I touched hands and wished each other good luck.

We both kept an eye on each other's movement while crawling slowly towards our first hut, all went well as I set up the charge and buried my fuse wire as deep as I could while slowly crawling back and covering it with vines. Giving the thumbs up to Dave to acknowledge one down and on to the next, Dave was in his element setting the charges, you could guarantee he had done a good job as we progressed to the next two huts doing the same with great care before moving on to the next one that we each had to do. It was slow and painstaking as we moved slowly along doing our job, with the last one to be done I signalled to Dave that I would do it as I was a little nearer to it than he was. I got to the hut and just crawled under it with Dave melting into the jungle just behind me to wait with his pistol ready, so I had Trevor, Robert and Dave giving me some cover and I felt very secure with that.

Just as I got under the hut the door banged open and I froze to the spot, I could then see six pairs of legs coming down the steps it seemed like an eternity as I waited. They stopped about twenty feet away from me, passing the cigarettes round to each other, eventually they lit up and walked towards one of the other huts, I gave a sigh of relief and proceeded to set the last charge covering the fuse wire as I headed back to where Dave was just behind me in the undergrowth.

Dave said that was a close call because if they had dropped anything on the ground and with the huts being raised there would have been a good chance of them seeing me, then all hell would have let loose and we would have had to try to get our man with no preparation at all, but we had got away with it.

As we buried the end of the last fuse wire near a tree, marking the spot as we had done with the rest by cutting a small mark in the bark, we made our way back to Robert and Trevor ready to go back to base and a nice soak in the stream.

It seemed a long crawl back because we could not move very fast through the undergrowth, also we had the fear of being heard or seen, as there were plenty of rebels wondering around the camp at the present time, but we arrived back okay and set off back to our base with more caution than normal.

Once we were clear we moved as fast as the undergrowth would let us, we radioed in to say that we were clear of the camp and on our way back, Dave jokingly said to Brian, "Run the bath for us, mate."

Brian uttered some comment back to him, so we pushed on until we reached the base. As usual we all went down to the stream first to wash the mud and insects off our clothes and bodies, then we had a good soak, it sure felt good, the warm water running against us whilst washing our clothes ready to hang out while we had dinner. Pulling on a pair of shorts we finally climbed out of the stream and headed with clothes in our arms ready to hang out. Dinner smelt good again the guide had done us proud, another great pot of everything that not only smelt good it tasted great. We then had bananas and some other fruit to eat so we were getting well fed if nothing else.

After dinner we radioed in to say we were all okay and on target to carry out the exercise and hopefully get the man back. Captain Rennie said, "good show, well done lads, come back safe." He really was a father figure to us all. Tony said he was one of the best officers that he had come across and we all agreed with him. He was a guy with compassion who really cared about his men and there was a lot to be said for that.

After dinner we decided that we would move in on the rebels' camp the next day to have one last day watching the comings and goings at the camp. We would also use this opportunity to set some plastic explosive further out on the trail back, this would be just in case we had to do a runner and get out of there fast, but our intention was to radio in for a helicopter to come into the rebel's camp to pick us all up from the huge clearing in the centre of the huts.

It was tailor made for a helicopter to land safely down in the dense jungle, but this would only happen if we had cleared all danger from the camp itself, if not, we had a back up plan to go back to our base and arrange another pick up from there. The only problem with this was that we did not know what sort of shape the man we were rescuing was in. If he was too weak to walk out, there would be no way that we could carry him all the way back to our base, except if we took turns to carry him, but that would be very slow, taking hours. That would leave us wide open to attack and someone following us back putting all our lives in real danger, but if that was the only way that we could do it, then so be it, we would have to give it a go.

Trevor said, "let's make sure, guys, that we take out the full camp and that will solve all our problems."

So next day we were going to have one last look at the camp, this was to make sure there was no unexpected problems waiting for us, we could then move in the next day with a big bang. Everyone of us was very uptight with adrenalin building up in our bodies as we talked about the mission. The good thing was that we were a real team of guys who would never let each other down when we were in a dangerous situation.

~*~

Next day it was heaving down with rain as we set off to the camp to spend the day observing all movements from a distance through our binoculars. It took us a long time to get through to the camp with the torrential rain coming down, when we finally got there we took some cover so we could observe everything that was going on.

Trevor and myself were going to check that all the fuses were still covered near to the spots we had left them and not been washed away, so we crawled in the sloppy mud and could not be seen from the camp because all the fuse wire was well hidden near to trees in the thick undergrowth just out of the clearing of the camp, the only thing that bothered us was the wire that we had buried under the huts. We hoped that was safe, unless anyone decided to go for a walk for any reason and spotted the wire if the rain had uncovered it, but with weather like this we did not think that would happen or so we hoped.

It was a good job that we had decided to check because the torrential rain had washed the leaves off some of the fuse wire and exposed it to the human eye in a few places, so we quickly re-covered it making sure that we had it well hidden this time, doing the first few we headed round to check the rest at the far end of the camp most of them were still covered, so job done we headed back to the rest of the guys.

There was no movement in the camp at all with the rain coming down still, we were soaked and our clothes seemed to weigh a ton but we were warm. After about an hour the sun came out and the steam was coming off the jungle floor, a group of men came out of one of the large huts to stretch their legs we counted the movement of about twenty two rebels with small weapons. Staying another hour before we decided to go back, we were satisfied that we had observed all we could for today. The next time we came would be to carry out the rescue and get out of here safe and sound, God willing, we hoped.

It was very heavy going with water running everywhere, Dave said the pools around the streams will be very deep tonight when we get back. We were all absolutely exhausted as we struggled into the base, hopefully for the last time, we all piled into the pools fully clothed as soon as we arrived back. They were overflowing once again with the amount of rain that we had had in the last few hours. It was great as we all shed our clothes and fooled around for the next hour, we then just lay relaxing in the pools to rest our tired and aching bodies as the fast running water pummelled us, we certainly felt better for it as we reluctantly pulled ourselves out for the night. We went to get our food, once again cooked by the two guides for us, the rain had virtually stopped now so that was a blessing, because the waterlogged undergrowth and mud would have made it worse for us in the morning.

We all sat round the fire eating our so called stew out of our Billy cans chatting to each other about our loves and lives beyond the forces, Dave went on about the women that he had left behind, telling us what a good time he used to have, the rest of us sat there intrigued by his exploits.

Robert said, "you don't do too bad now, Dave."

Brian was definitely not as bad as Dave because at least he had some feelings for women, Dave just did not care about their feelings one bit, the rest of us seemed to have lived very sheltered lives compared to Dave. I knew Brian from school and he was not too bad at all before he started competing with Dave.

Trevor and Robert chipped in and said it would not do for us all to be the same, and there were many women around the world who would never settle with one man, just as Dave will never settle with one woman unless he changes his attitude. Tony said he would never take Dave home with him as he could not be trusted. I said, "I would just tell him that I would beat the hell out of him if he showed me up in anyway, or abused the hospitality that was shown to him."

Dave looked across at me with a knowing look, saying nothing at all as I looked straight back at him. Later on Trevor said to me that Dave had told him he saw the emotion in your eyes as you stared straight at him and that told him more than a thousand words, do not try it ever. He said he knew that you would not hesitate to do what you said. Your eyes are always a dead giveaway in your emotions and they were very cold and calculated as you looked at him and he felt them boring into him. He said Brian confirmed the look by nudging him in the side, after the minutes silence with that little bit of tension we were all soon laughing together and joking around with each other once again. It was late as we retired to bed for the night under the mosquito nets.

~*~

Next morning the rain was heaving down again as we prepared for our trip, taking everything with us, just in case we were to be picked up at the clearing, we changed our plans and decided to get closer to the rebel's camp for the night then make a judgement on the attack of the place, depending on the rain when we arrived there, it would be certainly easier than going there to have to come all the way back again. We decided it would have to be real special circumstances for us if we had to come all the way back because if this rain kept up as it was we would struggle to make it back as the ground was getting heavier and heavier. It was making it very difficult to hold our balance in the mud and slime with heavy loads on our backs, at least if we got closer to the rebels' camp we would have a better chance. The two guides were to carry all our spare ammunition for us so that took a bit of the weight off our shoulders, we were very grateful for that in this atrocious weather. We were falling to our knees sometimes and then having to struggle back up and it was not easy, and with being soaked, we were carrying a lot of unnecessary weight along with us.

Dave said, "this is crazy, we will be exhausted when we finally arrive just outside the camp."

We all agreed and said that we would decide on what we were doing as soon as we reached our destination, it may be too dark to do anything but set up some sort of cover and hide ourselves away for the night. We stopped at a small clearing for a little breather, this was where we decided to radio in to Captain Rennie to let him know that we were doing okay up to now, and also to tell him that we were going to go for a pick up at the rebel's camp due to the inclement weather we were having just now, so unless anything went drastically wrong for us, that was the plan. He agreed and said, "take care lads, we will be waiting for your call, an helicopter will be with you within half an hour at the latest."

After that call we carried on through the mud and rain with aching limbs, all of us calling on the extra energies that we had trained for, both physically and mentally. We reached about half way before we had a break for about thirty minutes, really glad to get the loads off our backs for a little while at least.

We had a drink and managed to, at least, have a laugh at the state we were all in, covered in mud and slime; a sorry sight. Our spirits were still high as we set off once more, the rain was not easing off at all, if anything it was coming down with a real vengeance on the jungle, we had never encountered rain like this for a long time.

Robert slipped and vanished out of sight down a slope towards a stream. Trevor and I dropped our packs and scurried after him to help him back up the treacherous slope. He rolled all the way down and had a few cuts and, I would think, many bruises, he was stunned when we reached him.

I went down to the stream edge and took my shirt off soaking it in water after rinsing it out a few times, I brought it back to where Trevor was checking Robert over to make sure that he had not broken anything. I rinsed his face and washed the mud and slime out of his cuts, then taking a field dressing out of my first aid kit, wrapped up a large cut and then I sprinkled some penicillin powder on the other smaller cuts. Once we got to our destination we would clean them up properly for him. We were pleased that he had not broken anything but was just shaken by the fall. We then slowly made our way back up the slope with me helping Robert and Trevor carrying his pack. It was not too bad getting back up as we had plenty of vines to pull ourselves up with and hold on to so we did not slip back down the slippery slope.

Back at the top Robert said he was okay to carry on, but we gave him fifteen minutes to recover as we shared out his heavy stuff between us giving him just himself to carry along for a little while. He said, "thanks guys, I love you all." He was grateful for the load being taken off his shoulders for a time. The guides said that we should be looking for a place to stop to make camp in the next forty minutes or so, we were all on the lookout with great relief that our trek was nearly over, eager to rest our weary limbs, hopefully near to one of the many small streams so we could clean all the mud and slime off us and our clothes.

Shortly after Brian pointed to the right where there was a large pool with a small stream running through it and what looked like a decent place to spend the night as it was soon to be dusk, so we quickly descended down to the small clearing, dropping our packs and jumping in the pool with all our clothes on as the usual practice, shedding them in the pool, once again to wash all the mud and slime off them.

Robert had a lot of bruises on his legs and arms but was okay other than that, we would tend his cuts later, we had to make sure that they were clean and then had antiseptic put on them as you could not really afford to get an infection in a wound out here. It felt good to have all the pain of the journey washed away with the feeling of relaxation in the pool.

The guides were preparing something for us to eat then they would go into the pool also, it was amazing how, after soaking in the pool, our bodies seemed to recover from the arduous journey back and forth to the rebel's camp. It was a good job we had decided to get a lot nearer so that we would not have so far to go when we decided the time was right to get our man out of their clutches.

Dave and Brian were fooling around in the pool wishing that they had some women who could give them a scrub down in this pool. Trevor threw a soggy shirt at them saying, "that's all you two think about, women and sex, it will bounce back on you one day."

Tony and Robert were just laid there listening to the banter between us, enjoying the comfort of the pool and the running water. We must have laid there about an hour before we decided to get out and hang our clothes to dry. Robert got dry and Trevor said, "come here mate, let's get some antiseptic on those cuts after cleaning them with some spirit." Luckily he only had the one large cut that I stitched for him, the rest were only small and did not need stitching, so that was a plus, just as long as we made sure that they were well and truly cleaned. We ate some food and then discussed when and what we were going to do to get the man out and also, if anyone had any doubts about the plan, we would re examine it again that's why we involved everyone to make sure we were all happy with it. None of us had spotted any problems with what we had proposed to do, so we decided that four of us would go round the back to the fuses, light them and then come back quickly so that we could then move in on the huts that bordered the hut were the prisoner was being held. We hoped that they would think that the attack was coming from the other side of the clearing, giving us a few minutes to carry out our task. We decided also that we would hit at first light, hoping everyone was in the huts apart from the guards on duty. Trevor and I were to go and get the prisoner out, Tony would cover the compound as Robert would cover the other huts in case anyone got out. Dave and Brian were to cover us as we moved towards the hut that our man was in, the guides were staying put with our kit hoping that we came back.

If not they were under instructions to destroy everything and get the hell out of there before they were captured and killed, these people would show no mercy to them at all, but the guides knew this as they had dealt with them before and lost family members, life was so cheap in the eyes of these evil people.

So as long as the weather was okay and clear enough for a helicopter to land and pick us up, we would do it tomorrow, before they decided to move the guy once more. So we then made sure that we cleaned our weapons and packed plenty of ammunition in our pockets, we also checked the radio once more with a quick call to Captain Rennie to let him know that we were going in tomorrow all being well, saying that we would want a helicopter on stand by to come into the rebels compound, this was once we gave the all clear that it was safe to land there.

With that out of the way we decided to get some rest and be up at dawn ready to move in and, hopefully, do the business. I lay there thinking of how I loved all my mates and how happy I was to have spent time with them all even though in some difficult circumstances, we had a lot of good and happy times together also. I wondered what would happen to us if we decided to leave the forces at any time in the future, I knew one thing, we would all be friends for the rest of our lives, the bond was cemented between us now, we would be there for each other in any time of need as we were now. I must have fallen into a deep sleep as I felt someone shaking me, it was Trevor saying, "come on mate it's time to get up and get on our way."

The weather was okay, just a little cloud. We all got dressed and made sure that we had everything before we moved towards the rebel camp, intending to leave the guides about a hundred yards away from the compound with the rest of our gear and the radio. It did not take us too long and we were all on edge with the adrenalin pumping round our bodies eager to get on with it. We helped the guides to set up then we decided to go have a look to see how much movement there was. Tony and I went to observe for a few minutes, when we got to where we could see the huts and the clearing we watched for a little while and it was still, apart from a couple of guards outside the hut our man was being held in. So pulling back we agreed that it would be best to go in now, while we still had the advantage of surprise on our side.

Wishing each other the best of luck and a safe return, we had shown the guides how to send a quick message to Captain Rennie saying 'mission failed' just in case. They were told to do that before destroying everything and then getting out as quickly as they possibly could for their own safety, it was no good them sacrificing their lives when there was no need for them to do this because they would be needed to help again, we were paid to take risks and were trained, this was our occupation, to fight and defend our country and Commonwealth.

With that we proceeded with great caution towards our objective, it was the same as when we had looked before with just the two guards being on duty, hopefully Trevor said this will go well for us.

Brian and Dave were to go round and light the fuses, these were on a slow burning fuse to give them chance to get back into their positions before the huts went up in the sky, what a wake up call the rebels would get.

Once Brian and Dave were back with us and as the huts blew up, Trevor and I, after working our way towards the hut that was our objective, would kill the two guards then storm the hut, while the other guys took care of what was outside for us. Clasping hands with Trevor he said, "good luck, brother." As we made our way round to the hut from where we were to get the prisoner.

Once we were in position we waited for the rest to get back to give us some cover, Suddenly, there was an unearthly explosion as the huts started to ignite in flames, before the two guards could move we shot them both. We could hear other shots as we burst into the big hut, shooting anyone that moved, it was bedlam with the noise and shots whistling around us. I heard Trevor wince as he caught a bullet in the arm, another guy came towards me with a knife so I shot him between the eyes. We dived behind a cupboard as a couple of shots came out of the room at the end of the hut where our quarry was being held, crawling on the floor we had to

208

be careful now in case we shot the guy we wanted to rescue.

We observed where the shots were coming from and fired in that direction, hearing a thud, the door opened and a voice shouted, "don't shoot." I shouted, "come out and throw your weapons on the floor in front of you so we can see them."

This he did and he then walked out on his own shaking like a leaf, we must have shot the rest. There was a lot of gunfire outside the hut as we ordered the prisoner to free up our man, then telling him to lay on the floor, the guy that we wanted was okay and so relieved to see us. There was lots of gunfire outside as we tied up the rebel and told our man to stay low until we had made sure it was all clear. Trevor and I then lay low as we dropped over the steps of the hut and scurried underneath, setting some plastic and fuse for when we left. The shots were coming from a hut to our left and we could just see about five guys at the windows firing at our men, they hadn't seen us at all as their concentration was on the rest so we lined them up in our sights and quickly shot two of them and then sighted up two more which we also took out, this was before anyone caught on to where we were hidden under the main hut.

The other guy we could just see vanished out of our sight after seeing his mates go down, with the sound of rapid gunfire to the right of us, we decided it was too risky to move out just yet with the captured rebel and the man that we had been sent to rescue. We thought it would be better to keep them there for a little while longer, but realising once the rebels that were left found out that we had control of the hut and their prisoner they would do all that they could to kill the man that we had come for, rather than let us get him out of there. So with all the gunfire around us we decided to get back into the hut and get them out of there somehow.

Pulling ourselves up the side of the steps and keeping low, we managed to get into the hut, our man and the prisoner were still laid low.

I went into the back room leaving Trevor with them both, at the back of the hut, facing the jungle, I was going to put a little plastic explosive on a short fuse to blow a hole in the back of the hut so that we could get them out of there before anyone started to throw grenades or hammer it with gunfire. I set the plastic and lit the fuse, moving quickly back into the front part of the hut and closing the door to the back room behind me, going to ground just as the explosive went off with a blast that shook the hut.

We quickly ushered the rebel and our man into the back room I said to Trevor that I would go out first to cover them, once they were out and under cover in the undergrowth, I would join them.

Dave and Brian sounded to be under a lot of fire themselves just then, I dived through the hole in the back of the hut and rolled into some long grass quickly looking around with rifle ready, not seeing anything as everything had happened so fast, I then beckoned to them to come out.

First was the man we had come to rescue, followed by the prisoner and then Trevor. I shouted for them to get into the jungle and I would soon follow them, just as they were going, there was a couple of shots came our way, I could not see anyone and fortunately the three of them made it into the dense undergrowth and out of sight. I decided to follow them with my heart pounding away, a shot went over my head into a tree but I too was soon out of sight.

Trevor and I decided to get them safely to where the guides were so at least they could take the guy with them and kill the prisoner if we had trouble, it seemed a lifetime getting round to where they were, even though it was only about ten minutes, we could still hear the gunfire in the compound and wanted to get back there to help the lads as soon as possible.

We briefed the guides quickly on what we wanted them to do if anything went wrong, knowing that we could depend on them to carry out our wishes, we then melted back towards the compound to see how the guys were doing, it seemed as though one of the huts had a good few rebels in, and they were causing a few problems for our guys, as they had them pinned down with the amount of fire that was coming out of the hut.

We knew that we had a bit of an advantage as they did not know that we were there, just in the jungle out of their immediate sight, so Trevor and I split up, to skirt round the edge of the camp just out of sight in the undergrowth armed with a few hand grenades. We could see a few bodies laid around on the compound as we made our way round the camp, this told us that they were not getting all their own way with our boys. Getting behind the huts we looked across at each other, stuck our thumbs up and pulled the pins on the grenades throwing them into the huts through the windows, then quickly withdrawing under cover with rifles ready.

With the couple of grenades we had tossed into each hut, there was suddenly a great explosion as they blew holes in the huts, exposing the inside to us, we then rained fire on them so now whoever was left in there was getting it from both sides. Hoping that we had done the trick and taken some pressure off the guys, a couple of rebels bolted out of the front but were quickly brought to ground by the guys, who then had some freedom to move as we all made our way to a small pocket of fire at the far end of the camp, but before Trevor and I got there, Tony and Brian had taken care of the situation, we just lay low for a little while watching for any sort of movement at all.

I asked Trevor how he was, he said, "it's just a flesh wound I will be okay."

He then asked how I was because he had spotted that I had blood oozing down my left trouser leg, I had cut my leg and torn my denim bottoms as I dived out of the hut to give them cover. We could not see any more movement so we slowly moved out watching out for each other, with us coming from different directions it was easier to watch all the clearing with caution. The huts were burning away as we crossed the clearing to where we would go into the jungle to get the guides and the guy we came for plus the prisoner.

Brian and Robert were to go get everybody and just wait in the jungle on the perimeter of the clearing, just out of sight in case there were any rebels still around, because we could not now take any chances of loosing the guy we had come for now that we had got this far. As soon as they got to them they were going to radio in to ask for the helicopter to come in and take us all out before any more rebels came in, if there was any around. The rest of us lay low watching and waiting for them to come back, all of a sudden there was some heavy mortar fire landing in the clearing and around the area, it seemed as if the rebels had got a radio message out to some one as the shells exploded all around us, they were coming from the east of the camp. We guessed that they were being fired from the back of a truck or something as there was a well used path in that direction, that was all we needed just now.

Trevor and I decided to set off with caution down the track with some plastic explosive and grenades to try and cause some disruption and give us some breathing space as we had no idea how many men they had out there. After about two hundred yards we set some plastic explosive at the bottom of a large tree that was leaning over the track, we also buried some in the ground about twenty yards further on from there, this was the only way for a vehicle to get to us, but we were now very worried in case they could muster any air cover before we could get out of there. Suddenly we heard the heavy drone of a labouring truck, we quickly withdrew back behind where we had laid the plastic explosive and fed the fuse into the jungle with us. It seemed like an eternity, waiting for the truck or trucks to come round the bend in the track, we were very nervous and adrenalin was running high while we waited patiently for them to turn the corner, I had my rifle ready and Trevor had the fuse wire ready to ignite as soon as they were in sight, there were two trucks and they came lumbering round the corner.

We could see about six rebels on the back making eight with the drivers, they had no idea what had hit them as the plastic explosive sent the tree right across the track stopping the progress of the first one. At that time I lobbed a couple of grenades under the first truck that was now stationary, it was blown over onto its side with the explosion. The rear truck was just going to go over the plastic that we had buried in the track as Trevor set off the second charge, it lifted the truck off the ground and it burst into flames as I was picking off the guys in the first truck. They did not have any idea where the gunfire was coming from as they tried to scatter into the jungle, it was too late for a few of them as both Trevor and I picked them off with our shots, this was apart from two who had spotted where the gunfire was coming from and were returning our fire.

I said to Trevor, "you pull back, mate, round the bend and I will keep you covered and once I hear your fire covering me, I will pull back also."

So Trevor made his way back down the track while I kept the

rebel's heads down, after about five minutes I could hear Trevor now opening up on them, so I then pulled back to where he was.

I said that these two guys are being persistent they must be frightened of the consequences if they go back and say they lost everything. Their bosses will say that they ran away to save their own skins, we really needed to take care of them before we go back to the guys. We decided that instead of having a stand off from here that could take ages, one of us would stay here and keep them busy while the other one skirted into the jungle and around them so that we had a better view of them and maybe able to take them out, or at least flush them out from behind the wreckage of the trucks.

Trevor would stay here for the time being, and I would head into the jungle and try to get behind them, it seemed like a lifetime as I made my way through the undergrowth and vines, it was difficult with the mud and I was slipping all over the place, whilst concentrating on trying not to make too much noise as I progressed towards my objective, it was the first time that it flashed through my mind, 'what if I was shot and killed?' But then I thought, 'well this can happen anytime at all with the job we were in.'

I eventually got to a point where I had guessed I would be behind them, so with great care and rifle ready I cut back towards the path moving very slow, I came to a break in the undergrowth where I could see the track and the two blown apart trucks, looking for the guys who were returning Trevor's fire, but I could not see them just yet, this was because they had positioned themselves well in the wreckage.

I decided to move further down hoping that they would not spot me as I did so, and also hoping that I did not pick up a stray bullet from Trevor as he could not see me, but it was a chance that I had to take so we could get the hell out of there.

Making my way towards the trucks I caught sight of one of the rebels tucked near the wheel arch, I quickly took aim and shot him in the side of the head the other guy must have seen me as he returned my fire as I went to ground, that was his mistake also as Trevor must have seen him turn towards me because I heard the crack of Trevor's rifle and the guy fell to the ground with a thud as he hit a bit of tin off the side of the truck. Cautiously I moved up to the truck to make sure that they were both dead, they were lying very still in a pool of blood, I quickly tossed a grenade in the remains of each truck just to make sure they would take a good bit of moving for anyone to get down the track, and taking care of anyone hiding out in the wreckage. I then legged it back up the track knowing that Trevor would cover me if there was anyone else around. Reaching him I said, "well done, brother, let's get back to the clearing and hope that we are soon lifted out of here."

Everyone was ready and waiting when we turned into the clearing for the helicopter to come in and get us out, we waited on the edge of the clearing not realising that nearly all of us had blood running somewhere on our bodies where we had been cut or hit by something, it was strange how you never really took any notice of injuries while the adrenalin was pumping through your body. We decided to have a look at who was hurt and needed stitches, Robert had been lucky as the bullet that he had caught went straight in and out of the fleshy part of his leg, Trevor had a flesh wound on his arm and a few cuts here and there, as did Tony, Brian and Dave. My leg would need stitches also but that would be left now until we got picked up, we just put a temporary field dressing on the wounds that were bleeding a good bit, as none of us had life threatening injuries, it would be better for them to be washed and dressed when we got out of here to save any infections.

The radio crackled as they asked if it was clear to come in and land with a cheer from us all. Trevor said, 'it's a go we are all waiting complete with our man and a prisoner.'

Saying they would be with us in five minutes we dragged all our stuff into the clearing whilst a couple of us kept our rifles ready for any intrusion that may occur, but we thought that we had done a good job and it would be a good while before the rest of the rebels got there and found out that their prisoner had gone, there would be all hell let loose for someone, but that was not our problem we had done what we came to do and more.

Just then we heard the drone of the helicopter as it came into view, we breathed a sigh of relief as it landed and we got the two guys on board then followed with all our equipment. Dave said, "just a minute guys." As he lit a fuse and said he had placed some plastic explosive under each of the remaining huts to make sure that there was nothing left.

We just got into the air and away from the clearing when the huts blew up with timber going everywhere, Trevor said, "nice fireworks, Dave, that must have kept you out of trouble while we were gone."

After circling the area the pilot said he was going to take us into Manila as he had been told that there would be a plane waiting for us all to take us on to Changi. It was only a short flight but the medic that was on board cleaned and stitched up our wounds, not one of us had any serious wounds, we were very lucky. The main thing was to have them cleaned and stitched.

Arriving at the airport, we were quickly transferred to the Royal Air Force Hastings aircraft. We looked across and there were Philippine soldiers surrounding the plane that we were to board, we were escorted from the helicopter along the runway to our transport that would take us to Singapore as soon as we were on board, this guy must be someone very special with the attention we were getting to look after him.

As we boarded the plane we fastened ourselves in and we were soon taxiing down the runway and up and away to Singapore, it was a pleasant flight and we were all ready to have a few beers tonight all being well, and a few home comforts, like a hot bath and a decent bed to sleep in. As soon as we landed in Singapore the guy and the prisoner were taken away from us and whisked away in a car, then a couple of Land Rovers took us and our equipment to Changi.

# Chapter 14

On our arrival there Captain Rennie was waiting with a smile on his face saying, 'welcome home lads.'

He said he had prayed for our safe return, shaking all our hands, "well done you guys, I knew if anyone could pull this one off without too much fuss it would be you motley crew." He added, "but I have to admit I was very worried about this one."

He went on to say go get your wounds seen to by the doctor, then I guess you will want to clean up and have a few beers tonight we all echoed what he had said.

Deciding to get cleaned up first and have a soak in a hot bath knowing that would do all our cuts and bruises good and would clean them up for us, ready for the doctor to have a look at them as a precaution, then it would be down to the NAAFI for some food and a good few beers before hitting the sack for the night. We must have all been in the bath for about an hour before Dave emerged knocking on our doors to see if we were ready to go to the medical officer, then we would eat and have some beers. He must have got fed up in the bath and decided to make us all get a move on. I said to him that he need not think that we were going into Singapore tonight we were tired and just wanted to be alone with each other, thankful that we had all returned safely back here. I hoped that I was speaking for the rest of the guys but if anyone wanted to go into Singapore they could go with Dave and keep an eye on him, if not he could go on his own and suffer the consequences if he got himself into any trouble with sailors in the clubs. I was proved right later in the medical centre for saying what I did, even Brian said that he was not going out of the camp tonight and would leave it until tomorrow, by then we would all have had a good night's sleep and be refreshed ready for a night on the town. It would then be a different story as we would all go in and have some good food and go to a nightclub or whatever anyone wanted to do. Dave changed his mind and said, "okay guys, I will stay here with you and look at all your ugly mushes all night."

"Don't you try to kid us," said Tony, "your eyes will be everywhere but on us Dave, you will be looking at the NAAFI girls and anyone else who will be sat in the bar, no matter if they are with someone or not."

"Yes," Trevor said. "No scruples, Dave followed by a short head by Brian."

Everyone was laughing, even Dave and Brian at that remark.

One by one we went in to see the doctor to have our cuts and bits checked over, as soon as that was done with we were down to the NAAFI for a good drink and some food before having a good night's sleep.

When we reached the NAAFI there were quite a few people in there eating and drinking, so we sat down and asked what was on the menu tonight. It was roast pork and vegetables, so we all went for that for our first course, along with a Tiger ale each.

With plates piled high we got stuck in to what was a very substantial meal with the pork being very tasty with all the crackling on. Just before we finished in came the girls with their parents, they walked over to us and asked if we wanted to play darts with them once we had finished eating, we said sure we would love to, at least it would brighten Dave's evening up and he would not be mooching around all night.

They asked where we had been and we said just over to Darwin in Australia to pick up some parts that we had asked for, they were delivered there because it was a base we were going to work on, we said also it did not take as long as we thought.

That seemed to satisfy them anyway so we left it at that, we decided to all play darts and go round the board on doubles then trebles as that would take us a long time and everyone could play, sitting and talking while waiting for their turn.

We pulled some tables near to where the dartboards were and we enjoyed our game, watching Dave eyeing up the girls which added to the fun, spoilt for choice, they gave him as much banter back. They started to tease him but he did not bother about that, it was egg and milk to him, he just loved it. Asking them if they always went everywhere together they said, "yes, to avoid guys like you who want us for one thing only."

217

Dave said to them that he was very considerate and caring, we nearly fell of our chairs with that remark from him. One of the girls said; "yes, I bet you are until you get your own way or what you want, then I bet you drop a girl like a stone in a river."

Dave gave up then and just concentrated on trying to win the dollars that we had put in the kitty for the winner. We were all having a good night with good company playing and drinking, but as we were very tired, we decided to call it a day after Robert had cleaned up the kitty. So with Robert putting the money in his pocket we all said goodnight to everyone, and departed for a good night's much needed sleep after arranging to go into Singapore in the morning sometime when we decided to arise out of our beds.

Brian said he would not see daylight until about ten or eleven in the morning at the earliest, I think that was all our intentions, to have a good lay in as we were bushed.

~*~

Next morning it was twelve noon before any of us was ready to go into Singapore for the rest of the day.

We found out from one of the girl's mothers that they had already gone, she said they would meet us there. Just as we were preparing to leave Captain Rennie caught up with us, he said, "sorry, you guys, we want two of you to escort the prisoner back to Manila."

He had served his purpose by giving them a lot of information and he was to help in the future if it was needed, as no one knew that he had been captured it was up to us to get him back in a dishevelled state so that there would be no suspicion that he had betrayed them. Captain Rennie said to me, "I am not going to ask for volunteers, it is to be you and Trevor, you should be back in a couple of days."

We were disappointed as the other guys went off into the centre, wishing us both good luck and a safe journey. We went to get ready as we were to leave for Manila late afternoon, then we would be dropped off by helicopter near to the camp that we had destroyed, from there we would take the ex rebel as far as we could down the track to meet up with his friends before coming back to the clearing

218

to be picked up once more. Captain Rennie said it is a chance that we have to take to get him back with his people, the big danger is that if he blows it for us and tells them we are heading back towards the camp, but that is the risk that we have to take, then we would have real problems but it would be easier for two of us to avoid capture and get back safe. We both said that there would be no other person that we would rather be with than each other in a time of danger. After getting everything that we needed, we were taken to the airfield where the prisoner was waiting for us. We boarded the plane and were soon airborne and on our way back to Manila. Trevor asked if I felt nervous, I replied that I was and asked him how he felt, knowing that his answer would be the same, I think it was because we were not sure that we could trust the prisoner, so I thought I would take it in my own hands and have a word with him on his own.

I went over to where he was sat and said to him quietly, "I hope that you are not going to betray us?"

He said, "no boss I will not."

I got my wire out of my pocket, with its two small wooden handles and showed him it and said, "do you know what this is?" As I held a handle in the palm of each hand and stretched the wire out, saying to him, "if I find that you have betrayed us and we are not killed, I will come after you myself hunt you down and one dark night I will wrap this wire round your neck and take it to the bone while cutting your throat."

He squirmed in his seat and said, "I will not betray you boss."

"Good," I said and went back to my seat.

Trevor said, "his face drained of all its colour, what did you say to him?"

When I told him he said, "bloody hell no wonder the poor guy went white, he must have nearly filled his pants with fright after looking into your eyes and realising that you would do it to him."

When we arrived there was an helicopter waiting for us to take us to the camp, the prisoner was falling over himself to be nice to us, so we guessed that he had got the message that we would not mess about with him if he did let us down. It was only a short ride to the camp where we would spend the night in part of one of the huts, if there was any still standing to give us a bit of cover. As we landed the pilot wished us good luck saying that he would pick us up tomorrow evening if everything went well.

He was soon airborne again and on his way back to Manila where he would wait for the okay to come and get us out of there. The prisoner was okay as we sent him to check the huts out, to see if there was anything reasonable left for us to spend the night in. We watched with rifles ready for any trouble.

He went from ruin to ruin until he waved that one hut had a small room that would be okay for the night at least, we cautiously went to have a look and see if it would suffice for us. It was okay and the best of what was left in the clearing so that was to be it. It was getting dark so we told the prisoner that we were going to trust him not to run away because if he did, we would hunt him down and kill him, and if we did not get him someone else would.

He promised that he would not run away as he went white again with fright, so we got our heads down for the night after eating some cold chicken and having a drink, we did not expect that anyone would come here during the night, but I had put some trip wires on the only track in and out with grenades that would soon alert us to any intruders that tried to come into the clearing.

The prisoner did not know this because I had been and set them up saying I was just going to look round the camp to see what I could find, coming back with a couple of the rebels' rifles that were lying on the ground and some ammunition that I had gathered. With that we felt reassured even if the prisoner made a run for it, but we were also going to have him tied to the side of the hut just out of reach of us for the night. He was happy with this saying that he understood how we felt.

We were all soon asleep and with nothing happening during the night we arose at first light and prepared something to eat, looking around the huts for any rations that had been left, we found some tins of food in one of the huts and brewed up some coffee that we had also found.

We then set the prisoner free again and he seemed happy enough and a little more relaxed with us, so we ate and drank our fill of coffee before deciding to head off down the track with the prisoner.

I went and dismantled the grenades so he did not see me as we may want to set them later as a precaution. Going down the track with caution we came to the burnt out trucks, they were a tangled mess, but it was a job well done we thought as we made our way past them.

Making good progress the prisoner told us that there was nothing for the next six miles except very thick undergrowth then there was a small village where he would be safe and be able to get back okay. So we decided to take him there and leave him near to the place with us keeping out of sight, not allowing anyone to see us with him because that would get him killed for sure. It was a hard slog until we got within a few hundred yards of the village where we shook his hand and warned him again of the consequences of betraying us. We lay with rifles ready and watched him walk into the village as a precaution, then we decided to get a move on back to the clearing as fast as we could, just in case he did betray us.

I said to Trevor, "just think of all the little trouble spots in the world caused by greed and people wanting power at any cost with no feelings for human life, it makes me cringe at the thought."

"Yes," he said, "but we are doing what little we can to help in our own small way."

We had gone a couple of miles before we decided to have a sit down just off the track as we had been going at a good pace, Trevor told me that he would be glad to go home soon and see Elsie. He then turned to me and said, "she always asks after you and if you had a girl friend yet, but knowing you as she did, she said that you would not want to get tied down with anyone."

She said, "Ann is always asking after you and said she hoped that you would write to her sometime soon."

I said, "yes, Trevor I will, but you know that I don't like writing letters but I will, to save them getting at you."

We had been sat there for about fifteen minutes and no one appeared down the track so we guess the guy had kept to his word, though as Trevor said, I did put the fear of God into him by saying that I would find him and kill him and showing him the wire. Then we decided to set off once more just hugging the side of the track so it would be easy to dive in the jungle undergrowth if we heard anyone coming along.

Just as we were turning a bend in the track we heard a noise, we stepped into the undergrowth and lay very still with our sights on the track in front of us. We could now hear talking and whoever it was did not expect to see anyone because they were not quiet, they got within about fifty yards of us and we could see that there was five of them and they all had rifles and all of them were smoking away as though they did not have a care in the world, they must have been drinking also as one of them fired a shot off into the undergrowth. We were worried in case they all started as we could get hit if they started fooling around, we did not know where they had come from but there were small villages all over the place so we guessed that they were from one of them, but we didn't know if they were rebels or not.

I said to Trevor, "you keep me covered as I step out and see what reaction we get from them, we can't chance them hitting us if they all start fooling around and firing at will into the jungle around us. If they raise their weapons we can't take a chance, I will dive straight back into the undergrowth and hope that their reactions are slow with the amount of drink that they seemed to have consumed. We will have to open fire on them."

Not knowing what to expect I walked out a yard so I could just be seen by them, they stopped in their tracks not expecting to see anyone out there on foot, I asked them if there was any small villages where I could get something to eat as I was lost. One of them asked what I was doing here so far from the city, I said that we had been hunting and our vehicle had broken down, and I had left my friend with it while I tried to get some help. They were being cautious and did not know what to believe, I guess it was a new one on them, white men hunting! Even if they had seen the blown up trucks and camp they would not expect to see anyone coming towards them. One of them walked up to me, the others staying where they were. He asked if I had any money, I said no, it was with the land rover that I was in. I had my knife in my hand, clutched near to my sleeve, ready if it turned nasty. He then saw my watch on my other hand and said give me that now. I watched his eyes change to a mean look and I thought this is going to be a problem. I knew that Trevor would

222

have the other four covered, His voice changed and he said again, "give me the watch", so I reached with my hand towards him for him to take it, he walked forward to take the watch off me.

Once I was in reach I hit him across the throat with my blade so hard, he went down like a sack of spuds gasping for breath as the blood spurted all over, I dived into the jungle for my rifle as Trevor had opened fire and shot two of the other guys, it all happened so fast they did not know what had hit them, as I shot one, Trevor took out the remaining one. The guy whose throat I had cut was laid in a massive pool of blood, Trevor shot him and put him out of his misery because he would bleed to death.

We checked that they were all dead, we could not afford any prisoners anyway, they were not village people because they were well armed, also after we had searched them we found plenty of dope in their pockets, so we guessed that they had been plundering the village people of whatever they could and most likely raping their women in the process. We did not feel bad about this anyway it was us or them they would not have shown us any mercy, I suspect that they would have tried to kill me anyway and steal what they could from me, then go looking for the vehicle which I said had broken down.

So after pulling them off the track into the undergrowth we made our way on to the camp hopefully to be picked up as soon as we sent a message from the radio we had left there ready for us to call in.

Just then the heavens opened and it was torrential rain we could not see fifty yards in front of us, within seconds we were soaked right to the skin but we continued on hopefully to get some cover and get our clothes off and try to dry them. It took us about another hour to get back, with the mud and rain the track looked like a running river and we were slipping and sliding all over the place. We arrived back and entered the hut that still had a little bit of shelter from the weather. Trevor was going to light a fire as I went and set the booby traps on the track once more, it was only a matter of re-tying the wire to the pin on the grenades, this would give us a little security just in case anyone came, it would warn us and maybe kill some of them in doing so. I fell flat in the mud and water while fastening the last trip wire back across the track, once I had made sure that they would all work, I slipped and slid back to the hut were Trevor had a fire burning away and some water on the boil.

I said that I was going down to the stream to wash all the mud off my clothes first and he said he'd join me so off we went to get the thick mud off our clothes before hanging them up to dry in the hut.

We spent about fifteen minutes in the stream with the rain still pouring down on us before we headed back carrying our clothes which we hung out to dry and then hunted around in the huts for some more food, we found plenty of tinned stuff that we could make a meal from.

Once we had eaten our fill with the rain absolutely pouring down, it was then that we called in on the radio asking if we could be picked up but we were not very optimistic with the present weather situation.

This was confirmed to us and we were told that the weather was too bad really to take a chance as a high wind was also forecast, so it was left that we would now be picked up at first light in the morning, hopefully if the weather cleared up enough for them to come and get us. We decided to make ourselves as comfortable as we could for the night, we did not mind as the comradeship we had between us both was second to none, Trevor and I really were like brothers and both had a similar nature, the bond that had grown between us we guess would be there for the rest of our lives, we would always be there for each other in time of need, no matter where we were in the world.

Settling down near to the fire we had a beer each which we had found in one of the huts. It was so peaceful Trevor said, "apart from the pillaging rebel's around the place after anything that they could get, abusing the village people and taking their women for their own satisfaction. We have gone through a lot together and been very lucky at times."

I agreed saying, "I was really scared when we destroyed all those poppy fields, I thought that I was going to die."

"Don't worry, you are not alone, I get those feelings also," Trevor said.

We had a few beers then got our heads down listening to the rain

224

pounding on the roof, this was the only bit of the hut that was left with any cover at all but we were thankful for that, hoping that it would stop during the night and we could get the hell out of there back to civilisation and a decent meal or two in Singapore.

"I bet Dave and Brian are enjoying themselves while we are away and not there to dictate to them about their morals and right and wrong." Trevor added, "has he always been like this?"

"A little," I said, "but nothing like he is now and I guess Dave will never change. I pity anyone that he marries he will drive the girl mad. I'm sure that Brian will settle down sometime and be loyal to the person that he falls in love with and marries, but as for Dave, I don't know, I think that he is a lost cause now and there is no hope for him. He has no respect for women at all but I do hope that he turns out okay because he is a great mate to have around in times of need."

"Yes, I have noticed that and I don't think he will change at all, any woman married to him will surely have her work cut out keeping her eye on him where women are concerned."

The rest of the guys had morals and respected a woman's view and were always well behaved round them, but Dave and Brian sure made up for us all.

We eventually fell asleep, and the next thing we knew was a loud noise of a helicopter overhead, as we looked out of the hut we could see a couple of machine gunners peering over each side ready for any bother. The sun was beating down and there was our ride home, just hovering above, waiting for our signal, this felt really good, we were both very relieved that the weather had broken and they had come straight for us. Trevor went outside and waved for them to land, we quickly gathered our clothes which were dry, pulling our pants on somehow while carrying everything else so that we could get out of there as fast as we could. I just remembered the booby traps and shot off to dismantle them because we did not want innocent people getting blown up by them. If we could have been assured that it would be the rebels, we would have left them in there as a nice surprise for them, to remember that we had been there.

After I had done that I made it back to the helicopter as Trevor was putting the rest of our gear on board, once we had it all on, thank God we were soon in the sky and on our way back home. We were to be taken to Manila once more then catch a flight to Singapore which would be waiting for us. The pilot and his mate asked us if it had all gone well and we said 'yes, just as we wanted it to.' not mentioning the men that we had killed because this had become something that we did not talk about, we just said that we got the prisoner back safe and sound.

It was a short flight and we had to wait in the airport for our plane back to Singapore as it had been delayed slightly we were told. We waited in a room that had been set aside for us and there was coffee on the boil so we helped ourselves to it and some cake that was there. We were only waiting for about thirty minutes when someone came for us to say our ride was here and whisked us out of a side door to the waiting Royal Air Force plane and on route to Singapore.

Trevor said to me that he was very relieved that we had not got tied up into too much conflict and that everything had gone well for us.

I replied by saying, "I know Trevor, I am sure that God is looking over us as we go about our tasks.

I know just how you feel, you need a rest away from all this as we all do and I believe that your rest should be back in Blighty with Elsie. You would be able to go away for a week somewhere together, that will do you both the world of good I'm sure."

He turned round and asked, "what do you want to do, will you come with me? You can always ask Ann if she will come along, that will make the four of us and we could have a great time together."

"No, Trevor," I said, "I am just happy having a leave here, somewhere closer to Singapore. If I ask Ann, or Elsie does, where will that lead to? Something that I will not want to cope with just now, our relationship is based on us being great friends and nothing else, like mine with Elsie, but I do need to wind down like you and, I guess, the rest of the guys do too. I think that I will go see Tank and Robin in Aussie, it's not too far and soaking up the sun on a little beach, that will do me fine."

"I don't like going home without you as we have become part of each other," Trevor said, "but you are right, we are all ready for a rest before our next assignment wherever that may take us all."

With our minds made up we were going to see Captain Rennie and request a couple of weeks leave as soon as we arrived back in Singapore, we guessed that the rest of the guys would also want to go away for a couple of weeks to get away from it all and recharge our bodies, both physically and mentally.

Trevor said with a chuckle, "I bet Dave and Brian stay in Singapore for their leave with free board and lodging and able to spend their money on whatever they liked."

"I am not sure but we will ask everyone what they want to do before seeing Captain Rennie so we are clear who wants travel warrants and who does not."

After a pause I said to Trevor, "do you think that you will marry Elsie when you get out of the forces?"

"I'm not sure, we need to spend some time together first and really get to know each other away from any pressures, so this would be an ideal opportunity, going away together somewhere in Great Britain."

"Where would you like to go?"

"I wouldn't mind going to Cornwall, or the other extreme Scotland, but I will telephone her and ask for her views on where she would like to go, if she can get the time off work, though I don't think that would be a problem because she has been saving up her time for when we came back home on leave."

"I will bet you she picks Scotland, in the mountains somewhere away from the crowds, I know her too well, so you can have space together away from the holiday crowds that you would get in Cornwall during the summer months, at least in Scotland you can get away from it all and be alone together."

"Well," he said, "you know her better than me so we will see if you are right, I wish that you would come with Ann and then we could all be together and have fun."

"Ann's idea of fun would be different to my idea of fun, and there is no way am I going down that road, I would be more stressed than anything when I came back here."

"She is a good looking girl and her father has lots of money."

I was getting a little angry with his persistence even though I knew he was only thinking of me, so I said, "Trevor, bloody hell, I have grown up with them both and I know how they think, they would both be plotting together for Ann to get me committed in some way. I do not want to get involved with any woman while I am in the forces, after that it will be my choice."

He knew that I was very angry so he said, "okay mate, let's leave that one, there is no way that you and I are going to fall out over a woman, anyway, you are so right, you do know how they both think with going to school and growing up together, just as they know all your moods and feelings. You all have such a wonderful friendship and I don't think that anyone will ever break you up. From what Elsie has said to me you have been like a big brother to them through their lives, been there for them and protected them and they both love you to bits, knowing how they feel, I class you as the brother that I never had, so no way do I want us to argue over silly meaningless things. I was being selfish with this one just wanting you with me and Elsie but you can't blame me for that can you?"

I calmed down and said, "sorry Trevor, I was out of order, I should not have blown off at you for just wanting me with you and I treat you also as a brother and know that you would never do anything to hurt me as I would never do anything to hurt you either. We have developed a bond between us deeper than any ordinary friendship and that is too precious to lose."

Trevor said, "I would rather lose anything but our friendship, it is so very precious to me, more than anything else I could name or wish for, it is something that you cannot buy. In the short time that we have known each other we have come to know each other's likes and dislikes and built up such a wonderful caring attitude to each other, it's just that I will miss you by my side, looking after me, just knowing that you are around gives me a great feeling of safety and contentment."

"Trevor, you will have a great time with Elsie, she is a bundle of fun, you will never be bored in her company I can vouch for that, you both will have the time to get to know each other and the last thing that you would relish is me and Ann around you causing problems."

He turned to me and said, "you know that your eyes speak for you when you are angry, happy or sad, Brian was right, when you are angry your deep blue eyes soon let everyone know. No wonder he said you have ice eyes, when you are angry you sure do show it. Wearing your heart on your sleeve as usual." He continued, " Dave is different again to you but he still cares about us guys, Brian is loyal to you but you have grown up together and built up a trust. Robert and Tony are also great guys to have around that's why we are such a well balanced team together."

The plane must have been approaching Singapore as we were told to belt up and prepare for landing, the time had passed quickly with us chatting to each other, the good thing about what Trevor and I say to each other, it is always strictly confidential between our two selves, especially personal stuff, it is never mentioned to anyone else.

The plane shuddered to a halt and we quickly disembarked into a land rover that was waiting on the tarmac to take us back to Changi. It was refreshing to get back there, it was becoming our second home while we were in the Far East and we loved the place.

The driver dropped us off and told us that Captain Rennie said that we were to have a rest and he would see us both later, all I wanted was a good soak in a nice hot bath and that's where I went. Trevor said that he was going to do the same before we went to see the guys and ask if they were going to put in for a couple of weeks leave along with us.

It was heaven laid in the bath I nearly fell asleep at one time because my body was so tired.

I got out and laid on my bed and must have nodded off because next thing that I knew was a loud banging on my door and it was Trevor saying, "are you there my mate?"

Waking with a start I shouted, "just a minute Trevor." As I went to open the door to let him in, I quickly got dressed. Opening the door I said, "sorry Trevor I just nodded off and was dead to the world, I will not be a couple of minutes."

"No worry, I could have done the same but I wrote a letter to Elsie to say I may be coming home and would she like to go away for a couple of weeks or ten days and, if so, where would she like to go."

I was soon ready and we went down to the mess room to get a drink and see who was around the camp. Asking where the guys were, the barman said that they were all down at the pool waiting for us to come back, so we headed down there and as they saw us approaching they cheered and jokingly said, "where the hell have you two been?"

After they had finished ribbing us, we sat down and immediately asked them what they thought of applying for a couple of weeks leave, saying whoever wants to go back to the UK can do? We explained we could all get travel warrants or hitch a lift on one of the Royal Air Force planes that flitted between the UK and Australia, and surprise, surprise, everyone of them wanted leave.

They asked what Trevor and I were doing and I said that I have thought of going to see Tank and Robin in Aussie, soak up the beaches there and having a change of scenery.

Trevor said, "I am defiantly going back to Blighty, my mind is made up."

Dave and Brian wanted to go to Bangkok for a week and then go on to Aussie as two weeks would be too much there. Tony said he wanted to go home to England and Robert said he would like to go with me to see Tank and Robin.

So with our minds made up we decided to ask Captain Rennie when we saw him for some leave. We spent the rest of the day lazing round the pool in the very peaceful surroundings before we went to get changed to go for some food down at the waterfront that had become our second home. Brian said that he had seen Captain Rennie going into the mess as though he was looking for someone, guessing that it was us we made our way there deciding to ask him now if he could arrange our leave for us.

He said it was no problem, "I was going to suggest that you all have a break away from everything for two or three weeks."

He asked where we wanted to go and said that he would make the arrangements within a couple of days. He then congratulated me and Trevor for taking the man back and coming back safe and sound, thanking us for going at such short notice.

I said it was our job and if ordered we would have had to go, so it was a pleasure to do it for him. He asked where we were going tonight and Robert quickly said the waterfront for a meal and a drink, he said, "do you mind if I come, the food is on me tonight?"

So he came along with us and we went to a good seafood restaurant that we knew which had exceptional food, we had never had a bad meal there yet. We all sat outside as the night was very hot and dry and ordered drinks and looked at the menu, everyone started with grilled prawns and most of us followed with lobster, apart from Brian and Robert who had fish done in a sauce so we were all very easy to please.

The food was absolutely wonderful, Captain Rennie said it was the best he had ever tasted and he knew now where to bring anyone for a decent nosh. We all thanked him as he got up and said "have a great night you guys get another beer each on me and I will settle the receipt before I go."

Tony said once again what a great guy he was, no airs and graces, just one of the best. This was echoed by us all, we have never met anyone like him, he brought the best out of people with his caring nature, not the run of the mill pompous officer that you came across so very often born with a silver spoon in their mouths. He was just one of the lads and he could be strict with people when needed. He settled the receipt saying goodnight and his parting shot was, "look after yourselves guys, see you all tomorrow."

We sat there looking out at the Straits between Singapore and Malaysia, Tony said he would like to spend a few days in Kuala Lumpur on one leave if we could, we all agreed we'd like to do the same, we had heard that it was a decent place to visit from some of the Royal Air Force guys in Changi. You could see all the ships anchored for the night as we looked across the water.

"They must have an enormous amount of trade from all over the world call in there discharging and swapping cargos," said Brian. "The shipping lanes must be some of the busiest in the world with the amount of ships that turn round here in this small island."

Sailors from all over the world both commercial and Navy boats all spending their money in this small island taking gifts home with them to wherever they came from.

"How peaceful it is sat here," Robert said, "you would never believe a few days ago we were all in the jungle with the chance of getting killed, and you two have been back in there, thank God you both came back safe and sound."

Dave said, "look who is coming down the street." As we turned to look, there was Gwen and her friends with their husbands and, too late they had seen us. They asked if they could join us and we said sure, no problem. Gwen pulled a chair up next to Dave and the rest sat where they could. Gwen's husband said, "anyone want a drink and something to eat?"

It was a couple of hours since we had eaten, so we said we would just have a snack and another beer if he didn't mind. They ordered the works while we just had some grilled prawns to pick at. They asked us where we had been hiding, Trevor said we had been to a base in Australia for a few days to do some repairs on the runway. Dave chipped in saying, "did you get the message that I had left for you all?"

Gwen said, "yes, thank you David, it was nice of you to let us know that you were to be away for a little while." Then she said that they had been to Hong Kong for a few days, and had decided to come back here for another week before going onto Australia themselves to meet up with some of their friends.

Trevor gave me the eye and I nearly burst out laughing as I looked at Dave's face, it was a picture because Gwen had her hand on his leg under the table and was teasing him something rotten. You could see he was very uncomfortable with it for a change but had no say in the matter. He made the excuse to go to the toilet just to give himself a break, hoping that the food had come by the time he got back. Trevor smiled at me while the guys were holding conversation with Gwen's husband and his friends.

Dave was very lucky as the food was being brought to the table, I would bet any money that he went in the restaurant and chased them up with the order to give him breathing space, maybe he was getting a conscience after all, or was I just dreaming.

Whispering it to Trevor he said, "you are dreaming, Dave has no conscience he will be thinking how he can get Gwen away from the table for a bit of fun with him before much longer, you just watch him.

So Dave was the centre of our attention, all of us knowing what he was up to. Everyone else said how wonderful the food was and that they had never been here before but would be back again.

With that Gwen said to her husband, "come on darling, take me to the shopping mall I want to have a look around at some rings."

He turned and said, "I am still eating and I'm not going to the mall, I hate shopping." Turning to us he said, "will one of you escort my wife to the shops and make sure that she is safe?"

Dave immediately said he would take her, Gwen's husband replied "You don't know what you are letting yourself in for young man, she will take ages." Then he carried on eating, not giving them both a second glance as they left for the shops.

"Like hell," I thought, "they will be going to no shops, or maybe a quick visit to buy something to bring back as though they had been wandering around for hours."

I guess all the guys were having a little chuckle to themselves with the same sort of thoughts as mine.

We all got stuck into the massive plate of grilled prawns that had been brought for us, with refills if we wanted them, Gwen's husband said as he stuffed himself with lobster washing it down with beer.

He was a generous sort of guy and I guessed he must have had an idea what his wife was up to and did not particularly care, as long as she was out of his hair letting him do what he wanted to do without any interference from her. I suppose that she was happy also, spending and having fun with Dave with no strings attached.

We sat there watching the world go by, Trevor said that he could not wait to have a couple of weeks back home and was really looking forward to seeing Elsie. Tony joked with him and said we don't want you getting married without us lot being there with you.

Brian retorted, "yes, I can't miss Elsie getting married."

"Yes," I said, "we all want to be there for that, he has a great woman there fun to be with and always very happy."

Trevor said, "no way would I get married with you not being with me anyway, give us a break you guys we are only going away for a few days together, just to get to know each other more."

Brian leered, "yes, I bet you are going to get to know each other."

Gwen's husband joined in, "you don't want to be getting married you guys, at your time of life, you want to continue travelling the world without a woman breathing down your neck. You need to be enjoying yourselves without having a commitment to anything at all, the world is your oyster so go out there and enjoy it."

Little did he know we diced with death everywhere we went but we loved it and the adrenalin rush we got while helping the vulnerable. It was a feeling that you could not explain when you know you have helped little children have a better sort of life in most cases.

Robert said, "look there is Dave and Gwen coming back."

Gwen's husband said, "could they not have taken longer, I am enjoying myself with you guys."

Tony said to him they have been gone for nearly two hours, and his reply was, "I told you time flies by when you are enjoying yourself!"

Trevor whispered to me, "yes and I bet Dave and Gwen have been enjoying themselves too."

Gwen walked up and said, "Look what I have bought darling." Showing him a ruby ring that must have cost a fair bit of money, he glanced at it and said, "that's nice darling, sit down, I will get you a drink."

Thanking Dave for his time, and being a gentleman, taking his wife to the shops for him saying do you now want to eat and drink something, they ordered oysters and lobster. Dave winked at me and Trevor and just turned his thumb up to us with a grin on his face.

It got to midnight so we all then decided to get back to camp while the rest got a cab back to their hotel saying we may see you tomorrow at Raffles.

"As soon as I get back to camp," said Tony, "I'm going to hit the sack for the night."

In fact we all chipped in with what a good idea, an early night for a change, as we flagged down a couple of cabs to take us back to our camp. We were well fed and well oiled, we knew that we had drank plenty as we stood up and started to walk towards the cabs that had stopped for us.

Dave came into the cab with me and Trevor so we guessed that we would get the run down on what happened with Gwen and him.

234

He started by saying what a jerk Gwen's husband was, "she is red hot for sex."

Trevor said, "maybe that's the problem, she will not leave him alone, poor guy."

Dave told us they had quickly gone to a jewellery shop and bought a ring that she had seen before.

She was stroking his thigh as they waited for the man to wrap the ring up after putting it into a presentation box for her.

She then said, "come on Dave, we are going to book in the next hotel we come across and I am going to undress you as fast as I can, then make love to you like you have never had before."

He then said she was some crazy woman, but an excellent lay, who knew just what she wanted from a guy, he said that she had asked him to take her away for a couple of days, because her husband has some business to attend to in Kuala Lumpur and will be away for about four days. She was not going with him as it is always boring and she would rather be with me.

I asked what he was going to do and he said that he was going to arrange to go with her somewhere, even if they stayed in another hotel other than Raffles because her friends would still be there.

Trevor said, "that would not bother you Dave would it?"

"No," he said, "I don't have a problem with it in fact I may suggest that we stay there and I sneak into her room, but we will see what she really wants to do. She will be paying for everything and more." He chuckled, meaning she would be spending plenty of money on him as well.

Before he could say anything else, to our relief, as we had heard it all before, we arrived at our camp, we both dived out of the cab and said, "pay the man Dave you have money coming to you."

He was cursing as he said, "I will get you two back."

We laughed at him as we shouted goodnight and went to bed, I could still hear him cursing as he walked past my door slamming his door behind him.

Next day at breakfast we had to endure him again telling the rest of the guys about last night and adding the bit about us leaving him to pay the cab driver, everyone laughed at that and Dave was not amused. Robert said, "Add it to Gwen's receipt for your services,

Dave."

He replied, "I bloody will, don't you worry and plenty more as well."

He soon got over it and was laughing with us about everything. Captain Rennie walked in for breakfast and after saying, "good morning guys, did you have a good night after I had left?"

"Yes, and thank you for the meal once again."

"No problem guys you deserve it," he then said, "you are all okay for a leave."

We cheered him and said thanks we needed to have a rest before coming back on duty, he told us that he was also going home for a couple of weeks, so everything would be arranged in the next few days as we were all doing different things and the flights had to be arranged for those of us that were leaving Singapore.

Trevor was over the moon, I could see by his face that he was overjoyed at the thought of going home to see Elsie. Tony also said he couldn't wait to have a good break away from the stress and everything, but he had a lot to forget and I think it was a good bit of time before he trusted another woman again. He was sentimental as far as women were concerned, not like Dave, here today gone tomorrow.

We finished our breakfast and Robert said, "let's all go round the pool for the morning before going to Raffles in the late afternoon." Everyone agreed to do just that and relax around the pool, so we went to gather our swimming trunks and towels. It was overcast but very hot and humid, typical weather in Singapore and when it rained it came down in torrents bouncing off the footpaths.

We laughed and joked with each other round the pool playing a bit of water polo and diving to the bottom of the pool looking for coins that we had thrown in to recover. We then just laid there chatting away about the good times that we were going to have at the various locations that we had chosen for our leave.

Tony said he had a score to settle, but I told him to leave it until we could all go with him.

He said, "I can't, it's the deceit and the lies, and it had been going on a few months while there is me thinking everything was great between us. If she had not wanted to carry on why on earth did she

236

not tell me on my last leave in England? I truly thought that she loved me, the worst part is that I know the guy and he took advantage of my being away, so I just want to give him a good hiding, then I will be satisfied."

"If you go," Trevor said, "do it straight away, I will come with you just in case his mates are around."

Tony thanked him saying that would be great and that he would appreciate Trevor being around if he didn't mind.

"We are here for each other, so say no more," said Trevor, "you would be there for me in time of need."

"Tony," I added, "remember, it takes two to tango, she had only to say no to him, but you are right, I would give him a good hiding for old times sake and just to get it out of my system, so if that is what you want to do, go ahead, if Trevor is willing to go with you to watch your back, I only wish you would wait until we all got back to England, but if you decide to go ahead with it when you get there, do it and then get the hell out of there, go to London or something, or come back to Aussie and catch up with us, that way it will not eat away at you, but if you stay around it will cause you to have a very unhappy leave, so whatever you do, please take my advice and get away from them all."

He said, "I will, the last thing I want is you worrying about me like you do so I promise you that if I do give him a good hiding I will get my butt out of there straight away."

I reminded him that it is a long way to go for a couple of days.

Dave said, "once Gwen's husband has gone we will not waste anytime, we will be off booking in somewhere else I would think, if that's what she wants, she will pay dearly for me being with her." he said with a laugh, "my time is precious."

Robert said, "we will have a great time with Tank and Robin in Aussie."

"I'm sure that we will Robert," I said, "at least we will be free and safe in that environment, and able to do what we want without watching our backs all the time."

We were going to meet up in Adelaide and go from there. Tony chipped in and said, "I may fly straight out so stay there a few days and I will catch up with you because Elsie and Trevor will not want me around them for very long." He looked straight at Trevor.

"Being honest, no, my mate, I do not want anyone around us, especially my dear brother looking at me knowingly with a smile on his face."

We then all dived into the pool to have a game of water polo to cool down because it was very hot and sticky, we stayed there a couple of hours more, diving in and out of the pool before deciding to go and get a shower and change ready to go out to Raffles for the night and live with the filthy rich.

Just as we were leaving the pool Captain Rennie came across to tell us that everything was fixed. "Trevor and Tony will catch a plane to England in three days time, we have fixed for Tony to spend a couple of days in England then there is a flight, if he needs it, to Adelaide via Darwin and of course the stops on the way." Turning to Brian and Dave he said that they could go to Bangkok any day that they wanted if they still wanted to go. Robert and I were to fly via Darwin with a night stop over there before flying on to Adelaide, in two days time.

We all thanked him for arranging everything for us and said we would all come back refreshed and ready to get back to work, as he walked away he said, "I know guys, you all deserve a break so make the most of it as I will mine."

Feeling very happy with ourselves we arranged to have our showers, then meet up in about an hour and half to go to Raffles.

Trevor said to me, "I just can't wait, my brother, to get on that plane to England and to see Elsie."

He was so excited, like a kid with a new toy, but knowing Elsie she would make him very happy, as she was a very bubbly girl and so full of fun. I was very happy for them both of course, having grown up with Elsie I knew that she would be good for him or else I would not have given him her address so they could write to each other.

I decided to fill the bath and have a good soak before getting dressed to go out making sure that I did not fall asleep in the bath which was becoming the norm with me. All dressed and ready, we caught a lift to Raffles from one of the guys that was delivering some stuff there which saved us the cab fare. When we arrived the place was pretty full but we were beckoned by Gwen's husband to the table that they had and asked the waiter to pull another table up for us to join them.

He said, "join us for a meal you guys as I am going on business tomorrow and will not see you for a few days."

With that Trevor said, "thanks we would love to join you all."

As we sat down Tony told Gwen and her friends that we were all going to have some leave and that he was going to England with Trevor before flying back to Australia to meet up with us and some friends.

Dave then said that he was staying around here with Brian. With that Gwen's husband said, "good you can keep my wife company and keep her out of trouble if you don't mind?"

The look on Dave's face was a picture, Brian said nothing.

Gwen leaned over to Dave and Brian saying, "you guys don't mind looking after me do you?" Kissing them both on the cheek.

Tony, Trevor and Robert all looked at each other with disbelief with Gwen's husband condoning everything that Dave wanted without batting an eyelid.

The menu came and we all ordered plenty of food and some drinks with the knowledge we would not have to pay these prices. We all had a great time drinking and eating in such good company, once we had finished, Gwen's husband said, "well, I am turning in now everyone, as I have an early flight out of here."

We thanked him for his hospitality saying that we hoped to meet him again, if he was around when we came back off leave.

He said, "no problem guys, I am staying in the Far East for a couple of months so we should meet up again when I get back."

He was laughing as he said, "and of course, you keep Gwen out of my hair for me!" He strode out of the restaurant saying good night to everyone.

We stayed another hour before going ourselves thanking Gwen and her friends for their hospitality.

We would all be leaving in the next couple of days so had to get packed ready to go tomorrow because sometimes the flights were a little early going out, if there was some urgent cargo, so it was going to be a parting of the waves for a couple of weeks for us all,

I was quite sure that we would all miss each other, but would all return refreshed ready to start our work again.

# Epilogue

Trevor and Elsie really got to know each other when he went back to England on leave, and continued to correspond with each other on his return to Singapore. Love blossomed and they were married, surrounded by all his mates, when he left the forces.

Brian eventually met an Australian girl whilst he was on leave there and she certainly pulled him into line, he changed completely and spent every leave that he had with her at her home in Perth, Western Australia. When he left the forces they were married in Australia and live there to this day.

Robert went to live in Canada and married a Canadian girl. He became a policeman.

Tony went to work in the Middle East as head of security for an oil company.

Dave was the problem, he never changed. He married a girl who had plenty of money and became a school teacher in England. Though she threatened to leave him on numerous occasions for his exploits with women, he actually left himself when he met a wealthy Canadian woman and travelled the world with her.

And I, Bill, left the forces and worked in the security service after marrying my childhood friend, Ann. I have devoted my life to helping people have a better life, particularly young children in different countries around the world.

More great books from
Mediaworld and Best Books Online
can be seen on our publishing web site at
www.bestbooksonline.co.uk

**Publish with us in electronic book form,
traditional form, or both, and
your work receives world-wide listings.**

E-mail publishing@bestbooksonline.net
or call us on
08451661104 within the United Kingdom, or
+447092103738 from outside
(24 hour voicemail facility)

Mediaworld PR Ltd,
Yeadon, Leeds,
West Yorkshire.
Words and people that mean business

**We are a specialist company offering
much more than traditional publishers.
We deal with our authors personally
and provide all editing and marketing services
on a one to one basis.**